5-FIGURE AUTHOR CHALLENGE

Playbook

Alinka Rutkowska

5-FIGURE AUTHOR CHALLENGE PLAYBOOK

ISBN-13: 978-1-943386-18-5

Congratulations
5 figure author in the making!

You are one of the elite few
who gets what it takes to succeed
as an author in 2017 and beyond.

Enjoy the contents of this
mystery package!

When you apply what you've
discovered here, you'll get a taste
of what is possible...

... and that's when I'd love to
talk more about YOU
(last pages of this book)
Keep turning the pages, Alinka

DIRECTORY OF 5-FIGURE AUTHOR WINNING STRATEGIES

PART 1: WRITE A BOOK THAT SELLS

PART 2: MARKET LIKE A PRO

PART 1: WRITE A BOOK THAT SELLS

THE SECRETS OF PLOTTING VS. PANTSING YOUR WAY TO A 5-FIGURE BOOK (LIBBIE HAWKER)

WHO'S LIBBIE?

Libbie writes historical and literary fiction featuring complex characters and rich details of time and place. Although the majority of her books are self-published, she also partners with Lake Union Publishing on select titles. Libbie's writerly influences are varied, and include Hilary Mantel, Vladimir Nabokov, Annie Dillard, Michael Ondaatje, George R. R. Martin, songwriter Neko Case, and mixed-media storyteller Chris Onstad, among others. She has held a broad and bizarre range of "day jobs" while pursuing a career as a novelist. Included among these are zoo keeper, show dog handler, bookseller, and yarn dyer.
Connect with Libbie at www.facebook.com/libbie.hawker.

THE GOLDMINE

Alinka: Libbie! You are a bestselling fiction and non-fiction author, and as such you have some secrets that we want you to spill. What we want to know is, what are the secrets to plotting versus pantsing your way to a five figure book? Because you've done both.

Libbie: I think the biggest secret to writing a book that's going to be commercially successful like that is making sure you have everything organized before you begin. Of course that's not the case for every author. Some people really can just write a really killer book without having to plot it out in advance, but that doesn't tend to be the case for most people.

Most of us sort of need that organization early on in the process.

Most of us sort of need that organization early on in the process, so that we can be sure we're using our time as efficiently as possible, because you know, time is money. If you spend months and months writing a bunch of stuff that you have to delete later on, because it just doesn't fit in with the overall plot of your book, the overall arc of your story, you've spent a lot of time that you could be getting [recouped 00:01:07] in book sales.

Yeah, making sure you have an efficient process from the beginning, and also making sure the structure you use for the story is going to be one that's very compelling to readers and really draws them in and makes them excited to keep reading the book, is going to be crucial to building a commercially successful story.

Alinka: Shall we divide it into fiction and non-fiction?

Libbie: Sure, you can.

Alinka: All right, so let's talk about fiction first. How do you work? How do you suggest that authors work to create a successful book?

Libbie: If your goal for that particular book is that you want it to be commercially successful and it's not a project of the heart or something that you want to do for creative or artistic reasons, my suggestion is always that people outline from the beginning, and that you specifically structure your outline to focus on the character arc. Instead of focusing on like really exciting parts of the plot or the rampaging dinosaurs as I said in my book, 'Take Off Your Pants'. Instead of focusing on these external things that are happening sort of outside of your character's personal experience, by focusing on what your character is going through and what they're trying to achieve within themselves and overcome, that hero's journey that you always hear about in literature courses and whatnot, you're really connecting with readers on this sort of primal, instinctive level, to where we respond to that so strongly.

We're social animals, we are really drawn to other people in most cases. When we see a person who is struggling with something and trying to achieve something that we deem noble or valuable or worthy, we really get invested in that. We want to see them succeed. By putting the character's internal struggle as a sort of the central focus of your book, no matter what else is going on plot-wise, as long as you have that central personal struggle that they're facing, you're kind of putting a secret little like magic hook in there that sort of holds the reader right through there, and doesn't let them let go of the book.

Alinka: We should focus on character arc, the hero's journey, rather than the plot?

Libbie: Right, and the plot is also important, that adds a lot of unique elements that maybe somebody can't find in another book. Like maybe it's a really cool space exploration story in addition to this really great character story, but that character story is what's going to suck in readers and really lock them into the story, and make it difficult for them to put it down and walk away from it. I think that's what really leads to a lot of financial success as a writer, you want to make people feel like they can continue to connect to your characters and your stories over and over again, no matter what else is going on in that story.

That's what really leads to a lot of financial success as a writer, you want to make people feel like they can continue to connect to your characters and your stories over and over again, no matter what else is going on in that story.

If they come to your books because they love sci-fi space exploration stories, and then you decide to write this other thing that's more kind of a like a Tolkien-esque fantasy or something, they'll probably trust you more and give it a shot, even though it's not what they normally read, if they know that they can always connect to your characters and feel an identification with what ... Not an identification, an identity with what's going on with those characters in your book.

Alinka: Can you talk a little bit more about the hero's journey? How do you figure out what it should look like?

Libbie: Yeah, I'd actually distill it down even more than you'll find it distilled in books like 'The Hero's Journey', for example, or 'The Hero with a Thousand Faces'. I actually like to kind of condense it even more, into what I call the story core, which is like a five bullet point checklist you want to make sure you have organized in your head before you even start to write the book.

Every good, compelling story, whether it's a book, whether it's a movie, whether it's a really great essay-style article in a magazine, all of these things have five common, key criteria, that they all share in common. That's, number one you have a character, obviously. It's not much of a story if there's not someone to kind of watch go through this experience.

Number two, the character has to want something. There has to be something they're after. If it's just, you know, "This is my life, and I'm going through it and everything's fine," then there's no enough conflict for it to be interesting.

Alinka: No tension.

Libbie: Yeah, exactly, they have to have that tension. Number three, something has to stand in the way of the character achieving that goal easily. If it's just, "I have to check my mail to see if the check arrived," and they walk out to the mailbox and the check is in the mail, that's not interesting.

Alinka: You need an obstacle, a series of obstacles.

Libbie: Right, something has to stand in that character's way. Whether it's another character, an antagonist, or whether it's the environment they're in, like in the Martian, Andy Weir's book, or it's some kind of psychological block they've put up for themselves, sometimes they can be their own antagonist.

Number four, they have to fight against that force and try to overcome that obstacle.

Number five, they either succeed or fail. It's perfectly valid to have a character fail within the context of a book. I hope this isn't a spoiler for anyone if I talk about Ned Stark in Game of Thrones. He clearly was going on this hero's journey, many people who first started reading that book expected him to be like the big hero who saved the day, because the signals of the hero's journey were so clear. He did not succeed in the end and that's perfectly valid. It can still make for a very compelling story.

Alinka: It got to that point, that was so…

Libbie: Sorry.

Alinka: Such a sad moment. Yeah, what do you think, how do you think readers react to a book that doesn't have the happy ending? Do you think it's a good commercial strategy or it depends on something?

Libbie: It really depends on a couple of different factors. First of all you have to take into consideration what readers expect within your genre. A book that doesn't have a happy ending is not going to fly in romance. Those readers, it's all about getting to a happy ending for them. That happy ending is what they expect out of that book.

In another genre a happy ending might actually kind of buck the trends, and it might be so weird that people are like, "What's going on here? What is this?" I write a lot of literary fiction. That's usually about kind of big issues that people struggle with internally. There are seldom clearly unambiguously happy endings in that genre. Usually an ending is kind of a mix of happy and sad.

It really depends on what your genre expectations are. It also kind of depends on what brand you've built for yourself. If you have built up a brand like that thus far, if you're kind of established in your career and you usually do happy endings and your readers kind of expect that, it might not be wise to deviate from that too many times, or too dramatically. On the other hand, if your readers expect you to deliver these shocking, not so happy endings, like George R. R. Martin, maybe you want to keep doing that, because that's what they expect at that point. It depends, you're going to have to kind of analyse your genre and your own books and your own readers' expectations before you can make that decision.

Alinka: Okay. You said that you're a plotter.

Libbie: Yes.

Alinka: How do you, you do an outline ... How do you create that outline? How much time does it take for you to create it? How closely do you stick to it?

Libbie: Personally I stick to my outlines very closely. That's not necessary for everybody. If you kind of do a sketchier outline and it just sort of acts as a general kind of guidepost to get you through the book, that's totally cool too. That can still be very effective in helping you maintain your time efficiently and still stick to the guide that's going to create a compelling book for you.

Personally, I find it useful to really get specific and my outlines and to stick to them very closely. Generally it takes me, by this point in my career, because I've written and outlined so many books, I'm working on my 29th novel right now.

Alinka: [crosstalk 00:08:55]

Libbie: Yeah. I've written so many that now I kind of have it honed a little bit and I can write an outline in like one to two hours, for a book that's going to be 90-130,000 words.

Alinka: Wow.

Libbie: When you're first-

Alinka: Incredible!

Libbie: Yeah, [crosstalk 00:09:09] it's like riding a bike, it's really-

Alinka: Some people say that it takes them months to create the outline.

Libbie: It can, to start out with. It's a skill, it's storytelling. Outlining is really just distillation of storytelling.

Outlining is really just distillation of storytelling.

Storytelling is a skill that you have to learn and practice and build up over time. It's not something that you can just pull out of the air and ta-da, you can do it perfectly! It's something you should expect to put a little bit of investment into before you can get it down.

that's what really leads to a lot of financial success as a writer, you want to make people feel like they can continue to connect to your characters and your stories over and over again, no matter what else is going on in that story.

It may be that starting out it takes you a week to get your outline to a point where you like it and where you feel comfortable with it. Maybe it takes longer than that, but every time you outline another book, it's going to come together a little bit faster, because you start to sort of pick up these elements of story that are key in al stories, almost by instinct. You're like, you'll just kind of, without even having to analyze it, you'd like, "Oh! I need an antagonist to come in right here. This is a point where I should have like a little plot twist that shows up." You'll just sort of develop that instinct for it and it'll just come together much quicker.

Alinka: What does your outline look like? Do you do like an Excel spreadsheet, where you say, "Okay, so this is like the halfway point and this is the mid-point, the halfway point, is the same thing as the mid-point, and this is where there should be a big problem." Do you have this sort of structure and then next to it you write what exactly is happening? How do you do that?

Libbie: I don't do that personally. I don't go based on like, "I'm at 30% of my book now, I need to have this type of thing happen here, and at 60% this type." A lot of other writers use that and succeed. I haven't found that it works for me personally. I've developed a method, which I detail in my book, 'Take Off Your Pants', so if other people want to try it out for themselves, they can try it too.

I start with, I outline those five bullet points that I talked about before as kind of my story core, so I have my basic guideline of like, "All right, what's the main focus of this story?" From there I'll sort of envision a picture in my head, like it's a little movie playing, what the opening scene is going to be, what's going to be the inciting event for this character, what do I need to have happen to her in order to set her on this path where she'll face this particular antagonist I've picked out, and where eventually these conflicts will lead to this type of conflict that I've detailed in my story core. Where it will eventually get her to this point that I am envisioning as her final sort of destination in her character journey and in the plot itself.

I actually start with, "My opening scene is this," and I write that out and then, "The antagonist appears at this point. This event that's happening in her life, or whatever, she encounters her antagonist." Then I'll sort of detail, "Okay, next she's going to try to get this goal that she wants to achieve, but she's going to come up against this problem." Usually I have my characters go through at least three attempts to achieve their goal and then get thwarted in that.

Then I actually have, a really crucial character I found, in my books and in an a lot of other stories too, is an ally. They have this friend or a family member or somebody who's important to them on a personal level. It's this person who has emotional leverage over your main character. When they start to kind of turn away from the true path of their hero's journey because they get so discouraged by all this stuff, their ally steps back in and says, "No! You have to get back in and fight! You've got to fix this and finish this quest and get it done!"

I have that point where I outline where my ally steps in and kind of what they say in general terms that can force this character back on their path. Then they have sort of the big climactic battle, which is in my books, since I write a lot of historical fiction and literary fiction, is not usually literally a battle. It's more of an emotional struggle, where they finally confront all their problems head on.

At the end of that big confrontation, that enables them to finally achieve this internal change that they're looking for. Then in concert with the internal change they also achieve this external goal, or sometimes they don't achieve that external goal. They arrive at this final scene of their book, where you sort of see in this big grand picture like, "Ah! It all comes together!"

That's just kind of how I do it. I take what my character needs to change within themselves and how they keep sort of butting heads with this antagonist, until they finally just deviate off the path, get steered back on by their ally, and then ta-da! The big climactic final scene! That's kind of how my books come together.

It's a simple enough style of storytelling that you can find it repeated in stories from every culture around the world. It's very basic, it's very kind of primal, I guess you could say. It really speaks to us on a simple, kind of baseline level. It really reaches into human hearts and kind of grabs hold of you and goes, "Oh! This is an important story!" You can make it more elaborate, you can make it more dramatic if you want to. Or you can keep it a real simple kind of tale of this person who just keeps trying to do something and failing, and finally they get the but kicked into it and they make it happen. [crosstalk 00:14:06]

Alinka: You make it seem so easy.

Libbie: Once you start doing it it is pretty easy. Once you start putting it together you're like, "Oh, yeah." You can kind of see these logical ways where a character's action leads to this logical consequence, and that consequence leads to another logical thing they can try to do. It just sort of pings back and forth between what's logical and rational for a character to attempt in that situation, within that world that you've set up for them. It's a lot easier than people think it is.

It's also, it's tough to do it first because you'd never done it before. Like anything else you've never done before it can be a little bit tricky and intimidating to start. Once you do it, I think people will be surprised at how easy it actually is to plan a book before you write it.

Alinka: It's impossible to do until it's done.

Libbie: Yes, but then once you've done it one time it's way easier the next time.

Alinka: Yeah. Do you do research for your books and how much time does that take you?

Libbie: Yeah, I do a lot of research for my books, because writing historical fiction, the research has to be a big part of it. That's one of the tropes I guess, if you will. Historical fiction readers want to see a lot of historical detail from that era and that setting incorporated into the story. They want to pick up all these little tidbits of what people wore and what they were eating, and what political issues were going on in the background. If you don't have those in there, and if they're not accurate, [oh 00:15:26], look out! Readers are very sharp about this stuff in this genre.

I do a lot of research for my books. Research can kind of be like a sinkhole too, it can distract you from doing the actual writing. You can get so sucked into it and then so hung up on whether you've got everything right, that you forget to write, or you just avoid writing because it becomes so intimidating, because you're like, "Oh my god, I'm going to get it wrong!"

Alinka: When do you do that? During the plotting? During the outlining part or while you're writing and you're interrupting yourself? How does it work?

Libbie: It's a balance of doing during specific research time that I set aside for myself, and interrupting myself occasionally to pick up minor details. What the overall preparation for a historical novel looks like for me is, I have specific writing time that I set aside every day. During that time I do nothing else but write.

Then during my free time during the day, when I would normally be reading like really good novels my friends wrote or something cool I found on BookBub, instead I'm reading tons and tons of non-fiction which relates to books I plan to write at some point in the future. Right now I'm really immersed in reading about the 16th century Ottoman empire, because I'm thinking about maybe doing some novels on that at some point in the future, but I don't have a set date for any of that yet. I'm not even sure I'm going to write it, but I need to prepare for it now if I'm going to, so I'm reading all these biographies and historical accounts of the era and whatnot. That's how I spend my free time.

When I know a setting for a book well enough that I can write a complete outline and get all of the aspects of that setting into the outline, [dur 00:17:10] going to play directly on that character's personal journey, that's when I stop doing my specific research on that era. When I know enough about the Ottoman empire to be able to plot a coherent story of somebody who's living in the Ottoman empire, then I'm done. I don't dedicate any more reading time to that particular subject.

At that point I'll outline the book, and then when I'm ready to start working on that book, which might be the next day or it might be next year, whenever I can pull that one out and start actually working on it. Then I just follow my outline and I just go along, I write out the scenes that I've kind of planned for myself.

I'll come across little bits and pieces that I know need to be injected in there, but maybe I didn't pick up specifically during that research, so what would somebody's shoes have looked like in this era? Or how would they have fixed their hair to go to a party? When I hit those points in my manuscript, I actually just type little brackets, those little angular brackets around stuff.

I'll be tying along like, "Ugh, she walked into the feast hall, wearing her," bracket, whatever she would have worn, close bracket. Then I'll just keep up going on with the scene, so I don't stop myself. Then when I get to a point when it's time to do revisions I do a 'Find and replace' search for brackets. I'll go through and pick up anything that I now need to go back and do slightly more in-depth research on. I'll just really quickly plug those things in. I'll go back, I'll take [crosstalk 00:18:30]

Alinka: That's really smart. A really smart [crosstalk 00:18:31], really smart advice.

Libbie: Yeah, It works really well, I [crosstalk 00:18:32] go back [crosstalk 00:18:33] and I'm like, "Ah! I need to figure out what a noble woman would have worn in this time and era." I do that research on Google and go, "There we go. Bingo!" Put it in, move on to the next one.

That's how I've streamlined the otherwise massive time-suck that can be writing historical fiction.

Alinka: Yeah. It's awesome. How many novels a year are you able to produce?

Libbie: It has increased every year since I have started writing full time. Which is good, I guess you want to keep growing your business if you're going to own a business.

Alinka: Right.

Libbie: I may have reached maximum saturation, because in 2016 I wrote 12 books.

Alinka: Wow!

Libbie: [crosstalk 00:19:10]

Alinka: That's incredible all 100,000 word novels?

Libbie: No, no, not all of them. Thank goodness. I mean, if I really wanted to drive myself crazy I probably could have written 12 90-100,000 word novels. A lot of them were novellas and a lot of those were actually for one of my other pen names, which is urban fantasy. Those are less research intensive, you can make up a lot of stuff, because it's fantasy, you know? Whatever rules you want to put into that world. They were much quicker to write, and simpler, and they were shorter. They're like 50,000 short novels or novellas.

I did write some pretty big beasts during that year too. Like one of my books was 130,000 words. One of them I got like 85,000 on that one. I've written some big books this year, but I'm now at the point, I guess, where I'm cranking out like a book a month. Ugh. I don't want to keep producing at that rate if I don't have to, because it's a lot of work. It's very busy.

I'd like to get down to like six books a year. I think that's ideal. It's a nice balance of like-

Alinka: [crosstalk 00:20:07] your retirement?

Libbie: Yeah, yeah. It's a nice balance of like maintaining profits, but also enjoying your life. [crosstalk 00:20:13]

Alinka: Yeah. Do you think series, do you produce series? Produce, do you write series, or you think single books?

Libbie: I have found that series are a much, much better use of my time. The return on investment, on time investment that I put into a series is much greater than the return on time investment that I put into a standalone book. Even though I can write six standalone novels in the same amount of time it takes me to write two trilogies, I see more profits from the two trilogies than I see from six standalones.

The return on investment, on time investment that I put into a series is much greater than the return on time investment that I put into a standalone book.

I have made it my goal from this point forward to release at least one trilogy per year, just because it keeps the money coming in. Series are a powerful marketing tool. You grab somebody with that first book and then they really want to keep finding out what happens to those characters. You might as well, if your goal is to become a five figure author, or to write a five figure book, you might as well take advantage of the sort-of built in hook that's in a series and use that to your advantage. It is really a powerful tool.

Alinka: Yeah. When I said series you said trilogies. I actually heard that the latest data from Amazon is that the series that sell most are trilogies, so that you get all these incremental sales, up till the third book. Then from the fourth book it sort of drops. Yeah, trilogies is what sells right now, and it's been selling for a while now.

Libbie: Right, yeah, that [crosstalk 00:21:44]

Alinka: Yeah, at least when you [crosstalk 00:21:44] marketing-wise as well, but you know [crosstalk 00:21:47]

Libbie: Yeah, yeah. Definitely. Yeah, there are some genres where they really welcome, the readers really want more like open-ended series. That's like cozy mysteries and stuff like that, where you have the same character in each book, but it's a different story in each book. She's following a new mystery, or this detective is going after a new criminal in each book. It's still the same guy, it's technically still a series, but it's kind of just like a bunch of linked standalones. Those type of genres really welcome longer running series that go for 20, 30, 100 books. A lot of other genres like sci-fi or fantasy, or historical fiction, a trilogy or maybe four books tends to be more profitable.

Alinka: This is awesome. We know what to do with fiction, what about non-fiction? How do you ... I mean, you wrote an excellent book for authors. How did you create it?

Libbie: I created it basically by kind of seeing that there was a need for that. I was receiving a lot of emails from other authors, asking me how they could improve their productivity and sort of get to the point where I was in my career, where they could write full time. I found that the more I would talk to them about what their situation was like and what their writing process was like, I was finding more and more that there was this lack of knowledge among them, about the benefits that outlining could bring to their business model.

That's why I wrote it, to kind of try to teach as many other authors as I could that, "Hey, this is what worked really well for me. I can't necessarily say it's going to work that well for you, you've got to try it, but this is why it works and this is how it works for me." In my experience, the key to having a successful non-fiction book is first of all, identifying what that market is for it, and why there's a need in that market for the advice that you can give.

Then once you understand how to effectively give something that will kind of fill that hole in that market, then you can really market directly to those people who are looking to that specific answer to these questions they have. I mean, I think if you were just to do a very open-ended kind of, "This is how to write a book," type of a non-fiction book, it could be useful to some people, but unless it addresses a really specific question people have, it's going to be a lot more difficult to find the individual readers who need that information.

Alinka: Yeah, so you did something really savvy, that a savvy business person does. You-

Libbie: [crosstalk 00:24:11]

Alinka: -understood who your market is, what your market is and what they want. You niched it down and you created what they wanted. You answered that specific need. Can you tell me how you came up with the title?

Libbie: Take Off Your Pants! It's kind of a funny title, I know. I came up with the title because there's a saying among people who write fiction, it's the most popular question that gets asked on writing forums, "Are you a plotter or a pantser?" Pantsing refers to flying by the seat of your pants, or in other words, just making it up as you along.

There are these two kind of general approaches. You can sort of divide up most fiction writers into these two camps of people who plot things out in advance with an outline and people who just make it all up as they go along and fly by the seat of their pants, and we call them pantsers. Take Off Your Pants is the sort of call to arms to challenge people who have always pantsed before to get rid of their pants entirely and try a totally new method. That is my title in a nutshell.

Alinka: It's an incredible title and it definitely draws a lot of attention. When I first saw it was a book for authors, "I need to see what this is all about." Yeah, when you explain the whole philosophy behind it, it really makes sense. It's excellent marketing strategy to get people to notice and the book.

Libbie: Thank you. I've actually, in my experience, I think titles and covers of books are incredibly important to financial success of them. Whether you're writing for a non-fiction audience or a fiction audience, I really don't think the importance of those two factors can ever be overstated. I think titles and covers sell more books than the books themselves do.

Alinka: Now that you mentioned this, do you have a title before you start writing your book, or does it come later, after you've written it?

Libbie: I've had that happen both ways sometimes. Often I have a title in advance, sometimes I even will come with just, like a phrase will pop into my head and I'll be like, "Oh! That would make such a good book title!" Just write it down in a file and hopefully use it later in the future. I've only done that with one title that just popped into my head, I later found a book for it that matched it. Often times I'll be like part way through the book, and I'll kind of write a phrase or something, or come up with an image in that book, and I'll be like, "Ah, there's the title that I need for that book." I'll just kind of stick that on and get rid of the working title I had been using.

When you're trying to think of what's going to work for a title you really have to pay close attention to genre conventions. What's currently selling books well in your genre?

It's very rare that I'll get to the end of the book and then be like, "Oh, I still don't have a title for this, I've got to come up with something," but it has happened on occasion, and I've had to just sort of brainstorm and kind of make a list of what's going to work. When you're trying to think of what's going to work for a title you really have to pay close attention to genre conventions. What's currently selling books well in your genre?

Don't look at other genres because you're going for a totally different audience. If you're writing romance, look at the best selling romance books and follow those charts for two or three months if you can. Really pay attention to what style of title is attracting readers, what books are hanging up in the bestseller charts for quite a while, and note the similarities between those titles. How do they speak to that group of readers? What kind of messages are they conveying?

You really have to pay attention and kind of do your market research, because your title and your cover are such crucial aspects to selling that book. You can't mess them up or you're going to have a flop.

Alinka: How did you have them envisioned before you start writing? While you're doing your outline? Or you follow the charts, as you're writing and while you're following the charts you look at the covers? How do you get them done?

Libbie: Both of those. I constantly kind of look at the charts in my genre anyway, just because it's exciting, and it's fun, and I like to see who's selling what. Yeah, I'll really keep track of what's selling well in books currently. I use Pinterest a lot, I have like private Pinterest boards where [fin 00:28:13] going to be doing a book on whatever subject in the near future, I'll lock down a Pinterest board so only I can see it, and I'll go and pin all the book covers I can find, that might grab that audience for that book. Then I'll look at them later, when it's time to design my cover and I'll kind of analyse, like, "All right, what do all these have in common? Is it the color scheme? Is it the way things are laid out? Is it the style of font?" Whatever. I do that a lot.

I also while, I'm really like a cover nerd, I have like an addiction to covers, it's terrible. I make a lot of my own cover art too. I'm fortunate to have some background experience in working with Photoshop and doing some design stuff professionally. I'm able to make a lot of my own covers, or at least do the typesetting on them sometimes.

While I'm working on a book, or like if I just outline a book that I know I'm going to write two or three years down the road, I'll make a cover for it too. It's really terrible.

Alinka: Awesome.

Libbie: Will just stick it in my file. Then usually by the time I actually get that book done and put it out cover trends have totally changed, so I have to remake it a little bit anyway, or like alter the design. Yeah, they're important enough to the success of a book that I think it's worth really watching those trends carefully, and always kind of having some idea in your head about what you would like to see for this book's cover as you're working on it.

That way, by the time you get to the phase where you're working with the designer, or if you design them yourself or whatever, you have a really clear picture of what you can describe to that person and how you can work together to kind of make that into a reality.

Alinka: This is fantastic. You're really business savvy and you understand your market and what they want, and you produce what that market wants. Obviously you're a successful bestselling author. I really loved what you shared and so many really concrete tips that people can start applying right now. This was fantastic, thank you to Libbie.

I know that a lot [crosstalk 00:30:02]

Libbie: Thanks for having me.

Alinka: Yeah, of course. Another, I know that a lot of people will want to connect with you, so how can they do that?

Libbie: If you want to connect with me on Facebook, that's probably the best way. I'm Libbie Hawker, L-I-B-B-I-E H-A-W-K-E-R. If you're just looking to pick up my book and learn more about outlining, you can find it on Amazon or other places where you like to buy e-books. Just go search for Take Off Your Pants. Hopefully it's the only book that comes up with that title, because I don't want to know what the other books are about.

Alinka: This is awesome, Libbie.

Libbie: Thanks for having me.

Alinka: Before we end, just one more thing. Our attendees are action-takes and you've delivered a lot of great content, but if you can give people just one, one thing that they can do right now to make sure that they have the highest chance to produce that five figure book, and be a five figure author, what would that be?

Libbie: I would say challenge yourself to try outlining your next book, or if you're already working on a book currently, challenge yourself to try outlining even the next few chapters before you write them. Just plot them a little bit in advance and see if it makes a difference in how quickly you can get through those scenes.

Alinka: Awesome. All right. We'll be doing that right now. Thank you so much, Libbie.

Libbie: Thank you, it was really fun.

WERE YOU PAYING ATTENTION?

Q1: How do you create a commercially successful fiction book?

Q2: Which element should you focus on when writing fiction?

Q3: What leads to financial success as a writer?

Q4: What are the five criteria the most successful stories have in common?

Q5: What does having a happy ending vs. a sad ending depend on?

Q6: What definition for outlining does Libbie give?

Q7: How many attempts does Libbie have the character go through before they achieve their goal?

Q8: What's an important character to create that has leverage over your main character?

Q9: What's Libbie's technique to keep writing without interrupting herself to do research?

Q10: What brings the best return on investment?

Q11: How do you create a good non-fiction book?

Q12: What is incredibly important to a books financial success?

Q13: What do you have to pay close attention to when choosing the title?

Q14: How does Libbie come up with the cover?

CHALLENGE

Challenge yourself on outlining your next book. Or if you're already working on a book currently, challenge yourself to try outlining even the next few chapters before you write them. Just plot them a little bit in advance and see if it makes a difference in how quickly you can get through those scenes.

THE GOLDEN NUGGETS

Q1: How do you create a commercially successful fiction book?

A1: Outline from the beginning.

Q2: Which element should you focus on when writing fiction?

A2: On your character, on the hero's journey.

Q3: What leads to financial success as a writer?

A3: Making people feel like they can continue to connect to your characters and your stories over and over again, no matter what else is going on in that story.

Q4: What are the five criteria the most successful stories have in common?

A4:

1) You have a character.
2) The character has to want something.
3) Something has to stand in the way of the character achieving that goal easily.
4) They have to fight against that force and try to overcome the obstacle.
5) They either succeed or fail.

Q5: What does having a happy ending vs. a sad ending depend on?

A5:

1) What readers expect within your genre.
2) What brand you've built for yourself.

Q6: What definition for outlining does Libbie give?

A6: Outlining is distillation of storytelling.

Q7: How many attempts does Libbie have the character go through before they achieve their goal?

A7: At least three.

Q8: What's an important character to create that has leverage over your main character?

A8: An ally.

Q9: What's Libbies technique to keep writing without interrupting herself to do research?

A9: Brackets!

> (I'll come across little bits and pieces that I know need to be injected in there, but maybe I didn't pick up specifically during that research, so what would somebody's shoes have looked like in this era? Or how would they have fixed their hair to go to a party? When I hit those points in my manuscript, I actually just type little brackets, those little angular brackets around stuff.
> I'll be tying along like, "Ugh, she walked into the feast hall, wearing her," bracket, whatever she would have worn, close bracket. Then I'll just keep up going on with the scene, so I don't stop myself. Then when I get to a point when it's time to do revisions I do a 'Find and replace' search for brackets. I'll go through and pick up anything

that I now need to go back and do slightly more in-depth research on. I'll just really quickly plug those things in.)

Q10: What brings the best return on investment?

A10: A series.

Q11: How do you create a good non-fiction book?

A11: By seeing that there is a need for it.

Q12: What is incredibly important to a books financial success?

A12: Titles and covers.

Q13: What do you have to pay close attention to when choosing the title?

A13: On what's currently selling well in our genre.

Q14: How does Libbie come up with the cover?

A14: She studies best-selling covers in here genre.

HOW TO CRAFT A BOOK IDEA THAT SELLS AND SUCCEED AS AN AUTHOR (NINA AMIR)

WHO'S NINA?

Inspiration-to-Creation Coach, Nina inspires people to combine their purpose and passion so they Achieve More Inspired Results. She motivates writers and non-writers to create publishable and published products and careers as authors as well as to achieve their goals, fulfill their purpose and live inspired lives. The author of "How to Blog a Book: How to Write, Publish and Promote Your Work One Post at a Time" (Writer's Digest Books), Amir is a nonfiction editor, book proposal and blogging consultant, blog-to-book coach, and book and author coach with more than 33 years of experience in the publishing field.
Connect with Nina at http://ninaamir.com or http://writenonfictionnow.com.

THE GOLDMINE

Alinka: Nina, as an author with more than 33 years in the publishing industry, you obviously know all the secrets. Please, tell us how can we craft a book idea that sells and succeed as an author?

Nina Amir: That's a big question with a fairly long answer, but I'll try to keep it concise. The main thing I think, and this is how

Traditional publishers, [...] require a business plan. We call it a book proposal.

I work with my clients, is to begin with a plan, a business plan. It doesn't matter if you self-publish or you traditionally published, if you go by the model used by traditional publishers, you're going to have more success. That's that they require a business plan. We call it a book proposal.

Even self-published authors need to have this kind of business plan because what it does is it helps you evaluate your market and the competition so that you can actually craft a book that's unique and necessary not only in your market with your readers, but also in the category where your book is going to be sold. What I suggest is that you sit down and write a pitch for your book and a list of benefits, so what you think your book is going to be.

It's a small summary that's compelling that you would tell somebody if they said, "What's your book about?" You would say, "This is what it's about." It would tell them that it's for them and that it has benefit. The list of benefits is helpful when they say, "Tell me more," you have a few more things you could say. This is a start to your book. This is the kernel of your idea really.

Then when you add in market research, which is who are my readers, what do they want, what do they need, where do they live, how can I find them, all that kind of information, to the competitive analysis, which is what other books exist already that somebody might buy instead of mine, or even complementary books. What books would they buy in addition to mine?

You then begin to be able to craft that kernel of an idea into something that's much more saleable, much more marketable because it's unique and necessary, both in the category where it'll sell and with the readers so those are the big parts of actually creating the idea that will sell, but beyond that I always suggest that authors create their table of contents and then go a step farther and actually do chapter summaries which would be required in a book proposal.

I suggest this for everyone, fiction and non-fiction, everything I'm saying I would tell anyone who's writing in any genre. Your chapter summaries, if it's just for you, if you're an indie author, you would just go ahead and you might do bulleted items, "These are the things I'm going to cover," and maybe those become your chapter subheadings if you're writing non-fiction.

See whether that content is going to sync up with your market.

Then if you're going to go a little farther, you would actually write a few sentences about each one of these bullet points. Now when you're done with that, you can actually see whether that content is going to sync up with your market, with the competitive analysis you did with the pitch you wrote and the benefits you said you were going to offer. If all that syncs up, there's what I call the "precious moment" when you say, "Ah, that's it. I have a marketable book idea, a really good book idea, and not only that, I'm ready to write. I know exactly what I have to write. There's no sitting in front of the computer and wondering. Every day, I sit down, I have my chapter summaries and I'm ready to go."

Now, in my book The Author Training Manual, I talk about one other step to this process. Well, actually two. One is the evaluation of yourself. What people forget to do is to ask themselves if they're prepared to be an author, if they have what it takes, and that's not just the desire or the ability to write but are you willing to do all the things necessary because today, it's not just about writing. It's about building author platform and it's about promotion and doing all the things that, if you're an indie publisher, that you have to do like manage a team. You're going to have to manage editors and designers and many, many things.

Plus we all need to have websites so if you're not willing to do these things, then it becomes very hard to succeed as an author. You have to have that willingness. I talk about author attitude, so this is part of the evaluation. Do you have the willingness to do what it takes? Are you optimistic? Because if you're pessimistic, you're going to have a very hard time. Pessimists fail more often than optimists. Optimists succeed more than pessimists, so you want to be optimistic about this process.

You also want to be objective so you need to be able to take objective criticism of your work. You need to be objective about yourself. You need to be objective about your idea and whether or not it really is marketable, so you need to see it through the lens of perhaps an acquisitions editor or an agent, no matter which way you want to publish. You need to be tenacious. You have to not give up. You have to refuse to fail, so these are all aspects of becoming a successful author.

The other thing that I didn't mention, one other step is actually promotion. You need actually a plan within a plan for your promotion. If you're not willing to do the promotion and if you don't have a strong promotion plan for your book, it's not going to sell no matter how good it is. That's a lot of stuff all wrapped up in one.

Alinka: Yeah. I love it, how structured you are about this. I have one question here. An author who's trying to get published traditionally would submit the book proposal first to an agent, right? He would be the first gatekeeper who decides whether he would try to get it sold or not. What about indie authors, do you recommend that they show their book proposal of their market research and all the elements that you talked about? Do you recommend that they verify it by showing it to somebody and if yes, who?

Nina Amir: It is a good idea because we're not always as objective as we would like to be. It can be hard for us to put ourselves in the shoes of an acquisitions editor, who's the person who acquires a manuscript for a publishing house, or an agent and to see through their eyes. There are several places where you can, there's some online sites, I can't think of the name right now, where you can actually post some work and get feedback.

If you go to conferences, it's a good idea to go to a conference and pitch, like a writer's conference and pitch to agents, see what they say. You can still self-publish. It doesn't matter. You don't even have to tell them that you plan to self-publish. Just see if they think your idea's marketable. Of course, you want a lot more analysis than just look at it. If it goes into a publishing house, there's a whole team of people who are evaluating, for instance your competitive titles to see how many books they've sold, how many copies they've sold because this is an indication of whether or not your book will sell.

Also there are a few places where you can actually hire an agent to look over something for you. Sometimes you can just contact an agent. I have a few agents that I send work their way for them just to evaluate in that manner. "Would you please look at this?" Just give the author some feedback. It's not about pitching you, it's just feedback on the business plan. Tell them that, they plan to self-publish and they just would like feedback on the business plan.

It's not really a book proposal at this point because it's not polished and ready to be dissected by someone on a really fine level because they want to be published. It's just been done for them. It's a sort of loose business plan, so you can give that to an agent and have them give you feedback.

Alinka: Perfect. Let's say that after a couple rounds of polishing, the thing is now, it's been positively reviewed by an agent or by an acquisitions editor and then you decide to self-publish. You're a certified high-performance coach. What is your advice for people to actually get the thing done once they already have a good idea and they did the ground work?

Nina Amir: That's a great idea because a lot of people get stuck at that point or before that point. A lot of aspiring authors talk a lot about being an author and don't write. Some of them won't do the business plan either because that's scary and it's business. They don't see it as a creative process, which it is. Anyway, so what they need to do is to first get very clear about their goals and their deadlines. What do they really want to accomplish and by when?

They've already gained a lot of clarity from the process of doing the business plan. They know exactly what they're writing. They're ready to go, so now they need to get clear about, "When do I want to have it done and how am I going to achieve that?" Some of that has to do with showing up every day at a specific time. Scheduling, blocking out time to write ever day, and then you show up there with the energy and the courage to do the work.

A lot of authors get stumped. They think that they have writer's block. They don't. They just have fear and it could be fear of putting their work out there, fear that it's not good enough, fear that it won't get read, fear that they'll be judged, lots of fears. You have to have courage to sit down, put the words on paper, and then to share them later on.

You also have to show up with the energy to do the work. A lot of times I think people show up their desk and they're lethargic, tired, they're not breathing so they're not oxygenating their brain, they're not drinking enough water so there's a whole physiological aspect to this of showing up with the energy to do the work because it takes a while to write the book anyway. You have to have that energy.

We talk about clarity, energy, and courage. Then, of course, there's productivity. You really have to begin to evaluate what helps you be more productive. Some tools as a high-performance coach that I recommend are to first of all come with that energy but to trigger yourself. Come to the desk, do some deep breathing, maybe move your body a little bit, maybe do some affirmations or declarations of, "I'm ready. I can do this. I have a good idea. I'm a writer." Then sit down and write.

Write for a period of time, either 30 minutes or about 50 minutes and then take a break. This is another issue that a lot of writers have is they think, "Okay. I've sat down and I'm writing and I'm in the flow. I can't stop and I have to sit here for 3 hours until I finish." The fact is, at about 50 minutes, your productivity drops off, so you're better off setting a timer and getting up every 50 minutes and taking a break and getting another drink of water and taking some deep breaths so that you're giving your brain what it needs to be productive.

You're showing up like that on a consistent basis. That's going to help your productivity enormously. So will the clarity because you're not staring at the screen. You have these chapter summaries and you know what to write. You don't have to wonder about what to write. There's also some things about blocking time for research as opposed to writing. There are lots of productivity hacks out there.

Then last, I really think it's about influence, so these things that I've talked about are the 5 pillars of high performance: clarity, energy, courage, productivity, and influence. Influence, we talk a lot about influence in the writing world in terms of creating platform, that we need to influence our market so that they see us as an influencer, so that when we hold up a book and say, "Please buy my book, it was just released," they actually listen to us. They trust us, they know us, they like us, and they do what we say hopefully.

There's also influence over yourself and so when you're done with that business plan, you have to be able to influence yourself to sit down and write. You have to influence yourself to build platform. There's this whole other level of being persuasive and that has to do with persuading yourself to do what's necessary and to be willing to do it and to do it eagerly because all the things you're doing are contributing to you being a successful author.

Alinka: This is excellent advice Nina. I wanted to touch a little bit upon writer's block. Obviously if you want to write a book that sells and succeed as an author, you can't blame possible failure on the fact that you're blocked. You mentioned a few tricks that authors can use to not to suffer from writer's block, but can we go a little bit deeper into that? What is it really and how can people get some more tips to overcome it?

Nina Amir: The first thing I would say is stop calling it writer's block because then you're giving it power. You're saying, "I have writer's block." It's like, "I have cancer," God forbid. It's, "I have this thing that is a problem in my life, and it's stopping me from writing." Stop giving it that kind of power. It is not writer's block. You are not blocked, you just have something going on emotionally that is stopping you from writing which is usually fear.

Stop calling it writer's block because then you're giving it power.

You could spend some time figuring our what you're afraid of and evaluating that and coming up with affirmations. All that's fine and it works. I suggest just write it because that is the biggest chewer for not writing is to write. We always talk about writer's write. Stop saying you're blocked.

Sit down and write anything. Just start writing because once you're in the action of writing, you're going to build some momentum and you're going to see that you're not blocked, you can do this.

The more you think about being blocked, the more you get blocked. The other thing you can do is to visualize. "I just released a book," create a visualization for writers. Visualization is enormously powerful. Athletes all over the world use it as well as actors and musicians. They visualize. Athletes are always a great example, so they visualize themselves, let's say, running a marathon. It's a marathon runner and he or she visualizes the race beginning and having a good start, and they visualize the middle where they start to struggle and how they're going to overcome that.

They begin to program themselves and their mind to overcome this tough part where they are tired and their legs are aching and their lungs, they don't feel like they can breathe. They program themselves to say, "I can do it," instead of "I can't do it." "I can do this. I can do it. I have the energy to go to the finish line," and they begin to generate that energy because we're like power plants. We can generate any emotion or energy or thought we want. We just have to decide what we want, so this is what they're doing and then they visualize themselves having that burst of energy at the very end of the race that send them forward past all the people who've been running ahead of them to win the race.

What's happening then as they're visualizing this? Their mind is actually triggering their muscles. Their muscles are firing just as if they were running the race, but they're also convincing their unconscious mind that they can do this, that they can do it, that they have the strategies to get through to the end of the race and to win it.

The more you visualize in this way, so if we talk now about writers visualize, "I sit down every day. I put my hands on the keyboard. I begin to write. I produce 1000 words every 50 minutes. I get up. I take a break. I come back. I do it again. By the time 3 hours have passed, I have almost 3000 words done, and I see myself doing this every day," we are not only triggering the muscles of typing on the computer or on the keyboard, but we're also triggering our brain that this is what we do and this is what we can do and we have the ability and we do it every day. Then when we sit down, it get easier. Those are 2 things I would suggest.

Alinka: Perfect. I love the visualization approach. I have a few questions about it. First one is, is there a time of day that is best to perform this visualization and how long should it last?

Nina Amir: There isn't any right time of the day to do it or best time. I think a good time is at night before you go to bed because you're giving yourself, you're programming yourself and your subconscious is going to dwell on this while you sleep. It's also a good thing to do first thing in the morning but you could do it anytime. If you feel like you're struggling to write, visualize. What was the second part of that question?

Alinka: I'm going to add it now. Do you recommend that we visualize an intermediate goal or the final goal? Would I be visualizing holding my book in my hands, or would I be visualizing that I'm going to be writing today the 3000 words, or both?

Nina Amir: You can do both, and you can do them separately or together. I think that if we're talking about productivity, then I would be visualizing those hands on the keyboard and a timer and a word counter and seeing myself really racking up the words every day and producing the manuscript, the pages, printed pages piling up every day, something along those lines. Then of course maybe at night I visualize the actual book in my hands.

Alinka: I love the visualizations. They do work.

Nina Amir: Yep.

Alinka: Nina, you are the Inspiration To Creation coach. Can you tell us a little bit about what that's about?

Nina Amir: Well, that came about because I really needed branding. A lot of authors do not think about branding themselves, but

I was one of those creative people who just created a bunch of things so I ended up with 4 or 5 websites, with blogs. Before we started this interview, you were saying that I was quite prolific. Well, I have all these blogs I have to keep up with. I felt like I was a ... the people saw me like a split personality. I had a blog, I'm blogging and blogging books and I have the blog on writing non-fiction.

Then I had one on personal development and practical spirituality. Then I even had one about boys who dance because my son is a dancer. It's like, "Who the heck is this person and where do I actually find them because she has so many websites?" So I had to do a branding exercise and one of the things I was asked to do was to ask all the people who knew me or who I'd worked with or who read my blogs, what I did for them. Every single one of them said I inspired them in some way.

Even how to blog a book was inspiring, which I didn't even see it that way. I knew that was something that needed to be in my branding and then when I looked at all the different blogs and all my different websites and the reason I was doing what I was doing in each case, it came down to that I wanted to help people create something. They were either creating a book and a blog or they were creating a career as a non-fiction author or they were creating ways to become their best self, to achieve their potential, fulfill their purpose, create the life they want, live fully, become professional dancers, everything was about creation so that's where Inspiration To Creation came from.

Alinka: [crosstalk 00:19:33]

Nina Amir: -acronym for my name, Achieve More Inspired Results For Amir [inaudible 00:19:39]. That all kind of came together but beyond that, what I was doing, what I really believe, and this is at the crux of the Inspiration To Creation branding, is I believe that if you combine your purpose with your passion, you're going to get inspired. When you're inspired, you will know what action to take.

It will be inspired action, so we combine our passion and our purpose and then we get inspired to inspire to action and that's when we achieve those inspired results because we're in that flow of inspiration. That's sort of the whole picture of that, and I have a book that will later come out of this that I had started long ago, so that's figured into it and even a coaching framework that I use around this whole topic.

Alinka: Yeah. Let's talk a little bit about your coaching. I'm really curious about the number on struggle that people come to you with and how do you help them?

Nina Amir: Number one struggle? I think probably the number one struggle is that they have an idea and they don't know what to do with it. They don't know how to structure the book. They don't know how to carry it out in a way that makes sense and they're also afraid that they'll do it and it won't be right or it won't sell. It's this whole idea of getting started, so that's where the plan comes back in because even though they don't get to write immediately, they go through this whole business planning process and when they're done with that, they have the structure for their book and they know how to get started.

They also know how to become an author. They know what's necessary to be an author, so I think that that's it. It goes back to maybe a bigger problem and that's that people decide they want to write a book and they have no idea really what it means to be an author, none. They have no idea about the publishing industry, how the publishing industry works, and so suddenly they're totally overwhelmed because they have to, if they want to ... Yeah, everyone says it's easy to self-publish.

Well, it's relatively easy but you have to know a lot of things. You still need to have a website. You need to build a platform and even if you're a novelist, you need to build a platform. You have to manage the team, like I said, designers. Suddenly it's like, "Oh, everyone said self-publishing was easy but there's way more to it than just putting words on paper and throwing them up on Amazon." I think that's a big part of it too.

Also for the one who want to traditionally publish, there's a lot to be done in order to be traditionally published, so that's I think the overriding thing is they just don't really understand the industry and what it means to be an author. Then secondary to that is, "I want to write a book and I have an idea, but I have no idea how to carry that out."

Alinka: How do you help these authors who come to you and they're so overwhelmed? How can they deal with it?

Nina Amir: We chunk it down. If they don't go through my author training process then we just chunk it down into small bite size pieces. They can do personalized coaching with me, so they'll come and they'll say, "Okay. I understand I have to have a website. Let's dig into that," and we make that into little itty bitty pieces. Sometimes I do a whole career plan with them and we look at ... because that's another big mistake that authors make, both indie and traditional, and both experienced and inexperienced authors.

They go into being an author without a big picture of where they're going. They go, "Oh, I have this one book idea and I know that I have to create a blog to promote that book. I need to be speaking on the topic," and all this stuff, "I need to get the book done and published," and they don't realize that there's another book that follows it and another one that follows that. Then they brand a website around one book.

Kind of like what happened to me with, well how to blog a book had to be that way but it's very easy to say, "Well, now I need 5 websites because I have 5 books," and so they're not looking ahead. I help them see their whole career plan starting with their values and their passion and their purpose and their goals and their interests and, "Now how many books are you going to write? What will they be about? What's the theme that runs through everything," and now we go and say, "Okay. Now we're ready to brand a website and start a blog and create a blog plan," and think even about monetization.

Are you going to create courses or will you speak or coach or what will you do and how is your promotion going to fit into that? That's one of the things I do with people is give them a big picture view of where they're going and how to get there but we have it in little tiny pieces that they can [inaudible 00:24:25] down and take action on. Did that make sense?

Alinka: Made absolute sense. I love it. Nina, you mentioned that you have different ideas, different websites. I know a lot of authors who write in different genres and they're not sure if they should bundle it all up in one hub or have various different websites that they run simultaneously. How did you deal with this issue?

Nina Amir: Well, initially I didn't. I didn't know what I know now, so I created a lot of websites, one for every topic. What I now recommend to authors is to do what I just said is to go through this sort of career planning process and decide how all their books are ties together, who they really are as an author. When somebody says, "Nina Amir, what is it she represents," kind of like a Nike or Levi's, Levi's are sturdy. You depend on your Levi's to hold up, so what is it that you as an author bring to the table? What's the benefit you're offering people?

Then to trade a website that encompasses everything you do, so that you don't have to have all these other ones. If you go to NinaAmir.com, you'll see that I haven't gotten rid of the other websites. I've just linked them there in a way that makes sense to what I do, to my overall umbrella. Take some time. My advice would be to take the time to think about the future. What other books are you going to write? What are the themes that run through them and then create a website that encompasses that?

Now it may be that you can't ... it may be that its' difficult to write about all your topics in one place because to have your website rise up in the search engine results pages, you need to be writing about one topic. The more you write about one topic, the more Google gets that that's what you write about so when somebody puts in a search into Google, they're going to show up on your site because Google knows that this is your area of expertise because you're adding new content to your blog all the time on that topic.

If you start writing about 5 topics because you have 5 books on different topics, it's going to work for you generally but it's not going to work to push you up in the search engine results pages and help you be more visible, to be discoverable. That's something to keep in mind that it could be that you have some interest to write, a topic you want to write about that's not going to fit into that umbrella but the more you can have an umbrella and come up with a blogging plan that encompasses all the books you want to write, in some way, that Google will get so that it's just one topic or related topics that go with one theme, that's going to help you the most.

Alinka: Yeah. What you did, you actually niched down your different interests and then linked them all in this one hub site. This way you get the best of both worlds because all your different interests have their website and they get the ranking. Then if somebody comes to your main websites, they can see what you're all about. This is a way to get out of this, which you very smartly did.

Nina Amir: Right. I recommend they do that umbrella site first because I did it backwards, but I teach what I've learned so [crosstalk 00:27:43]-

Alinka: Yeah, but there's sometimes we come up with something new that we want to experiment in different genre, so I think we need to be a little bit flexible and allow ourselves to experiment and to discover ourselves. It takes time, as you said. When we split it up into chunks, it is much easier. The discovery process is also process, right?

Nina Amir: Then we're creative people, so writer's tend to be creative and it may be that you have an idea that just doesn't fit under your umbrella. You're going to find the dancing blog, my son can dance, a link to it on my site but do I ever talk about that on that site? No. Rarely because that site is a site all its own as well. Because I'm helping create professional male dancers with that site, it still fits into the Inspiration To Creation idea or branding, but it's separate.

It could be you come up with something, you're writing romance and you suddenly decide you're going to do a non-fiction on dog training and that just doesn't fit into your author website which is about being a romance writer and the themes in your romance novels. You have to start something new, you do, but then you also have to be willing to do the work it takes to keep it up with more than one site if you pursue more than one idea in different genres because it's work.

Alinka: It is. Nina, this was fantastic. We've learned so much from you and no wonder, after all, a certified high-performance coach and the Inspiration To Creation coach, and you're an accomplished author with over 33 years of experience in the publishing industry. Is that right?

Nina Amir: It is.

Alinka: Nina, I'm sure with such a resume, people want to know a run to connect with you, so how can we do that?

Nina Amir: They can most easily just go to NinaAmir.com. N-I-N-A-A-M-I-R .com. As I said, that's my umbrella site. You can find links to all my blogs there. It's set up by different interests, blogging and blogging books, non-fiction writing, personal growth, so you can just click through and find the blog and find my products and services. There are some books there in the personal growth area, I have a few books that aren't on Amazon, but then all my books also are on Amazon. An easy way to get to them is booksbyninaamir.com.

Alinka: Perfect. One last thing. Our challenge participants are action takers, so can you just tell us one thing that people can do right now to make sure that they craft a book idea that sells?

Nina Amir: They can create a business plan. They can sort of force themselves to sit down and do the analysis, the evaluation of themselves and of their idea so that they do craft a book that will sell. A book that sells gets read and that's the point. We want our books to be read and if you're writing anything that's inspirational or motivational or self-help, or anything like that, when it gets read, you're making a positive and meaningful difference in the world.

For those who are writing non-fiction, they can go to my website writenonfictionnow.com, writenonfictionnow.com and they can download an ebook there that will help them structure their book. It's called the Inspiration To Creation's Guide To Writing A Non-Fiction Book and it's free. They can go there and at least learn a little bit about structuring their book which is going to help them get going on the whole planning process.

Alinka: Perfect. Thank you so much Nina.

Nina Amir: You're very welcome and thank you for having me on. I was honored.

WERE YOU PAYING ATTENTION?

Q1: What does Nina recommend you begin with?

Q2: How do you craft a book that's unique?

Q3: What two things should you write before you write the book?

Q4: What elements of market research does Nina list?

Q5: What is a competitive analysis?

Q6: What are the two characteristics of a book that sells?

Q7: What two elements should you create for your book proposal?

Q8: What is the "precious moment"?

Q9: What skills do indie authors need on top of writing?

Q10: What are the characteristics of a successful author?

Q11: How should you get feedback on your book proposal?

Q12: How do you make sure you get your book finished?

Q13: What are the five pillars of high performance?

Q14: How to deal with writer's block?

Q15: What's Nina's advice on dealing with overwhelm?

PS_BX06670878

CreateSpace
7290 Investment Drive Suite B
North Charleston, SC 29418

Log in to your account at www.createspace.com and "Contact Support."

03/14/2017 12:12:17 AM
Order ID: 163939445

Qty.	Item
	IN THIS SHIPMENT
1	5-Figure Author Challenge Playbook 1943386188

Q16: How do you deal with multiple niches/interests in terms of branding?

CHALLENGE

Create a business plan.

THE GOLDEN NUGGETS

Q1: What does Nina recommend you begin with?

A1: A business plan (a book proposal).

Q2: How do you craft a book that's unique?

A2: You evaluate your market and competition.

Q3: What two things should you write before you write the book?

A3:
1) A pitch.
2) A list of benefits.

Q4: What elements of market research does Nina list?

A4:

1) Who are my readers?
2) What do they want?
3) What do they need?
4) Where do they live?
5) How can I find them?

Q5: What is a competitive analysis?

A5: What other books exist already that somebody might buy instead of mine.

Q6: What are the two characteristics of a book that sells?

A6:

1) It's unique.
2) It's necessary.

Q7: What two elements should you create for your book proposal?

A7:

1) A table of contents.
2) Chapter summaries.

Q8: What is the "precious moment"?

A8: When you know that you have a marketable book idea because your content syncs up with your market.

Q9: What skills do indie authors need on top of writing?

A9:

1) Platform building.
2) Promotion.
3) Managing a team.
4) Creating a website.

Q10: What are the characteristics of a successful author?

A10:

1) Optimistic.
2) Objective.
3) Tenacious.

Q11: How should you get feedback on your book proposal?

A11:

1) Post online.
2) Pitch agents at conferences.
3) Hire an agent.

Q12: How do you make sure you get your book finished?

A12: You have to get very clear on your goals and deadlines. What do you want to accomplish and by when?

Q13: What are the five pillars of high performance?

A13:

1) Clarity.
2) Energy.
3) Courage.
4) Productivity.
5) Influence.

Q14: How to deal with writer's block?

A14:

1) Stop calling it "writer's block" and giving it power. Sit down and write anything.
2) Visualize.

Q15: What's Nina's advice on dealing with overwhelm?

A15: Chunk it down.

Q16: How do you deal with multiple niches/interests in terms of branding?

A16: Create niched down websites on your different interests and then link them all on one hub site.

THREE DANGEROUS MISCONCEPTIONS PREVENTING YOU FROM FINISHING YOUR BOOK (ANDREA CUMBO-FLOYD)

WHO'S ANDREA?

Andi is a writer, editor, and writing coach. She's the author of the best-selling "Discover Your Writing Self: 31 Days to Deeper Understanding of Who You Are as a Writer". Andi recognizes that One-size-fits-all writing advice doesn't work for anyone and she helps you discover who YOU are as writer: from your fears through reasons for writing to the best time and the ideal environment for your writing practice. If you feel overwhelmed or confused by all the writing advice out there, Andi will help you sort through it in a way that is authentic and genuine for you.
Connect with Andi at AndiLit.com/wdido.

THE GOLDMINE

Alinka: Andi, as best selling author of "Discover Your Writing Self", you are the absolutely best source for writers to understand the three dangerous misconceptions preventing people from finishing their book. Shall we jump right into and can you let us know what these misconceptions are?

Andi: Sure, so I'll give them all to you guys and then we'll talk about them in more detail. The first is this idea that perfect is possible, when it comes to writing a book. It's a huge misconception. The second is that later exists. This idea that you'll just get to it later is a huge misconception. The third is that your book in unimportant, that people don't care about it.

You can monetize done. You can't monetize perfect.

Those are the three things that I think a lot of people really struggle with, and so the first is perfect is possible. It's not, it's not possible in any of life, so why would it be possible in writing a book. It's not possible to do every bit of research you ever wanted to do for a book, because there's always going to be more. I just finished reading Stephen King's novel, 11/22/63, which is phenomenal by the way, and then I listened to his little epilogue about it, and he's like, "Sure, I got some stuff wrong, I could have done more research, I could have read more things", but it's one of the best novels I've ever read, so you're not going to get to perfect when it comes to research, you're just going to get close. Also-

Alinka: Done is better than perfect.

Andi: Done is always better than perfect, because done is readable. Perfect doesn't exist.

Alinka: You can monetize done. You can't monetize perfect - undone.

Andi: That's right, exactly, so it's also not possible to get the style of your book perfect. You're never going to love every sentence you write. You're never going to get the book quite the way it sounds in your head because the way you're imagining it, that has more parameters to it. You might be seeing colors and hearing music, and a book only has words on the page, so that's never going to be possible. You're never going to quite get to where you want it to be, you just get it as close as you can, and then you're never going to get the grammar perfect.

I mean, hopefully you hire an editor and you hire a proofreader and you get it close, but-

Alinka: It's a must.

Andi: -it's just never going to be perfect, yeah. You can really slow yourself down as a writer by trying to be perfect, like be perfect as a writer yourself, but also be perfect in your book. It's just not ever going to happen.

Alinka: Let's dig into this a little bit. When do you know that you're actually done and not just being lazy?

Andi: That's a good question. For me, the way I know and the way I suggest that my clients know is that they have done everything they know to do for the book as of right now. You know, as of whatever deadline they set for themselves. That they have asked other people to give them feedback on the book, so beta readers or hired editors, whoever it is. They have taken that feedback and really sat with it and worked with hit as they think is right for the book. Then the final is that they put the book away for as much time as they can spare, some people can do this after a few days, some of us need a couple months, but you put the book away for a little bit and you let yourself think about it without being actively involved in writing it.

Then you figure out, "Oh, right, I meant to also add this", or, "No, I feel like I pretty much got it". Then that's it, that's all you could do, because you could continue to research, you could continue to tweak sentences, you could continue to play with headings and spacing and all that stuff forever. You just have to make a choice and be like, "I have done everything I know to do at this moment in my life. I'm going to put it out into the world and see what happens with it."

Alinka: Mm-hmm, perfect. All right, so now we know how to get it done rather than strive for an unattainable perfect result, that, you know, is in our imagination only but doesn't really exist. We sort of need to know when to stop. What's the other misconception?

Andi: Another one is this idea that later exists. I'm going to get a little time travel for you here. I feel like Doctor Who, this will work for you, but the idea that we don't have any promises of what's going to happen in the future. We don't know whether we're going to get sick and not be able to write, we don't know whether our lives are going to take big changes, our children are going to need more care, or our parents are going to need more care, or we're going to have to do a different kind of job.

That promise of later, like a lot of writers will tell me, "Oh, I'm going to write my book when I retire." What if you don't get to retire, or what if you're sick when you retire, or what if your partner is sick when you retire? What if you die? I don't like to think about that, but we all will at some point. Later's not promised, so we have to kind of work with now. There's also just no ideal time to write. If you're waiting to have completely clear days where nobody interrupts you ever, and you never get a phone call and you never feel bad, and you never get up to get a snack, it's never going to happen. That day doesn't exist.

You have to not keep waiting for that ideal. I know you have kids, Alinka, so I imagine you know what it is to try to work when you have little people around.

Alinka: I can totally relate to what you're saying.

Andi: Yeah, so you just have to choose to write now, and you have to choose to write in the way that works for you. There are all kinds of writing folks out there that'll tell you you need to write every day at this time, or you need to write every day of the week. I think you just decide what works for you, in your life, at this moment, but you decide to do it now. Not in six months when you think life will be easier, because it may not be, and you could maybe have a book out in six months and you would have missed an opportunity there.

Alinka: Totally. Yeah, I listened to a podcast recently where it was said that people are much less attached to future money than to current money, because it's easier to spend money in the future for something than right now. I think it's the same with time. There's the saying "time is money", and for a reason, so it's much easier to plan your, as you said, perfect writing conditions in six months, but after these six months, when the time arrives, you realize that there is no perfect, because this happens, that happens, there's this emergency, there's that thing that needs to be taken care of, so yes.

I've recently really seen time fly, and my calendar just flies under my eyes. I feel like I have to elbow my way to get things done and to show everybody that I have priorities here, and also for myself. The same thing with your book, you know I've heard stories of really good books being written on a train or on a bus while people commute. These are maybe not perfect conditions. It's bumpy and you have people walking by and there's a lot of distractions, but you can put some earplugs or listen to some music and just lose yourself in your own world of writing, and that commute will pass really fast when you're busy writing a book.

Andi: That's right.

Alinka: Yeah, we have to make time now.

Andi: We do, yeah, and I think that's the other piece of this, is this idea that you're not going to have to sacrifice something. I think we live in this world where everybody thinks they can have it all all the time, and the truth is hopefully we can have a lot of it, but almost everything requires us to sacrifice something else, so you have to set your priorities, and I'm not suggesting anyone sacrifice their family or their friends or anything to write a book, but maybe you help your children understand you need a half an hour in the evenings to write some, or maybe you help your spouse understand that you're not just trying to hide away and watch the Desperate Housewives or something. You really just want to get away and get some work done.

It's just a matter of choosing what your priorities are and then figuring out what you have to sacrifice.

Alinka: Yeah, I agree with what you said. It's showing your priorities to your family members. My husband and my kids, they know that there are moments when I close the door, put an "On air, do not disturb" sign, like right now, and when they see that on the door they don't come in. They don't disturb. Whatever is happening, they're able to take care of it, and also I think as a mom of two small children, I could basically spend my days taking care of them. One goes to kindergarten but the other one is still really small. It's a matter of organizing family to take care of the babies, the kids, they love it if you can do it, or a babysitter.

When you do have an hour or two that you have just for yourself, I am sure all moms will relate with this, when you have an hour and a half to yourself, you can accomplish more in that hour and a half than in four hours of a day where you have all the time in the world. I remember when I had all day to do something it's completely different, so it is matter of priorities, and you can do it. I know that many people watch TV and shows and soap operas and stuff. I do as well, on demand sometimes, or to wind down, but if it consumes two hours of your day, every day, then you maybe can cut half of it, for example.

Andi: Right, exactly. The number one thing for Americans, maybe it's a worldwide thing, is television. We spend more time doing that than anything else. If you practice, you can write easily 500 to 1,000 words in half an hour. You just lose a half an hour of TV. Don't lose sleep if you can help it.

Alinka: Sleep is so important.

Andi: That's right.

Alinka: Yeah, I was just listening to the same podcast on sleep. It was a sleep expert talking about how, he was talking about some sports team that was having their biggest game the next day, and they were jet lagged because they were playing at their, I'm really bad a sports, but they were playing at their opponents' field, and they were all jet lagged, but they had to do the practice before the next game though, the last big game. The sleep expert said lose the practice, let your team sleep.

They weren't really very enthusiastic about this idea, but that's what they did, they let their people sleep, the players sleep, and they won.

Andi: Right, there you go.

Alinka: Next year, both teams hired a sleep expert, because it's really important. You are much more productive if you do that.

Andi: That's right.

Alinka: There are ways to go around our busy schedules to make time. Stretching time, making it.

Andi: That's right, and I would encourage everybody to remember, everybody has 24 hours in a day. People that write six books a year, they have the same 24 hours you have, and so you can do it. You just have to choose to, and decide to put aside the excuses.

Alinka: Yeah, you either find excuses or you find a way to do it.

Andi: That's right.

Alinka: Awesome. All right, what's number three?

Andi: Number three is maybe the most important one, and it's the one that comes out of a lot of fear for a lot of writers, and that's this idea that their book isn't important. That what they have to say about parenting, or what they have to say about business, or the novel they have to write. It doesn't matter, nobody's going to care, why should they bother anyway. There's a lot of fear behind that. There's the fear of rejection, there's the fear of apathy, there's the fear of being the imposter, where you're claiming authority over something that you don't really have authority over.

That fear often gets magnified into this idea that, "why would I bother because nobody cares anyway?" The truth is, we don't know. We don't know who reads what we write, for the most part. Maybe 1% to 2% of the people that read what we write respond and tell us they liked it or got something out of it, but there's a whole world of people out there hopefully that are reading things, and they, just like more of us, don't write every writer all the time and say, "Oh, I loved that. That was so helpful."

People do care. We can't know who cares always, but they do care. The most important thing I think to remember is

You are the only person who can tell your story.

that each of us is an individual. Each of us has an individual story, and you are the only person who can tell your story. You're the only person that sees that business idea that way and would express it with those words. You're the only person that knows how to do that kind of cooking with this kind of budget and this kind of schedule. You are the only person that's going to be able to express that, and so you have to own that you're special, which is a hard thing for people.

We talk like we think we're special, but sometimes we don't own that. The reality is, we're all unique, we're all special, and so we have to share that with people. If we all walk around afraid all the time, we're not going to get books done, that's just not going to happen. You can't be afraid, you can't be convinced that what you have to say is not important. What I tell people is, "if you think what you have to say doesn't matter, try talking to yourself the way you talk to somebody you love. A good friend, your partner." You don't tell them, when they say, "Oh, I have this great idea." You don't go, hopefully you don't go, "What a stupid idea, nobody cares about that."

Hopefully you say, "I love that idea, you should do that", and encourage them. You have to start changing your self talk so that you are encouraging yourself in the same way you would encourage the people you love.

Alinka: Yeah, I love it. We're all authors here, or we all want to be authors, or writers, so we have this in common here at this challenge, but very often we're sort of isolated in our world. We gather online like at this event, but then in our home or at work, in our community, we're the only writer or the only author, or the only want to be author, so what advice would you give people who sort of want to get that book out but maybe they're afraid to vocalize that, or they're uncertain [crosstalk 00:16:00] type of internal fears?

Andi: Yeah, I think the number one thing is to find other writers. The internet is a blessed thing, as much as it can be a time suck, it is a wonderful thing too. There are tons of online communities that you can join. I run one, Alinka has some connections there. There's all kinds of people that have online communities where you can just go into a group.

The number one thing I think that happens is those online group especially is you realize that other people have exactly the same problems and fears you have. That can be really empowering.

If you are at a place where they have a local library, or you have one of those still existing local book stores, they often have writer's groups that you can join. I would just look for other writers. You just look for people that you really connect with, and then you try your best to be as vulnerable as you can, and share the reality and the struggles that you're having. Fear grows in darkness, so if you put some light on it and you share it, it tends to shrink a little bit.

Alinka: I love that. Awesome. What about authors who've got that manuscript sitting in their drawer, that they've had it for seven years or so, that they've been working on forever, but they've never actually done anything to publish it. We want to talk a little bit about, hear the aim of this interview to understand how people can get it finished. By finished, I mean published, out there. How do you get your manuscript out of the closet and online to sell it?

Andi: Yeah. If you're done, you've written the last page and you know the last word is done, and you should do that first of all, because finishing itself is a huge win, and once you get in the habit of finishing it's easier to keep going. Once you've gotten that finished, you send it to someone. You can start with, send it to somebody who will give you honest feedback if you can. Your mom may be awesome, but she's probably not going to tell you if she doesn't like something, so maybe pick somebody a little more critical than that.

Send it to someone and get some feedback, and do not work on it while it's gone. Let it go, and get some feedback. That's usually the first step, because ocne we let one person read it, you'll let other people read it. I recommend if you have something done that you hire an editor, because especially if you're going to self publish, if you're going to independently publish, because you need somebody else to look at what you've done and give you some feedback on it.

There are tons of editors out there. You can go to the editorial freelancer's association and find wonderful ones. Hire and editor and then submit it. One of the things that, if you want to traditionally publish, you need to do is send it out for agents to consider. If you want to independently publish, you just do it. There's not a huge ... Aside from editing and cover design, if you hire a cover designer, there's not a huge cost involved, but just get it out in the world. You can always, especially if you self publish, pull it down and change it.

If you find out later you've forgotten something or you want to add something, you can update things as you go along, but if you get it in the world then you have a chance of getting some affirmation for it, and some money, which is not a minor thing in the world. If it's just sitting in your drawer, there's no risk in that except a huge amount of regret later in life that you didn't send the book out and get it into the world, but there's also no way to be affirmed, there's no way to be encouraged, and there's no way to monetize something that's in a drawer.

I encourage you to hire an editor, if you're independently publishing. If you're traditionally publishing, send it out to agents. Get feedback. Just be brave. I think people don't finish things because they're scared. I think they're usually nervous, and I don't judge that because goodness knows I'm terrified 90% of the time when I'm writing stuff, but it takes an amount of courage and you just have to do it, because sitting in the drawer nobody can read it.

Alinka: True. You mentioned two ways to go to publish your book. The majority of people here will independently publish, and I've done this many many times, so we've got that part covered if anybody needs follow-up, but what about that traditional way? You mentioned contact agents. Do you have any advice on how to get an agent, because I know that that would be a first question for anybody who wants to try to get traditionally published. Do you have any-

Andi: Connection?

Alinka: -words of wisdom or just put yourself out there and try something?

Andi: Definitely put yourself out there. Query a lot of agents. If you know people, if you have read books you love by people you know of people you don't know and they have listed and thanked their agents, they often will in the acknowledgements at the end. If you write something like that book you love, it's definitely worth exploring and researching that agent to see if they might like your book.

Alinka: Super smart tip. Acknowledgements. [crosstalk 00:21:07]

Andi: I would definitely, yeah check that. If you have friends who have published books, ask them if they would recommend you to their agent, and then follow through and contact the agents. Just like submitting to a publisher. Very few publishers take un-agented manuscripts now, but some do. You have to follow the rules, so if an agent says they only want email copies or only the first chapter, or whatever, you need to do exactly what they say, because it's bad form to send them something they didn't want, and it probably will mean they aren't going to even look at the manuscript.

The biggest tip is to try to use your connections. That's another reason for being connected to a group a writers. If people can recommend you to an agent, it'll definitely help your chances.

Alinka: You could also try to use LinkedIn to search for agents, right?

Andi: You can, and agent query is another one. AgentQuery.com is another great agent list. Yeah LinkedIn is a great place, you can also do Twitter pitches. There's all kinds of places that you can query agents, contact agents, get to know agents, follow agents on Twitter, connect with them on LinkedIn. Build your literary community and you'll find that getting those resources to get behind you is a whole lot easier.

Alinka: Maybe a word of caution. An agent will never contact you saying "I love your blog, would you like to publish with my company?" That never happens. If something like that happens, red flags. Don't even respond.

Andi: Yes.

Alinka: Forward to me and I'll check it [crosstalk 00:22:42].

Andi: That's right. If an agent ever asks you to be paid up front, that's another big no-no. They get paid on commission when they sell your book and that's the only way they should be paid, yeah.

Alinka: Perfect, yeah. I'm glad we covered that because I know it's trap.

Andi: Absolutely, yes.

Alinka: Let's talk just a few minutes about your book, "Discover Your Writing Self". I asked you for three misconceptions, but you in your book you provided a whole list and we're not going to go into that whole list right now, but I have a tricky question that I don't know if you're prepared for. I wanted to ask-

Andi: Okay, I'll try.

Alinka: -how long does it take to discover your writing self?

Andi: That's an excellent and hard question. Here's the simple answer. The more you write, the more you'll know how you write, and who you write for, and the way you write the best. If you're just dipping in and out of writing on an odd Saturday every seven months or so, it's going to take you a whole lot longer to figure out what works for you and what doesn't work for you as a writer. If you're there regularly, every weekday is when I write, or three or four times a week, or even a couple times a week, you're going to quickly find out simple stuff, like, "I like to write to music", or "I can't write to music", or "I work really well in café", or "I work best alone in my house", or things like, "I really want to write for young people. I want to write a business book for young entrepreneurs", or "I want to write a fantasy novel for senior citizens."

The more you write, the more you'll know how you write, and who you write for, and the way you write the best.

Someone just told me about a book idea for senior citizens the other day. I was like, "that's awesome, you should write that." The more that you do the writing, the more you'll know who you are as a writer. That takes some of us very little time, and it's taken me maybe five or six years to really hone how I do this well, and what doesn't work for me. It does not work for me to have a ton of meetings on days that I write, because then I get all the ideas from meetings in my head, and I'm thinking about other things and I'm not focused.

What does work for me is [worth 00:24:57] writing before my day starts, because then I'm not distracted and I get everything done. I don't have children, so no one wakes me up at 5 AM that [need 00:25:05] to go to the bathroom, except my goats. Sometimes they do, I will say. I think it's just practice, and that's the best reward about writing, is that if you write you get to know yourself and get to know what you love and what you don't love, and that itself is a reward that you can control, because sometimes the other stuff harder to control.

Alinka: True. Maybe I'll share one minute what works for me, because it could work for other people.

Andi: Please.

Alinka: I really respond well to deadlines, and when I'm supposed to write a novel, for example, which I did under a pen name, but it's not something I'm focusing on. I did it on a dare, but I wrote the novel. My deadline was, I'll do it in 30 days, and I figure out that it's going to be 50,000 words, and in 30 days I needs to write, I think, 1,700 words a day, and I figured out that it takes me like an hour and a half to write these, so I basically set a time every day, and mornings work best for me as well, so I need to get my word count done.

I respond well to that, to my word count. When I get more words written and I'm closer to that goal, I feel satisfied. When something happens and I can't get that word count done, the next day I try to do two sessions so that I, you know, I like to be ahead of my own word count. I think that really works well for me. [crosstalk 00:26:34]

Andi: Yes.

Alinka: Music, I need music in the background. Classical. Yeah, so this is something that works really well for me, but you can't do it back to back, 12 months in a year. You can do that one month here, and then several times a year repeat it. Up to you. We've talked to some other authors on the challenge, and Libby Hawker said that six books a year is her sort of target, which is a lot, but she [crosstalk 00:27:08] even more, I believe.

Andi: That's high.

Alinka: Yeah, so that would be one out of every month. One month yes, one month no that you do that. You sort of have to, just like you're saying, Andi, when you get to know yourself and especially your writing self, then you can set your environment in a way that makes you thrive best.

Andi: That's right. Yeah, I wrote three books last year and it nearly killed me, so go Libby, goodness. There are some folks that work hard jobs five days a week, and so what they do as a writer is sort of their side job. Maybe they can't do 1,700 words a day, which is awesome, by the way, go you. Maybe they can do 500 words at night after they go home from work, and that's, you just have to know what's possible for you and plan for that.

Actually, I just did a video on this this morning, I'm like, "That was funny". On having a deadline and then working backwards from the deadline in terms of your word count, because that really does help you get, helps you have a goal that you're going to reach, which is a huge motivator to finishing, but it also makes it manageable and you can set that pace based on how much you can write in a given day.

Alinka: That's the goal. That's what I've done all my life. That's how I function. I've done this in high school for friends. I've written out their timeline and goals and what they have to hit when, to get into university, so I [crosstalk 00:28:35] study plan for my friend, yeah, that's how my mind works.

Andi: That's right.

Alinka: Yeah, when you figure that out, what you respond to best when writing, then you're going to get it done fast and well.

Andi: Right.

Alinka: Awesome.

Andi: Absolutely.

Alinka: Andi, I really love it because we have so many golden nuggets of wisdom here, so many that I'm not even going to repeat the whole list now, but yeah that's obvious and you're the author of "Discover Your Writing Self", where you go way way deeper into all these things, so people can conquer all their fears related to writing, because you've listed so many of them. That's really a great resource to pick up.

Andi, how can people connect with you?

Andi: I would love for people to get a copy of my other book, my other book called, "Writing Day In and Day Out". They can do that by just going to my website, AndiLit.com/wdido, which is writing day in and day out. They can download that, and then they'll be on my newsletter list, and I do a newsletter twice a month with writing tips or writing encouragement. Sometimes book reviews of books that I've just loved. Other resources, I link good stuff sometimes in there that would just help you with your writing life. I would love for folks to get that free book, and stay in touch.

Alinka: Awesome, perfect. We're all heading there right now. Just one last thing. Now our challenge participants are action-takers, so I know you listed a bunch of things that we need to consider, but if you could just say one thing that people should do right now to make sure they get their book finished.

Andi: Okay, so here it is. It's based actually what you said, Alinka. Look at what you've done for your book, and then set a deadline for when you're going to finish it, and then work backward from the deadline for how many words, say do a week if you can't write every day. A week you're going to write until it's done, and then commit to send it out to at least three people. Those can be three agents, or they could be three beta readers. Just three other people that are going to give you some feedback on the book.

Alinka: Perfect. Simple and easy system to follow. All right, thank you so much Andi, and let's get those books done!

Andi: Yes ma'am. Thank you!

WERE YOU PAYING ATTENTION?

Q1: What prevents from finishing their books?

Q2: Why is done better than perfect?

Q3: When do you know that you're done and not just being lazy?

Q4: Why doesn't "later" exist?

Q5: What's the best thing to sacrifice to make time for writing?

Q6: What's not recommended to sacrifice to make time for writing?

Q7: What types of fears do authors face?

Q8: Why IS your book important?

Q9: What does Andi recommend you do to deal with fears around writing?

Q10: What should you do if you feel isolated as a writer?

Q11: What's the next step once you've written the last page?

Q12: What does Andi recommend you do to get an agent?

Q13: How long does it take to discover your writing self?

Q14: What does Alinka recommend to get your book written?

CHALLENGE

Look at what you've done for your book, and then set a deadline for when you're going to finish it, and then work backward from the deadline for how many words, say do a week if you can't write every day. A week you're going to write until it's done, and then commit to send it out to at least three people. Those can be three agents, or they could be three beta readers. Just three other people that are going to give you some feedback on the book.

THE GOLDEN NUGGETS

Q1: What prevents writers from finishing their books?

A1:

1) The idea that perfect is possible.

2) Later exists.

3) Your book is unimportant.

Q2: Why is done better than perfect?

A2: Because done is readable. Perfect doesn't exist. You can monetize done. You can't monetize perfect – undone.

Q3: When do you know that you're done and not just being lazy?

A3:

1) You have done everything possible to make it your best work.
2) You've received feedback from beta readers and editors.
3) You've worked with that feedback.
4) You've put the book away for a while.

Q4: Why doesn't "later" exist?

A4: It's not promised. Anything can happen. We only have now.

Q5: What's the best thing to sacrifice to make time for writing?

A5: Watching TV.

Q6: What's not recommended to sacrifice to make time for writing?

A6:

1) Family
2) Sleep

Q7: What types of fears do authors face?

A7:

1) Fear of rejection.
2) Fear of apathy.
3) Fear of being an imposter.

Q8: Why IS your book important?

A8: Because you're the ONLY person with that point of view.

Q9: What does Andi recommend you do to deal with fears around writing?

A9: Talk to yourself the way you talk to somebody you love.

Q10: What should you do if you feel isolated as a writer?

A10:

1) Find other writers. Go online. Join a community. Contact one of the speakers at the challenge.
2) Join a writers' group at a local book store or library.

Q11: What's the next step once you've written the last page?

A11:

1) Get feedback.
2) Get an editor.

Q12: What does Andi recommend you do to get an agent?

A12:

1) Query agents authors thanked in books you love.
2) Use your connections, if you have any.
3) Websites like LinkedIn and AgentQuery.com.
4) Follow agents on Twitter.

Q13: How long does it take to discover your writing self?

A13: The more you write, the faster you'll know.

Q14: What does Alinka recommend to get your book written?

A14: Set a word count and stick to it.

THREE MUST-DOS BEFORE YOU HIT PUBLISH - NEGLECTING THESE WILL CUT YOUR SALES BY HALF (MICHELLE WEIDENBENNER)

WHO'S MICHELLE?

Michelle is the UNCOVER AGENT who helps writers uncover their stories so they can unleash them into the universe. She's a multi-award winning author, best-seller and a John Maxwell Team speaker and writing coach. Her books are "Cache a Predator", "Scattered Links", "The Canine Pandemic", and the "Éclair" series.
Connect with Michelle at http://michelleweidenbenner.com.

THE GOLDMINE

Alinka: Michelle, you're an award-winning and best selling author, and one of your books is even being optioned for a movie. How awesome is that?

Michelle: Pretty awesome, yeah.

Alinka: You definitely know how good books are created. This is what we need to discover. Exactly, we want to know what the three must-dos before we hit publish are. I know that these three must-dos are super important because neglecting them can cut people's sales by half.

Michelle: True.

Alinka: What are they?

Michelle: Well, the first one that a lot of people don't think about is they publish a book, and then it's the end of the relationship with the reader. I learned this from another author friend. He's like, "Your book needs to be the beginning of a relationship with your reader. It needs to be one part of your business." So, like a smorgasbord, your book is just one. You might think, "Well, I write fiction. How can that be like a part of a business?"

Oftentimes, every time, your book should have a message. Your book should have, your fiction even, a character arc. It's something that I really like to do, and work with writers on uncovering who they are and what their message is. If they can make their book's message, and focus their business around that message, it can be the beginning of a relationship with their readers.

Let me just illustrate that for you. For instance, I have a children's book coming out, and there are some messages for kids in there, there's a message for parents. I thought, "Well, how kids don't buy books. Their parents do." I thought, "Well, how I can bring value to parents, but use who I am, and what my message is?" I'm a leadership coach. I thought, "I am going to create this movement of bringing leadership skills to parents. So developing the leader within your child, and start this movement where it will promote [Wiley 00:02:28], my next book. Before I ask them to help me promote that, I will give them more in what I bring with my personality, and who I am to that."

You always want to bring value to other people before you expect them to promote you. The only way to do that is to earn their trust and to find ways that you can give them something that they need. I'm hoping that this is really going to be the start of something, rather than just, "Here, buy my book, and go buy it."

If you're listening to this, and you have a book, think of, even if it's fiction, partnering with some theme in your book. If it's about child abuse, how can you bring value to that theme? Think outside of just the book. Obviously, if it's nonfiction, then it can be a part of a business. You can use it as a business tool when you're speaking, when you're training. You can use it mastermind groups. Promote your book that way. Even in fiction, make it just a piece of the smorgasbord of all the different things you can offer as a business. Think of it as a business. That's one of the ways.

Shall I go on to the second way?

Alinka: I have a few questions.

Michelle: Okay.

Alinka: You mentioned a bunch of things that people can do with a book. What are some practical ways that an author who's launching their very first book, so maybe not so proficient in all these book marketing ways yet. What's a simple way to make this the beginning of a relationship, and not just a one-off experience?

Michelle: Well again, I think that before they launch that, they need to think about what the character arc is. What that message is that they are trying to convey to the reader. Make it fun.

Here's just another example. When I published "Geocaching", one of my children's book, was to teach kids all about geocaching. It was through a little girl's adventure with her eccentric grandmother. I planted that book in geocaching sites all over the US and Canada and the UK. People at geocaching.com can email me back and forth, and talk to me about, "Hey, we saw this book."

It's really tough for me to know exactly where each author is who's listening to this right now. I'm confident that each one of you has something in your book. Somebody who wrote romance novels, it was all about this jam factory in South Carolina. She partnered with them. They sold her books in the store. Always think about it from another perspective, from a business perspective. Even if you don't do that on the first one, be thinking about where you're connecting with people. If you have that in your mind, it's going to build.

Alinka: I have a fun question. Did you think about partnering with these websites before you wrote the book or after?

Michelle: Before. Well the geocaching-

Alinka: The savvy business person thing.

Michelle: Yeah. I know I'm good at that. I think I'm good at that. I like to do that. I'm an idea person.

Alinka: Yeah, that's very smart. That's the way to go.

Michelle: There are people out there that can help you. Listen to your family and friends ‘cause you'll say to them, "Well, what am I good at? What can I do with this?" Some people just undermine their gifts. They just don't think that they're gifted in any certain area, or they're giftedness is in an area where, "Who's going to value that?" Well, don't discredit that because you are made a certain way. That's where you're going to shine. That's where you have unlimited potential. I help people find that. But if you are just starting out, ask your family and friends. They're going to be astute to who you are and what you're great at.

Alinka: I love it. That's the coach in you speaking.

Michelle: Aw, probably.

Alinka: Perfect, awesome. What's the second one?

Michelle: The second one is something technical. I'm really funny about making sure I have a developmental edit of my books. There's a difference between a line edit, which is checking for grammar and typos and that kind of thing, and a developmental. I love to study "The Hero's Journey". I have the DVD series. You can plot your whole novel, if it's fiction, from the beginning to end, and include elements. I also go to movies. I will do in my mind movie biology. I'll dissect the parts. I'll think, "Well, why made that work?"

So many times, writers are in a hurry to get their book out in the market, but they're missing the boat. Because your character needs to have an arc. Who they are at the beginning is not the same person they are at the end, even if it's a child, even anybody. If they just wander from one place to another, and there's no goal, readers are not going to pick up your next book. They're not going to want to read it.

It's really important to save and to have a budget for developmental edit. I spend probably most chunk of my money pre-launch on the developmental and the line editing of my books because I want to make sure that the readers go along with the characters. They bond with them. They want to finish the story. They learn something along the way. I would say the second one is definitely investment in the developmental edit.

Alinka: Yeah, totally if you want people to pick up your next book, you need to make sure they enjoyed the first one they picked up. Excellent advice. What's the third mistake authors make that ... ?

Michelle: This is something you're so good at, Alinka, and why I love following you. That's building your email list. For 10 years, I used to own a blog. Well, I still own it. I used to blog all the time. People were coming there and getting information without opting in, without putting in-

Alinka: Those rascals.

Michelle: Yeah, imagine that. Over and over again, yeah. They're taking all my information, but they weren't leaving me their name or any way that I could have an ongoing relationship with them. I began to build landing pages where again, I'm giving people information that I think they need, just what you do. It gives me the chance to impact their lives every day by sending newsletters over and over again. Being a part of their journey. Because if somebody's going to buy from you, if somebody is going to follow you, they want to know that it's worth it. That you're not going to just scam them. You're going to give them information that's going to help them on their journey, maybe encourage them.

Gaining email addresses is difficult. Something I recently started doing was Google Ads, pay-for-click ads, and Bing

ads are a little less expensive. I'm taking classes on Facebook ads and how to- But I did notice that Amazon now, you can start paying for pay-per-click ads on Amazon. I'm waiting to hear back from the first ad that I'm going to try with them and see how that goes.

My point is that again, it's all about building relationships. This is just one part of a business. If you think you're going to write a book and it's going to become a movie, and you're going to become really wealthy, oh you're going to be disappointed. Because that doesn't happen. You have to continually build relationships. Email lists, build that email list so that you can let people know when your next book's coming out. Give them something 10 times more than you've asked for them to do something for you.

Alinka: I love it. Well, you've published a bunch of books. What are the things that went wrong in the publishing process with the first book? Things that you learned and that you improved in your subsequent books?

Michelle: Well, I write in multiple genres. I actually don't recommend people do that because my first book I published was a thriller. People that read that are like, "Awesome, I'm going to go check out her other work." Well guess what? I've written no other thriller since then. If they buy the next book that I published, it was a multicultural more women's fiction, even though it was a young adult story. It has nothing to do with crime or thriller. I guess I could say what I did wrong was I didn't stick with one genre.

Again, I'm all about staying true to who I am and my messages. Social issues are a big part of me. The first book was more about child abuse. The second book was about post-institutionalized children and attachment disorders. Even though they were fiction, they had those themes. I guess if I had to say what did I do wrong, it would be that I didn't stick with one genre, and I didn't build an email list early on.

Alinka: Yeah, but most authors don't think about it. Especially with the first book, it's a labor of love that you want to really focus on that book. Then you hit publish, and you're wondering what's going on, and why aren't people buying it? Why isn't it a New York charts best seller? That's usually when you find people like me to help out.

Michelle: Invaluable, yes.

Alinka: You're right. When you focus on one genre, it's much easier to build a following. When you start and have an email list, I didn't start with an email list then. I learned about that later. When you decide what genre works for you, because you might be experimenting. Many authors write more than one genre. Maybe you're really successful writing in one, and the others not so much. Many successful authors, once they've hit these really huge levels of success, then the readers started looking at their blacklists, books that were sinking. Then they wanted to read that as well because of the one book that was really successful. If you're in one genre, it's just so much easier. Because to acquire a reader is, as you said, because you're experimenting with all those ads, that's all ways of directing traffic to your book. In other words, traffic, those are readers, getting new readers for your books.

Once you've invested efforts, time, money, resources to get those readers, then it's really good to have something else to offer them once they're done with your book. We learn. We just cover ourselves, so let's give ourselves a chance to do that and to be a little more relaxed about all this strategy.

Michelle: I think if I had to say one thing that most authors do wrong, is they're always thinking about themselves. You've got to get out of your way. It's not about you. This is a product. This is about your customer. This is about your readers. You have to think how you can best serve them. It's hard because our egos are like, "Oh, somebody bought my book and left a five star review."

It's not about you. This is a product. This is about your customer.

If I try to focus on how I can, even if it's just to entertain, you have a responsibility to your reader. If we can get out of our own way, and make this about them, instead of about us, or our message, or our theme, it's so much easier. It takes away the pressure. A lot of times it will definitely take away the pressure of thinking, "Did I get this right?"

Because if you can focus on somebody else other than yourself, you're doing it for the right reason.

Alinka: Yeah, exactly. I couldn't agree more. Because people come online to do two things. They either want their problem solved, they're looking for information, they're looking for nonfiction, or they want to be entertained, fiction. Yeah, it's so much easier to sell a book if writing it, you're thinking about your reader. I'm not saying right now, "Write to market", although that does work. Wise thinking about your reader that you're providing value for them, rather than entertaining yourself as you write it. Althought it's important to enjoy what you're doing.

It is a complete mindset shift from "I" to "you". I've seen that happen in my business. The moment I shifted mindset from I to my audience, and I serve my audience, just everything shifted. The engagement really increased. I have started attracting more people, really amazing people. It's so much more rewarding. Business has improved. It all started with a mindset shift, which really does make sense, when you think about.

Michelle: Yeah, and I'm glad that you clarified. When I say, "think of your reader when you're writing fiction", I don't mean that you just write exactly what they want. For instance, if you're writing young adult, there are certain things that are expected in a young adult novel.

Somebody sent me their book awhile ago. He was all about it. The premise was really great. All of a sudden in chapter 24, the pig started talking in the story. What he missed was that in fantasy, if your pigs are going to talk in chapter 24, you got to make sure that in chapter 21, the reader knows this is fantasy, and that that could happen. That's a responsibility to your reader. There's certain things about genres that you need to understand before you write. That's what I'm saying. You think about your reader. When the pig started talking in chapter 24, it came out of nowhere. Readers are going to shut the book. They're like, "Wait, that's crazy."

Alinka: You need to set the rules for that at the beginning, right? Like in fantasy, it's a [inaudible 00:20:04] world, but you need to make sure that things out of the blue don't happen like that, that readers are prepared in advance.

Michelle: They should know that right from the beginning that what's going to happen so that they're less surprised by it.

Alinka: That probably would have happened if this writer listened to your advice. I think it was number two, piece of advice number-

Michelle: Developmental, yeah. Hopefully, he's taken time to go back and find an editor because that's what I did recommend. I said, "You need a developmental editor because of certain things." Not that I know everything because I totally don't. I'm just saying that, for me, I have responsibilities. I really try to get it right. Am I going to get all five star reviews and get it right with every person? No. That's another discussion isn't it? How we get over those negative reviews.

Alinka: Yes, but it's important to get those reviews. You will get many more positive reviews if you get that developmental edit. I wanted to stress how important the pieces of advice you gave because you just give them as if they were so easy. They're really impactful. Maybe people listening could say, "Oh, yeah, of course, sure." It's not, "Of course, sure."

It's you really have to do that because otherwise, there's a series of consequences. If you have these pigs talking in chapter 24, that they shouldn't be, then readers are really sharp. They're going to pull that out, and they're going to write it in the reviews. Your score's going to go down. You're not going to be able to get a really good BookBub ad because they see that. There's this whole series of consequences.

Michelle: You're not going to sell books.

Alinka: Right. You touched on reviews. It's an important subject for many authors. How do you deal with a negative review?

Michelle: Great question by the way. The first couple times I got one, I was like, "Oh", it just really hurt. This helps me. If I look at the person, and look at all their reviews, and I notice that they give everybody negative reviews, I pray for them. I know that sounds pretty crazy. It's almost like they are in a really tough place in their life. Sometimes people just are negative period. They miss the point. They miss something about what I was trying to convey in the story.

I also look at it like this is a product. Not everybody's going to like the same product. As long as I did the best that I could do, and I paid for my edits, then that's the main thing. That's what really matters.

Alinka: I also click on the reviewer to take what they review. If it stings- The first time it happens, it does, but it just means that you're really reaching more people. You've reached people outside of your direct circle of friends, and your parents. It's bringing in a negative review. It means a real reviewer read it. Probably it wasn't your biggest enemy playing that game. Most probably, it's your expanding your audience.

Michelle: That's a great way to look at it, yeah.

Alinka: You can click on any book that you love, and you will see how many negative reviews that book has.

Michelle: Right.

Alinka: Plenty.

Michelle: Sometimes they're selling way books and making way more money, so.

Alinka: Yeah, sometimes even the polarization thing that you're able to have a book that people talk about by-

Michelle: Controversy. Absolutely.

Alinka: I wouldn't stress it so much. To me, I'll just give two really quick tips to our audience what not to do and what to do. What not to do, I would never respond. Just completely ignore. Because when you respond, you give it more power. When you share it on Facebook, saying, "Look at what this terrible human being wrote," people started commenting on, it gets out there. You give it power. Don't do that. Focus on something else.

Something else that you can focus on is getting more reviews. The more reviews you get, the faster that review will sink in under all the other reviews. Then quantity at a certain point becomes really important, the critical mass. When somebody sees 100 reviews, nobody expects 100 five star reviews. Except for your book, Michelle, maybe.

But 100 reviews, it's normal that you're going to have a percentage like 10 or 20, 30% of negative reviews. When you have 100 reviews, people see it as social proof. They can tell that it matters. Of course, nobody's going to love the same product. That's why there are so many books. A lot of reviews, they're a really good thing, even if you have a bunch of one stars in there.

Michelle: Yeah, the higher the likelihood you're going to get more high reviews, the more reviews you have. Something else I do too is I try to focus on the positive reviews. With Kelly's book, a couple people said that they thought their life was over. They were in a really bad place. They read her book, and it changed their life.

Alinka: Maybe you can do a little summary of it because not everybody is familiar that you co-authored a book.

Michelle: Well, "Fractured, Not Broken" was written with a quadriplegic. She types with a mouth stick. She really couldn't type. She came to me and said, "Will you write my memoir?" I listened to her story. I was blown away by it. She used to be a nationally ranked athlete, and then she was hit by a drunk driver, and became a pelagic quad, meaning four. She can't walk. She can't use her arms. I was inspired by what she did with her life after that.

I actually got the chance to pitch that to a literacy agent. He said, "It's a great article, Michelle, but it's not a book. Don't waste your time." I didn't agree with him. I really didn't. I thought that it was going to change lives. At the time, I didn't even know how to self publish back then.

Then I spent 10 years learning the industry. Then I published six books. I went back to Kelly in "Fractured, Not Broken". I said, "Let's do this. I don't need anybody now." That's the one that's optioned for a movie. It's a true story. It's not typically the fiction I love to write, but here's the thing. When my editor edited that, she checked it against the fictional elements in the story arc. I still made sure that it had an inciting incident where something changed in her life. Then she had a character arc, who she was in the beginning was not the same person who she was in the end.

Alinka: This is fascinating. This is your sequence to writing a best seller because that book is selling like hot buns.

Michelle: Yeah, I know. It's an indie. That's the thing that literacy agent said, "Don't waste your time." Amazon actually featured it on their indie publishers list, or something. I was like, "Really? Okay, that's cool." Anyway, yeah.

Alinka: That's a great story of how you need to follow your part. What's inside of you rather than somebody's cold objective advice. There's so many stories like this, but I love that this one is in our self-publishing world.

Michelle: Thank you.

Alinka: And how amazing do you feel right now?

Michelle: Pretty good. It's just rewarding. Again, it's about them. Knowing that it's helping people, inspiring people. People are using it in bible studies, and all over. Wow, it doesn't get any better than that. For a while actually, I didn't want to write after that because I was afraid I was frozen. I was like, "I can't do any better than that." I've since unstuck, but it took me a whole year of thinking, "Do I really want to keep writing after that?" I do. I can't stop.

Alinka: Yeah, but the success like that different, because there's this thing that, "How are you ever going to do something better?" But that comes with anybody achieving success. How incredible is that? That's the reason people write. That's like the ultimate reward you can get. It's not their royalties. It's knowing is that you're changing people's lives.

Michelle: Yeah. It is. It's great. That's why I do it though.

Alinka: Perfect. Michelle, I can't believe that we just managed to go through the entire interview. It was incredible. We've touched some really profound things here. We've really talked about why authors write. You are a wonderful example of somebody who's done it successfully, and not just for yourself. That was the thinking about not yourself. We talked about this mindset shift. You were thinking about Kelly and about people whose lives will be changed when they read that. I think that's one of the reasons. Actually, I think it's the fundamental reason why this book is such a success because of the place that it came from.

Michelle: Yeah, well it's really, you know how they say stories sell. The bottom line is, "Is it a good story?" You can't make that up. It's a true story. She's an amazing, incredible woman. It kind of wrote itself, if you will.

Alinka: You made sure that it had all the parts you talked about.

Michelle: I tried.

Alinka: With the character arc and everything. Yeah, it wrote itself, but you directed writing.

Michelle: Well, this was so kind of you to invite me. Thank you. It's just a pleasure to be a part of your life, Alinka. I feel very blessed to have met you online and connected with you. Thank you. It means a lot to me to be a part of your summit. Thanks for asking.

Alinka: Thank you so much, Michelle. This has been so incredibly valuable, but-

Michelle: I hope so.

Alinka: After all, you're the uncover agent who helps [crosstalk 00:31:39] uncover these stories.

Michelle: If any of you need somebody to help you uncover your message, it's there within you, inside you. You just might not know what that is because you're humble, or you undervalue it. Trust me, you matter, and your stories matter. Unleash that story into the universe. Let me help you if you need help. Sure.

Alinka: How can people connect with you and get help from you?

Michelle: Just at Michelleweidenbenner.com. You can opt in for my newsletters. Everything is there. Michelle Weidenbenner. That's a doozy. You'll probably have that somewhere, how to spell my-

Alinka: That's under this video.

Michelle: Okay, yeah. Michelleweidenbenner.com. Or you can email me at michelle@michelleweidenbenner.com.

Alinka: Excellent. We've talked about, it's been so profound like an epiphany thing. We do this for every session. At the end, we want to have some homework, some actionable advice for people to go into right now. So that they make sure that they will launch their book, and it will launch them on this path to a five figure career. What's your advice? Something for people to do right now.

Michelle: Gosh, there's so many things. Maybe just soul searching about who they are. What inspires them where they're at. To ask their family and friends, "What do you think I'm good at? What do you think my book's message should be? How can I give to others?" Maybe do that homework. It's just homework on yourself. Why are you writing this? What is the purpose behind all this? Because I'm sure there is. Even if it's just to entertain, you're bringing a part of your personality to this. Maybe there's something in your story that can resonate with people out there who need something you can give them. There's your homework. Go find out who you are.

Uncover your message, it's there within you, inside you.

Alinka: I don't think it can get any more profound than this. All right, we're going to find out who we are. This has been amazing. Thank you so, so much.

Michelle: Thank you, Alinka. Have a great day.

Alinka: You too.

WERE YOU PAYING ATTENTION?

Q1: What is the first must-do before you hit publish?

Q2: How do you make your book the beginning of your relationship with your reader?

Q3: What should you do before you expect people to promote you?

Q4: What perspective should you be thinking about your books from?

Q5: What does Michelle recommend you do to determine what value you can give to your readers?

Q6: What's the 2nd must-do before you hit publish?

Q7: What's the 3rd must-do before you hit publish?

Q8: What advice does Michelle give authors wanting to write in different genres?

Q9: What is the essence of your book?

Q10: What does Alinka recommend you NOT do when you get a negative review?

Q11: What does Alinka recommend you do when you get a negative review?

Q12: What's the ultimate reward as an author?

CHALLENGE

Soul search for who you are.

THE GOLDEN NUGGETS

Q1: What is the first must-do before you hit publish?

A1: Know your book is NOT the end of your relationship with the reader.

Q2: How do you make your book the beginning of your relationship with your reader?

A2: Uncover your message and focus your business around that message.

Q3: What do you need to do before expecting people to promote you?

A3: Give them value.

Q4: What perspective should you be thinking about your books from?

A4: A business perspective.

Q5: What does Michelle recommend you do to determine what value you can give to your readers?

A5: Ask family and friends for feedback on what you're good at and what you can do with it.

Q6: What's the 2nd must-do before you hit publish?

A6: A developmental design.

Q7: What's the 3rd must-do before you hit publish?

A7: A landing page.

Q8: What advice does Michelle give authors wanting to write in different genres?

A8: Don't do it! Stick to one, build a following.

Q9: What is the essence of your book?

A9: It's about best serving your readers. It's not about you.

Q10: What does Alinka recommend you NOT do when you get a negative review?

A10: Don't comment on it, don't share it on social media.

Q11: What does Alinka recommend you do when you get a negative review?

A11: Go get even more reviews to bury this one under the new ones.

Q12: What's the ultimate reward as an author?

A12: Knowing that your book is changing people's lives.

BETTER THAN LONGHAND. THE ULTIMATE SHORTCUT TO WRITING YOUR BOOK FAST (DONNA KOZIK)

WHO'S DONNA?

Donna Kozik is a multi-award winning author and now shows people how to become authors themselves with the "Write a Book in a Weekend" virtual online events, private coaching and more.
Connect with Donna at freebookplanner.com.

THE GOLDMINE

Alinka:	Donna, you are the founder of My Big Business Card and, as such, you have the ultimate shortcut to creating a book fast. Is that correct?
Donna Kozik:	That is right. Fast and easy, that is what I am all about.
Alinka:	Perfect, so spill it.
Donna Kozik:	(laughs)
Alinka:	First of all, what genre are we talking about here?

Donna Kozik: I focus on non-fiction, where I show people how to write a book to use as that big business card, as a marketing tool for themselves. Although, Alinka, writing is writing and it is all a lot about butt on chair and getting things done, which I have some tips for as well.

Alinka: Perfect. Okay, how does it work? I know you have an online program on how you teach that, and it takes two days [inaudible 00:00:52]

Donna Kozik: You might hear my cat here a little bit, nothing I can really do about it.

Alinka: Perfect, we can teach the cat too. How does it work, can you sort of distill the main points of how it works in our 25 minutes here?

Donna Kozik: Sure, absolutely. First thing you want to think about is what will a book, a non-fiction book, how will it serve you? What is a good reason to have one? If you don't want to write one, then don't write one. If you do, you probably have some reasons as to why you want to do it. To add credibility, to position you as a thought leader, to have as a lead generator for something that you can give to clients, things of that nature.

What is a good reason to have a book?

To add credibility, to position you as a thought leader, to have as a lead generator for something that you can give to clients.

That is what a lot of people are after in getting a book. The fact is then why don't you have one done if it would serve you so well? I hear a lot of the same kind of rationalizations or excuses, depending on what you want to call them, about not having enough time, not knowing what to write about, maybe being torn on different topics. One second here, I am going to move [Felina 00:02:11] out of the way. Being torn on different topics, what to write about, how to get started, that is a big one, a lot of people don't know.

What my program does, and what I encourage people to do is really figure out for themselves, hone down for themselves, why they want to write a book. I do this with a process I call 'vision statement' to create vision statement. Reverend Michael Beckwith with the Agape Church here in Los Angeles says that the pain pushes us until the vision pulls us. We have enough pain as writers and of things we want to do, so that is how the vision pulls us forward.

What will your life be like when your book is done?

The first assignment I give my write a book in a weekend crew is to create a vision statement for themselves to talk about why they want to write a book, what their life will be like when their book is done, and that can range, Alinka, from doing book signings, to doing more speaking, to having the book on Amazon. It might be as something as simple as holding it in their own hands and saying, "You know what? I wrote this, I did this. This is mine, this is something that nobody can take from me." Or giving a copy to maybe a spouse or a kid, something to be proud of. It is kind of the adult version of having a coloring page that you put on the refrigerator.

Alinka: Yeah, so you work with hundreds of authors. Statistically, what is the main motivation that people have to write a book?

Donna Kozik: That is a great question. I think, from what I have observed, although we talk about it, and it is true, about having the book as a big business card, that credibility and that authority. I think for most people it is more of an internal gut feeling. I call it honoring the author within. It is this feeling of, "This is something I want to do. I am going to leave my mark here, leave something that is part of my legacy." Most people, I think, that is what draws them to writing a book.

Alinka: Perfect. How does that ... What did you call it? A vision statement?

Donna Kozik: Mm-hmm (affirmative).

Alinka: How does that work?

Donna Kozik: Basically it is taking a few minutes, or thirty seconds, if you have a paper and pen. I am all about taking action right away, just write down for yourself a little list about what your life will look like, or how you will feel when your book is done and you are holding it in your hands. I also call this a vision statement in that when you are working through the book writing process, you can go back to it, make sure it is congruent with what you are doing with what your vision is with what you want to do. It is also a touchstone statement. It is something that can be with you throughout the process to make sure ... It can act as your guiding light to make sure you are on the right path.

Alinka: Okay, I could be your student for this 25 minutes and I will be following your process. I am going to create my vision statement aloud. I'm going to write a book for authors where I show them how I sold 80,000 books. Does that sound good as a vision statement?

Donna Kozik: Right, and how will this make you feel?

Alinka: Oh, it will make me feel satisfied and happy that I will be able to share my expertise with a lot of authors.

Donna Kozik: Very good. Is there one moment in particular, looking forward to, someone that you are looking forward to showing off your book to or giving a copy of your book to?

Alinka: Yeah, I am really looking forward to sending my link to Donna and say, "Check it out!"

Donna Kozik: "See what I did?" All right, that sounds good. Yeah, see, also you bring some of that laughter and some of that emotion to it, that's what makes it seem real, rather than this is like an adult homework assignment that we have.

Alinka: All right so I have got my vision statement, what is next?

Donna Kozik: Next is creating what I call your reader avatar. Many times in business we talk and it is important to have a target market or a niche market, but the good news is that when you are writing a book, it can be much more intimate and personable. What I have my 'write a book for the weekend' students do is actually create a character sketch of someone who will keep them company, like an imaginary friend, throughout the book writing process, but this imaginary friend is also someone who will be asking questions about the subject, or saying tell me more, in a really friendly way.

A lot of writers, we have our demons, we have our inner critics and inner editor who just kind of ... Maybe even a fifth grade teacher who was very liberal with the red pen, that can just freeze us up when it comes to writing. This is the opposite, this is someone who is cheering you on, asking questions, really interested in what you have to say. I encourage people to create, again, just a one person reader avatar. Not a group of women ages 30 to 35. Instead, a woman, she is 44 years old, she has two kids, she loves mint chocolate chip ice cream. She lives in Portland, Oregon and she works at a corporate job as receptionist but she is looking forward to leaving that one day and starting her own nutrition company. Something, something very specific so you can almost see this person in your mind.

Alinka: Okay, so it is a person pulled from our target audience.

Donna Kozik: Yes, and someone, again, that you can have almost a pretend conversation with. Also, you will find when you speak to this one person, you actually speak to thousands of people because you are making it very real. When you are writing, it is almost like you are writing a letter to them, yet all of your readers will feel like you are talking specifically to them. It is a wonderful technique for making your writing feel more personable.

Alinka: Okay, so can I do it now?

Donna Kozik: Absolutely, go for it.

Alinka: My character is Linda and she lives in San Diego. She just retired recently and has more time on her hands and she wants to ... She started writing her book and, as she is writing, she is aware that she is going to have to market it so she is researching the topic a little bit while she is taking a break from writing and she wants to be savvy and aware of everything she is supposed to do to properly launch it and possibly get to a five figure income, starting with her book.

Donna Kozik: Very good. She sounds like a real go-getter, like someone else I know in this conversation who is blonde like you are and ready to go. I like this idea. Was it Linda, was that her name?

Alinka: Linda, yes.

Donna Kozik: Linda. Linda is ambitious, she wants to do things the right way. What you can add to that too, is a little bit of what are some of her fears and some of her worries that she has about marketing her book that she is almost afraid to admit to herself, but if you address them in your book, she will be like, "Yeah, this person gets me, this is totally what I am worried about." Maybe there is something there?

Alinka: Somebody could say, "Linda is not very technology savvy and she is worried that all of these super young writers who come out right now with their books will have an edge over her." That might be her biggest fear. We can address that saying it is not all that difficult and there are ways to overcome it and ways to outsource it and she can still make her dreams come true.

Donna Kozik: Right, I love how you have the solution at the ready. It is like, "It is going to be okay Linda. We are going to walk you through this. You are going to be fine." That is good but, again, going back to her fears, where I think it is good to recognize that she has this fear of being left behind. It is like there is all these tech savvy kids out there, all these whiz-bang things, apps, probably, "All this stuff going on, who is going to listen to me? I am a newly retired person in California in all that."

Of course, you wouldn't say in your book, "Newly retired from California," but you would say maybe transitioning after leaving a job behind and you want to do this and promote your own book. You probably have some theories that go along with that, including pure technology. "That is perfectly understandable, I am going to walk you through it," is what you will say, and reassure your reader avatar that, and your readers period, that you are going to be able to help them out.

Alinka: Awesome, so I have my vision statement, my reader avatar, what's next?

Donna Kozik: Next, what you want to do ... Let's see, there are a couple ways we can go, but I think I am going to go with what I call the power outline. I surveyed my audience and I asked them, "What is one of the biggest detriments, or one of the biggest hurdles that you have to get over to write a book?" The majority of them said doing an outline. I think that this is another one of those areas where we get caught up in what we had to do in elementary school, or grammar school or eight grade, middle school, about an outline then there were Roman numerals and then capital letters and little Roman numerals.

This is really confusing, it doesn't have to be that confusing. What I teach is what I call the power outline and it is one sheet of paper. On that sheet of paper, in no particular order, I want you to capture your main messages that you will be putting in your book. The things in that you feel are really important to address. Do you want to do that for your sample or [crosstalk 00:12:23]

Alinka: I will do a very quick power outline here. In the book I am going to talk about four very important topics. We are going to talk about the product or the book, how to write a good book, or what needs to be in the book so that it sells well, then I am going to talk about price, how to price it, so that you sell as many copies as possible. Then I am going to talk about place, which is distribution, so where you can sell it and where you should sell it. Then I am going to talk about promotion, how to promote it. These are my four key elements, the four 'p's. Product, place, price and promotion. Is that a good power outline?

Donna Kozik: That is a fantastic power outline, four items there. Enough on a level that you will have something significant to say about each one. Each one important to your reader avatar, to Linda and to others who would be picking up this book. What you can do also in your power outline is, I won't make you do this today, but when you write this down on your sheet of paper ... Again, four or five items that works, leave some space in between and underneath each item, list some of the sub-items that you will be talking about.

For instance, price. What is too high, what is too low, how to cover your cost, how do you end your price? Should it be .95, .97, .99? You can cover all those things and you want to almost make it a little outline. Jot down those things so then you can go to that and it will serve as a writing prompt for you when you are writing that chapter. What your power outline actually turns into is your table of contents.

Alinka: Yeah.

Donna Kozik: Another thing about this too is, probably, next is getting started in writing. How do you pick what to write first and a big mistake a lot of writers make, and wannabe authors, is that they start with the introduction. I think that is the worst place to start because you are introducing something that you haven't written yet. You and I both know that when you write, things change. You might take some thoughts deeper, you might branch off and talk about something you didn't realize was as important until you started writing. I recommend writing the introduction last. Instead, picking an item from your power outline that you are most interested in, or that you can write about easily. Where if I woke you up from a deep sleep at 4am and said, "Tell me about ..." You would be able start yakking about it. That is the item to start with for writing, from your power outline.

Alinka: Okay, just to get started, and once I started, I have to finish it. How do I finish it when the easy part is done?

Donna Kozik: Okay, so I am glad that you think the writing part is easy.

Alinka: No, I mean the easy part because you said to start with something that is easy for me to write and once I did that part of the book, I have to write the difficult stuff and I don't want to jump your process so let's follow your process and maybe fill out this question as you go.

Donna Kozik: Right. Say you chose price to get started with, that you are writing about. Just to mention about that, when you write, I encourage you to do what I call a popcorn draft. A fast draft of your writing, not worrying about statistics, and numbers, which would have a lot to do with pricing. Instead, just getting the content down about why pricing is important, here is how to thing about it. Those things that you know and leave blanks to go back and put in any numbers or statistics or something like that.

You want to write a draft really fast until you are about 80% done.

You want to write a draft really fast until you are about 80% done with that part of it. You are feeling like, "Okay, there is a little bit more here to wrap this up, but I know what that will be and I am feeling pretty good about this." Sometimes, some of my students, what happens is that that one thing that they picked to write about turns into their whole book because they realized that they have so much to say about it and it is easy for them to write about it. Aren't they glad that they picked the one item that was easy for them vs trying to start with something that they found difficult?

Once you get that 80% done and you say, "Okay, this isn't going to make a whole book, I better go to another one of my 'p's, you got and choose the one that is next easiest for you to write about. The point of this, Alinka, is to get some momentum to go [inaudible 00:17:21] you are writing to actually see some progress of what you are producing with your book. Excuse me, I have to cough.

Alinka: Perfect, sounds like a plan. Yeah.

Donna Kozik: Yeah.

Alinka: A great strategy.

Donna Kozik: Yeah, thank you. Again, the idea here is to just kind of keep going with this 80%, 80%. Ideally you have a popcorn draft of your entire book before you go back and do any kind of revision, so you have something to work with, it is almost like an artist that has their lump of clay in front of them, something that you can mold and you can work with.

Alinka: All right.

Donna Kozik: All right, do you want me to continue?

Alinka: Yes, please.

Donna Kozik: Okay.

Alinka: I am not going to write my draft here live.

Donna Kozik: Okay, "Hang on, I will be right back." While this is going on, a lot of questions I get at this process is, "What about the title? What should my title be, I don't even have a title yet?" I remember somebody joined the program and she was already freaking out about that. I am like, "It will come, it will come." When I first started teaching this program in 2008, when people asked me about their title, I got quite irate with them and I was like, "You don't need your title until you upload the book or you are ready to design your cover. Get the content down first."

I softened in my ways and after a few programs I realized that people like to have a name for the project so they can refer to it even in their own mind. I encourage people to come up with a working title and then, during the weekend itself, we play 'Title Idol' where we test out some of the titles that you are thinking about and I give feedback on them. I give you a formula that most titles follow and then we kind of slot it in there, always staying cognizant and keeping an open mind that you might write something brilliant in your last chapter and be like, "Oh, that is the perfect title for this book." It is a little bit of give and take and some play with it, but I think it is important to start thinking about the rhythm of the words and how you present yourself."

Alinka: Yeah, so for the book that we just outlined, the working title ... This is a book I actually wrote so it is easy for me to create it now, to pretend I am creating it. The working title of my book was 'The Four Ps of Book Marketing' and that was what I referred it to in my mind during the period I was writing it. Then when I did some research and I researched key words and what sells and what people are buying, then it occurred to me that that title is not as powerful as 'How I Sold 80,000

Books". That changed. The content is the same, but the title is just so much more powerful and you don't really need much of a description, or much of any explanation, because that title is so self-explanatory.

Donna Kozik: Exactly, it is a statement unto it own and it is still ... Your other title was well, but having a number in the title really works, it gives the brain something to latch onto. It is like, "Oh, I am going to learn something here." Just the how to part of it, "How I sold 80,000 Books," very appealing to a reader. Good job on that.

Alinka: Thank you, but I had the lame title all the time when I was writing it, but then I came up with a good one. As you say, I assure that everybody listening and watching that this is the case. You will probably come up with a better title towards the end, or even after you finish, which is ... You need to do some research and ... It will come, as we were saying, there's things coming. It is good enough to rush it and have something with a title that you are not sure about. It is good to research these things and the power words, what people click on. It is really interesting.

Donna Kozik: Yeah, you can, I never had. There is little a little secret from me. I admire people who do and I know you are a smart and savvy woman and I think that is great. I just don't have the patience for it or the interest in it so I am like, "Ah, I am just going to go with it."

Alinka: Yeah, but you know. You know everything, you know about the numbers, you know about the how, you know everything. Yeah, okay. Are we close to the finish line of the process?

Donna Kozik: We are. In getting your content together, and I just want to end with some information about revising because I talk about the power outline and the actual power core draft or the rough draft. Then the revising trips a lot of people up. Frankly, it is my favorite part because I have something to work with. I think that there is actually some work with revising, or some things that you could do to help your revision techniques that have nothing to do with working with your manuscript.

By that I mean reading some good stuff. I think it is good idea, when you are reading, whether it is a magazine article, a newspaper article or another book, you kind of read with two minds. One for the information that you are absorbing and the second to noticed how did the writer put things together? What was their sentence vari ... How did they vary their sentence length? When did they start a new paragraph? When did they ask questions, when do they make statements, when do they use bullet points? How do they end chapters, how do they draw a reader into the next chapter? If you kind of study it from that mind, it will improve your own revision techniques so when you go back to work on your own popcorn draft, or your rough draft, it just becomes a little bit easier and you kind of get in that mode of being an actual author and writer.

Alinka: Yes, so read [crosstalk 00:23:31] as every good writer should read.

Donna Kozik: Yeah.

Alinka: That is logical. What about .... What happens now that we have revised a book? What now?

Donna Kozik: Yeah, if you are ready to go, you have all the elements together, the table of contents, your acknowledgement to your dedication and your content, you put it together, I have templates that people just plug the content into the templates. You can just format it in such a way and upload it to a place like CreateSpace or, here in the States, we have Lulu, that can then get a copy of your book in your hands for about $5 a few days later. It is really ... It is a such a great little investment to make it real for you, to see that you can do this for yourself. That is pretty much the process right there.

Alinka: Awesome, sounds so simple and it can be when you know what to do. That is why we are having experts like you on the challenge to apply this. One other question, how does an author's or a business person's, life change once they have published this book?

Donna Kozik: I love this question. It is really something you want to experience, I believe, in this lifetime. That is why it is part of my mission is to get people published so they can have this feeling of holding their own book in their hands. For many, that is where the biggest leap happens. That is where the biggest shift in consciousness happens. When you went from not being an author, not having a book, to actually holding it in your hands. [crosstalk 00:25:22] See? Yay! Look at the smile on that face. Absolutely, absolutely.

[Publishing a book] is something that nobody can take away from you. You have accomplished this, it will be yours forever.

As you know, it is something that nobody can take away from you. You have accomplished this, it will be yours forever. I think that answers that call of the honor the author within that we started taking about in the beginning about why do most people sign up for a program like mine, or want to write a book? They want to give credit, or heed that call within so then that comes full circle to completion when they are holding their own book in their hands. Of course, there is all the added benefits of having the big business card and being on Amazon and making a name for yourself as an author. There is also the added confidence it gives you. Didn't you feel more confident in your subject after you published the book about it?

Alinka: Of course.

Donna Kozik: Yeah, exactly. That is what a lot of people are lacking, especially business owners. Some business owners, completely, with some confidence. Even if they really know their stuff, sometimes it is having that universal symbol of expertise, of having your own book, that really brings it home for them and for people around them and clients and prospects and leads. All good reasons to having a book. I really don't see a downside to it.

Alinka: Perfect, I totally agree. All right, this has been awesome and packed with value. If somebody doesn't have a book, I cannot see how they won't go and do what you told people to do because this is a great process. Obviously because you are the founder of "My Big Business Card' and one of the very best sources to write this non-fiction book. Please tell people, how can we connect with you and learn more, go more in-depth into the process?

Donna Kozik: Yeah, I actually have a planner, a book planner, that gives you a little bit of timeline and how to get started, even a place where you can declare your intention of being an author. You can find that at freebookplanner.com. When you register, make sure you respond to any of the emails, let me know that you know Alinka so I can thank her for sending you my way.

Alinka: Awesome, perfect. Before we finish, our attendees are action takers, so we just want one thing that we can do right now to get one step closer to creating that book fast and getting to a five figure income.

Donna Kozik: Absolutely, again I like grabbing a sheet of paper and a pen. I like this better than typing something on a document, and start your vision statement. It will just take you 60 seconds, but will start to clarify things for you, crystallize your dream. Just a reminder, answer the question, "What will my life be like when my book is complete?" Make yourself a little list of what you will be doing and, most importantly, how you will be feeling and then put that on the refrigerator so you look at it every day and feel good.

Alinka: I love it, awesome. This is the perfect ending to our session. Thank you so much Donna.

Donna Kozik: My pleasure, see you in the bookstore.

Alinka: See you in the bookstore.

WERE YOU PAYING ATTENTION?

Q1: What are good reasons to write a book?

Q2: What are people's main excuses for not writing a book?

Q3: How does Donna help authors decide what to write about?

Q4: What are the main reasons author write books?

Q5: How do you create a vision statement?

Q6: What is the next step after creating a vision statement?

Q7: What is a reader avatar?

Q8: What do you do after you have your vision statement and reader avatar?

Q9: What does the power outline turn into?

Q10: What should you not start writing your book with?

Q11: What should you start writing your book with?

Q12: How does Donna recommend you start writing?

Q13: What is a popcorn draft?

Q14: When do you need to have a title?

Q15: What is the last step of the process?

Q16: What does Donna recommend you do to improve your writing?

Q17: What happens when you publish a book?

CHALLENGE

Write your vision statement.

THE GOLDEN NUGGETS

Q1: What are good reasons to write a book?

A1:

1) To add credibility.

2) To position yourself as a thought leader.

3) To have a lead generator.

Q2: What are people's main excuses for not writing a book?

A2:

1) Not enough time.
2) Not knowing what to write about.
3) How to get started.

Q3: How does Donna help authors decide what to write about?

A3: With a vision statement: what will your life be like when your book is done?

Q4: What are the main reasons author write books?

A4:

1) Credibility
2) Authority
3) Wanting to leave a legacy.

Q5: How do you create a vision statement?

A5: Write down what your book will look like or how you will feel when your book is done and you are holding it in your hands.

Q6: What is the next step after creating a vision statement?

A6: Creating a reader avatar.

Q7: What is a reader avatar?

A7: A sketch of someone pulled from your target audience whom you know intimately (including her fears), who asks questions and who cheers you on.

Q8: What do you do after you have your vision statement and reader avatar?

A8: Create your power outline.

Q9: What does the power outline turn into?

A9: Your table of contents.

Q10: What should you not start writing your book with?

A10: An introduction.

Q11: What should you start writing your book with?

A11: An item from your power outline that you're most interested in or that you can write about easily.

Q12: How does Donna recommend you start writing?

A12: By doing a popcorn draft.

Q13: What is a popcorn draft?

A13: A fast draft of your writing, where you leave blanks on statistics or numbers or similar and get around 80% done.

Q14: When do you need to have a title?

A14: When you're ready to publish. Before that you can just use your working title.

Q15: What is the last step of the process?

A15: Revising.

Q16: What does Donna recommend you do to improve your writing?

A16: Read.

Q17: What happens when you publish a book?

A17: Your life changes.

PART 2: MARKET LIKE A PRO

WHY 72% OF SELF-PUBLISHED AUTHORS NEVER SELL MORE THAN 1,000 BOOKS AND WHAT IT TAKES TO BE A 5-FIGURE AUTHOR (KEVIN TUMLINSON)

WHO'S KEVIN?

Kevin is an author, podcast host, keynote speaker, and Director of Marketing for Draft2Digital. He helps will-be authors start their book businesses through his weekly podcasts and through books like 30-Day Author. Kevin has dozens of novels, novellas, and non-fiction books available and is producing more every day. Kevin—along with his wife and his dog—are traveling full-time in an RV, exploring the US as Kevin writes and promotes his books. The inside joke is that they are going on the worlds most far-ranging house hunt. They're only half joking.
Connect with Kevin at http://draft2digital.com or http://kevintumlinson.com/.

THE GOLDMINE

Alinka:	Kevin, as Draft2Digital's marketing director, you know the answer to this question that's bothering a lot of authors. Why do 72% of self-published authors never sell more than 1000 books? Do you think the statistic is correct first of all?

Kevin Tumlinson: I think it's fairly close. I actually think it's probably a bit higher than 72%. Going by Draft2Digital's actual numbers, I can say that within our service it's a little higher just because we have a great volume of authors and over 100,000 books listed. I'd say that 72% is probably a little conservative but it's in the ballpark.

Alinka: This is what we want to address during this session. This and what it takes to become a five figure author. You've been in Draft2Digital for a while and you're the marketing director. We want to know it all from you.

Kevin Tumlinson: Okay, I'll give you everything I know. I would think that as far as what does it take to be a five figure author, I think really mostly it comes down to strategy and marketing which is not something a lot of authors like to hear but it's just part of the business. I think a key component to a great success as an author however you're going to define your success. I think the biggest component is treating this like a business which means going out and getting an actual business education about what you're doing. That just means for the largest part studying your market, knowing who it is you're writing to, knowing what their buying habits are, knowing where they like to hang out, where do they shop, what is your ideal reader spend their money and spend their time. These are key components.

To be a five figure author, I think really mostly it comes down to strategy and marketing.

I think that the biggest reason that a lot of authors do not sell more than 1000 books or even reach that 1000 book benchmark is because they spent really no time researching their markets. I want to say that this doesn't necessarily mean write to market although that actually is a very good strategy especially when you're starting out. It's great to write to market in order to build your initial audience.

Researching your market means knowing who your ideal reader is, where they spend their time like what social media channels that they like to frequent, what events they might go to, what magazines they might read. You want to spend your time researching how to craft the message of your book or craft the message of buying my book so that it reaches that audience. I think that's key. It's not an easy pill to swallow though.

Alinka: When you say write to market, what do you mean?

Kevin Tumlinson: Right now it's very popular Chris Fox and a few other very well-known names in the indie publishing world are publishing books around this topic. Writing to market in a nutshell is going out and researching your audience and writing a book specifically tailored to that audience. It's almost the idea of chasing the fad in a way but it's a little more strategic than that. You are actually doing some research to find out what's hot right now. A good example would be if sparkly vampire romance novels are hot right now then you might write a sparkly vampire romance and put it out there.

Writing to market in a nutshell is going out and researching your audience and writing a book specifically tailored to that audience.

One of the big sellers for example in the Draft2Digital catalogue is shifter romance. If you write a shifter romance and publish through Draft2Digital, your odds of success go up. Your odds of selling that thousand books goes up. There is a component of righting the market in this. I would argue though that it's much better to not just write to market but choose the market specifically and then write for that market.

What I mean by that is rather than chasing trends for example the shifter romance. I can tell you that you can do fairly well writing shifter romance but rather than chasing that as a trend, go on and find the audience for the type of book that you would be happy writing. If you're okay writing shifter romance, it's no trouble. Just write the stories you would enjoy as a reader of that genre and market to that genre. It actually helps when you're a fan because you know what you like and you're probably a pretty good representation of what everyone else will think about the book. You can do that.

It's much more to your advantage, you gain a much greater advantage if you actually spend the time to research the market for the type of book that you will be most comfortable and happiest writing. That's a much better approach to the whole write to market strategy.

Alinka: Probably for people who see things in their mind's eye, these would be two circles. One circle would be passion and the other circle would be what the market is looking for right now. You would see how these circles overlap and a point of where they overlap. That section would be where you should be focusing your writing and marketing efforts, right?

Kevin Tumlinson: Right. That overlap in that particular Venn diagram is going to be your market. Then what you would do at that point is spend your time and energy researching that market. If you are writing thrillers, I mean this is something I've experienced recently in my own work. I recently started writing Dan Brown type thrillers. They have a large audience. They are popular but I had to enjoy that type of writing. In the genre of thriller, there are hundreds of different styles of book and hundreds of different styles of authors. You can go in a number of directions actually.

When I decided I was going to write thrillers, I had to pick the direction that worked for me that I felt comfortable with. Then I had to go out and find those readers. I had to make sure that when I did targeted advertising on Facebook for example, I was targeting the readers of those books and those authors. That helps a great deal because now you're spending your ad dollars in a place where your readers are hanging out. You're reaching more readers because you're being more targeted about the way you're reaching out to them.

That's something that a lot of authors forget. There's a real tendency to want to reach everybody. You want everyone to be a reader. I'm trying to fall back on the old … we call it a Fordism. When Ford first built the whole factory system for building these automobiles, there's a phrase. There's a saying he has that if everyone is your customer, no one is your customer. I think that's absolutely true. You want to be as niche as possible. You want to be so laser focused on your audience that you can almost narrow it down to a handful of people.

Alinka: Wasn't that Ford said you can have any color as long as it's black?

Kevin Tumlinson: Yeah. For the original I think the model …

Alinka: It worked for a while.

Kevin Tumlinson: Right. The limited choices make it much easier for customers to make their purchase. You can focus on quality. In that case the advice for authors if you're looking at that particular Fordism would be find your genre and stick to it. I'm a cross genre writer I will confess. I've enjoyed a little bit of success in this but it hasn't come easy. It's been rather difficult actually to build up a strong following. Another way to ensure that you're getting those 1000 books sold would be to have that laser focus. Go out and find the genre you're comfortable in and stick to it. Write as many books in that genre as possible.

Alinka: You want a genre also that people want, right?

Kevin Tumlinson: You want a genre that people want.

Alinka: More than [inaudible 00:08:36].

Kevin Tumlinson: Let's be clear on something. Almost every genre out there has a large enough body of readers that if you market well enough, you'll do just fine. For a great example, look at some of the more ridiculous genres out there like dinosaur porn for example. I should have given heads up. This is the non PG part of the discussion. There's a market for this stuff. There's people writing about big foot erotica. There are people writing these books.

Alinka: Oh dear I'm so ignorant. I have to research.

Kevin Tumlinson: Just because you write a lot of children's fiction. You [inaudible 00:09:21]. You're not in this …

Alinka: Yeah I know that. Keep talking about the dinosaurs.

Kevin Tumlinson: The point here is you can write on just any topic you like. You can write any genre you like. The key isn't what genre you write in, it's, is there an audience there for it and how are you reaching that audience? There's always an audience. The general wisdom is that if you have 1000 faithful readers, 1000 raving fans, then you can make a pretty good living. I can attest to this. If you got 1000 really good readers and you're putting out a volume of work every month or every couple of months, you're going to do okay. The more of those readers you can bring to the fold, the better. You can find that 1000 readers with big foot erotica. They're there. They exist. It doesn't actually take that much to nurture that audience.

Alinka: I heard that's a good genre to write that kind of … get it risen.

Kevin Tumlinson: You had to be comfortable with the fact that you're now writing that story and that some people are and some aren't. There are a lot of pen names [inaudible 00:10:30] that. I fall back on Obi-Wan Kenobi's wisdom. You must do what you feel is right. Yes, in that your goal is find your key audience and it's not generally that hard to find the key audience. For the most part we write the kind of stories that we enjoy. Go to the places that you enjoy spending time and look around and ask around. You'll start finding people who might enjoy your work.

Marketing is much more complex than that. Here's the secret to marketing no one ever considers. I never [inaudible 00:11:08] talk about this but here's the reality of actual marketing. Marketing is an odds game. It's about improving your odds and that's really all it is. The way we market our work is we start wide and we narrow focus. We start wide in order to see those hints to capture that fringe audience to see who's paying attention. Then we take that group and we narrow down. We want to find more people like that.

Marketing is an odds game. It's about improving your odds.

Facebook is a great tool for this because you can do these lookalike audiences. You can do the same thing in Google ad words. I always default to Facebook for some reason. You can find these lookalike audiences. If you start …

Alinka: Facebook ads, yeah.

Kevin Tumlinson: Right in Facebook ads. Facebook advertising has been a real boon for indie authors. Guys like Marc Dawson, his courses they've been fantastic for that growth. If you start wide and you find … let's say you post ads and you're targeting 30,000 people and you find 1000 people in there who are perfect for you. Who love your work and who respond to your ads that sort of thing, you clone that audience and go find hopefully another 1000. You just keep refining. You're narrowing and narrowing and narrowing until you have the perfect conversation for the perfect audience. That's what marketing is all about. It's about improving your odds of reaching the right people with your work.

Alinka: That's the people who already understand, who haven't … more or less they have an understanding of who their target audience is and they're finding and looking for more readers. What about somebody who's going to write their book either first book or they just want to switch between genres because they think their genre is not as hot? They want to write a book in a new genre. How should they find that genre? How should they decide? What should they take into consideration?

Kevin Tumlinson: It's really the same story. Whatever genre you're writing in, presumably you enjoy that genre. Look at where you go for more of that work. Where do you hunt for books? Who do you talk to? Then start building relationships within those circles so that you can start occasionally recommending. "Hey I've got this book. Would anyone like to pick it up for free?" Whatever your pitch happens to be until you can start building a little headway there.

You can also just flat out start advertising to markets that are similar to yours. Back to Facebook. If you want to target the readers of [James Rollins 00:14:00] there's a way to do that. You can have it advertised and say readers of James Rollins love the books of Kevin Tumlinson. You'll get some pushback on that. You'll get people who are offended by that but you'll also get that handful people who are curious and want to try it out. Everything starts at the bottom and everything starts slow. As long as you're aware of that, you can start growing exponentially over time.

You talked about the person writing their first book. A lot of the strategies you hear are aimed at people who have multiple books and that there's a reason for that. You want to give your reader somewhere to go once they've finished this work. Once they read that first book, you need someplace for them to go. Which means you need to probably have a minimum of three books. I actually tell authors frequently that if you can take it, if you can stomach it, write the first three books before you publish the first one.

There are multiple reasons for this but it is a big advantage to you as an author to have … when you release book one and you do all that marketing, you put all the energy into marketing, you're talking to people. You're posting about it everywhere you can think of. Maybe you pay for a book club. Whatever means you use to get some activity going behind in that book, it will go much smoother, much easier for you if you have a second book already waiting that you can mention right away. You could say, "This is book one of my trilogy and book two releases in two months or book two releases in 30 days." Whatever is comfortable for you.

There are strategies you can fall back on [inaudible 00:15:56]. If you're able to release a book every couple of months, you'll see some great momentum from that. That will help you sell 1000 books much faster. If people discover you and like you, they immediately want to go find something else you've written. If you've got one book out that's problematic. There's nowhere for them to go. Give them some place to go.

Alinka: Yeah that's definitely true. That is the business approach. Everything that we're talking about. You want to understand who your market is and what they want. That's exactly what people do in a successful business and that's what successful authors do when they sell a lot of books. There are these two strategies. One is to release three books simultaneously. The advantage is that people as soon as they find you and when you have everything set up like your funnel and the way you communicate with people.

Release three books simultaneously.

If you have that set up correctly and your books are optimized and everything, then it will go to your second and third books. That's fantastic if people like you but the second option is you just publish one book and you test and you see if people like it. What if the book is not as good as you thought and you published something people don't want to read. The strategy is [inaudible 00:17:31] if you've done your research first.

Kevin Tumlinson: We're working on the assumption first of all that you've nailed craft. Maybe that's a poor assumption. I feel like if you've gotten to the level where you can write three books, you probably have a decent grasp of craft. Trial your books before you publish actually. Get beta readers. Even if it's just family and friends, try to get some opinions on the work. Try to find as educated and opinionated as you can find. In the interest of time, I just want to assume you've got craft nailed. Work on craft first. The thing about releasing books nobody wants to read, that is a marketing problem. That is not a quality problem. If you're writing books that no …

Alinka: You haven't done your marketing research.

Kevin Tumlinson: You haven't done your marketing research. You haven't found the right audience. That's another tough pill to swallow because there's work involved here. I'm one of these people. You start out with, "I've got this great idea. I've got a book. I'm going to release it and then I'm going to kick back and watch it just take off." You don't think about marketing because that's stuff is hard. Getting out there and meeting and greeting people you just want to release a book and see it take off. Everyone wants that.

Alinka: I felt that way too.

Kevin Tumlinson: I felt that way with literally every book I ever published. That never goes away. The thing about marketing your work is that it's a conversation you're having with people. It makes it a lot easier when you start thinking of that way too. You want to form a relationship with the community of people that is centered on your work. That's what you're trying to build. When you start Facebook pages, when you get on Twitter, wherever you're finding your audience, it's really all about maintaining that momentum of conversation and building that community around what you're writing.

If you're putting a book out, if you put five books out and no one is reading any of them, then my answer to that is you haven't done enough research. You haven't found the market that supports that work. They're out there. I'll give you a great example from today. I'm publishing one of my books. It's been out for quite a while but I'm publishing it chapter by chapter on Wattpad. It's not getting a huge reaction because it hasn't quite been discovered yet. The people who have discovered it are very vocal and they love it. They're commenting. They're a community that's building up around this work. That kind of feedback is positive and great for me.

Wattpad in particular is a great environment for building up a community around your work.

If any of them were to say, "Look you've got some typos or whatever." That would help me as well. I can go and fix that stuff and release the book publicly or whatever. Wattpad in particular is a great environment for building up a community around your work. We've seen things like this. Hugh Howey, Andy Weir, you've got guys out there who have published and built an audience around their work through their blogs or through other resources. They were encouraged to go. That's a great way to go because one, you're working on craft while you're doing it. People will tell you if something sucks and you can go fix it. You're working on the work ethic because people demand to see that new chapter. They want that update. If you're not updating regularly, you're going to hear about it a lot.

You develop a work ethic. You develop the sense of responsibility you have to your audience. You're building a community. You've got now this group of people and the longer your work is out there and the more you're interacting with your audience, the stronger that group becomes. As you build this community and you say, "Look, the book is available on Wattpad but I'm about to release it on Kindle. I'm going to sell it for 99 cents. Can everyone here just go buy a copy and leave a review?" Then suddenly if you got … a friend of mine has 40,000 followers on Wattpad. The instant he releases that book on Kindle for 99 cents, he's probably going to sell at least 30,000 books that day and that's just going to skyrocket him. I think that's a great strategy.

Alinka: I've done Wattpad as well. I never got to 40,000 followers because I just did for a month [inaudible 00:22:01].

Kevin Tumlinson: Me neither.

Alinka: I don't remember the number. I did get followers and they did the comments. It motivated me to update every day and to get it finished. I actually did NaNoWriMo. When I did NaNoWriMo I did Wattpad and I was updating every day. That is motivating for authors and it has a great platform because you can then get those offers. You can take them with you on other platforms when published. You had a following.

Kevin Tumlinson: The thing about Wattpad is the audience tends to be younger and they don't have as much disposable income. They don't usually get to make purchasing decisions about things. Part of this is a long gain. I encourage everyone to work for the long gain. In fact, to the point of sacrificing your short term gains over long term gains. If you are talking to an audience of high school kids and they're digging your work and they're super fans, eventually they graduate high school. They get jobs. They buy books and they're going to remember the authors that they loved when they were younger. They're going to come back and buy your stuff. There's a future strategy at work that you need to be working toward.

The thing about the whole publishing business is it really is a long gain anyway. You can gain some short term success by going exclusive for example. For example KDP Select and get your book into Kindle Unlimited. Patriciate in the KDP Select fund that sort of thing. That's a great way to build some immediate traction but you have a fairly limited audience. That audience tends to want free books rather than paying you for books. There's a balance to strike there that's why the Draft2Digital our whole goal is to get people to go wide because we know that wide is the way you build a long term successful author business. There's a strategy to consider there.

Alinka: I really like what you said that we need to narrow down your niche down to write in. It takes market research to do that. Once we've got that figured out, we want to go wide at all the tunnels. Not just for eBooks but also for paperbacks. It takes a little bit of creativity. Just today I got an email from Skagway in Alaska because I have a book about two kids in Skagway in Alaska. The lady said, "You passed in my story like a few years ago showed me your book. How can I make a wholesale order?" You can just go with your book and tell people about it. You can get a response like two years later. When somebody does a wholesale order, a shop like that where every cruise passenger goes to and gets souvenirs back home, you can get those 1000 books sold just like that with one sale.

Kevin Tumlinson: What's interesting is that you goal is 1000 books. I remember early on I went and spoke at a couple of high schools. Within the first week I sold 1000 books. Just going every couple of days I would go and talk to either a high school group or a small reader's group or something like that and they always want to buy whatever it is you've written. If you got multiple books sometimes they'd buy multiple books. Selling 1000 copies didn't take that long. It makes an impact on you financially but the real trick is you want to build and sell that 1000 copies every week or even everyday if you can especially every day. If I was selling 1000 copies a day, you and I might not actually be talking right now because I'd be on an island somewhere.

Alinka: That you bought.

Kevin Tumlinson: Yeah that I bought. The goal here is not just to hit that 1000 book mark. I know that's a great benchmark because once you've hit 1000 books, you can look back at your career and you've got some usable metrics basically. You got usable data. You can see who's reading you. You can customize advertising. You can customize all your promotions. You get to know that audience a little better. It's a little easier to strategize around what to do next. 1000 books is a great target but it's not the end goal.

A lot of authors get hung up on, "I've got to make that first 1000 sales. I've got to make my first five figures. I've got to break the barrier." I can tell you from experience that you can break that barrier but if you don't have an infrastructure set up to repeat what you did, next month you're going to be struggling to break that barrier again. The goal isn't to break the barrier. The goal is, "How do I hit that number consistently and then grow from there?"

Alinka: Perfect. So a long term strategy and a system in place to have that.

Kevin Tumlinson: I think most authors do not think long term. There's a real tendency to look at where you are now and lament the fact that you're not making five or six figures each month. I'd love a six figure month. Haven't hit that yet. There's a tendency for us to look at where we are now and we can often become discouraged or we become … lax also is another danger. We're making pretty steady sales just with what we're doing and we never rethink our strategy. I think coming back to your marketing strategy, your business strategy frequently and making changes based on what you're learning is also key to success.

Alinka: Yeah, I couldn't agree with you more. It is.

Kevin Tumlinson: Yeah.

Alinka: This is perfect. I love it Kevin. Obviously it's perfect to hear the marketing director of Draft2Digital and you have your own podcast that you've been doing for a while that I have actually been on.

Kevin Tumlinson: You have. You have been a guest on the show which is how we met.

Alinka: Yeah that's how we met. Thank you for that. Please tell people how they can connect with you both on Draft2Digital and on your show.

Kevin Tumlinson: Draft2Digital its Draft, the number two digital.com if you haven't heard of it already. We're a publishing platform. You can come in and convert your book from a word document for example to an eBook very cleanly. We've got a great automated system for that. We aggregate several distribution channels. If you want to be on apple iBooks, Barnes and Noble, Nook, Kobo, we can help you with that. We do a great job. We have great customer service which is one of the reasons I was attracted to the company. Visit that.

You can also find me. Now the easiest way is kevintumlinson.com. That's where all things Kevin Tumlinson including the words from your podcast which you have been on. Visit that site. You can find my books. You can find information about me. Find my various podcast. I'm all over it. That's the two main ways to reach out to me. I would very appreciate.

Alinka: People can knock on your door and your RV.

Kevin Tumlinson: Yes you'll never know where I'm going to be parked. My wife and I recently …

Alinka: You could try. This is awesome Kevin. Our attendees are action takers. We just need one last thing. Something that people can do right now to make sure that they have the biggest chance to get to that five figure income.

Kevin Tumlinson: My best advice for you to get to five figure income is to start by analyzing your actual strategy. One second I'm sorry. Sorry. I'm glad I have a [inaudible 00:30:26] so I didn't have to do that in your ear.

Alinka: That's awesome.

Kevin Tumlinson: Look at your strategy as it revolves around exclusivity and wide distribution is my biggest advice. You can actually use exclusivity to help you move toward that five figure goal. It'll help you build an audience. It'll help you create a rapid revenue stream. What you want to do is assess your goals and determine when it will be time to go wide. Write out a strategy that includes benchmarks for taking each book wide. Some advice I can give in general is if you have only one to three books available, keep them exclusive. Keep them in KDP Select until you can double that volume.

Then each book you publish after book three, move a book into wide distribution and expand your marketing efforts to reach an audience for those specific channels. For example, if you've written three books in a 12 book series, publish the first three exclusively on Amazon. I would say do them rapidly one after the other. Publish one, get your marketing effort going on. Publish that book. Keep the marketing effort going by saying book two will be available on this specific date. Use preorders. Get everything set up so that you can keep momentum going.

Then once you've reached the third book and you've got the fourth one in the wings, as that fourth book releases, take the first book and go wide. Start your marketing efforts for those channels. This will help you build a nice momentum and some nice revenue. Just be prepared for a drop. This is why I tell people use the 80-20 principle or whatever people are calling it now, the Pareto principle.

Find the books that are past their prime as it were. Those are perfect to go wide. Use that strategy. That's an action arm. Sit down and work out like what your benchmark goals are for as far as income and sales volume over the next year to two years, to three years and then work out how many books you're going to produce in that time and precisely when you're going to release and when you're going to go wide with each volume. That's my best advice.

Alinka: It's perfect. Excellent. Complete advice that people can apply right now. Awesome. This has been fantastic. Thank you so much Kevin.

Kevin Tumlinson: Thank you. I'm happy to be here and always happy to offer advice. Draft2Digital in particular is all about helping indie authors. That's a big component in my career as well. Very happy to be here. Thank you for having me.

Alinka: Awesome, thanks.

WERE YOU PAYING ATTENTION?

Q1: What does it come down to if you want to be a 5-figure Author?

Q2: What type of education do you need to be a 5-figure Author?

Q3: What are the key components every author needs to understand?

Q4: What is writing to market?

Q5: What's a better strategy tan writing to market?

Q6: What two components should overlap for you to write the most successful book?

Q7: What's the problem with wanting to reach everybody?

Q8: What's the secret to marketing no one ever considers?

Q9: What's the minimum number of books Kevin recommends authors have before they start marketing?

Q10: What platform is great for building up a community around your work?

Q11: What's an example of a short-term gain?

CHALLENGE

Use kdp select for fewer books than three. Then go wide.

THE GOLDEN NUGGETS

Q1: What does it come down to if you want to be a 5-figure Author?

A1: Strategy and marketing.

Q2: What type of education do you need to be a 5-figure Author?

A2: A business education.

Q3: What are the key components every author needs to understand?

A3:

1) Study your market
2) Know who you're writing for
3) Know what their buying habits are
4) Know where they like to hang out

5) Know where they shop
6) Know where they spend their money
7) Know where they spend their time

Q4: What is writing to market?

A4: Researching your audience and writing a book specifically tailored to that audience.

Q5: What's a better strategy than writing to market?

A5: Choose the market specifically and then write for that market.

Q6: What two components should overlap for you to write the most successful book?

A6:

1) Passion
2) What the market is looking for

Q7: What's the problem with wanting to reach everybody?

A7: You reach nobody.

Q8: What's the secret to marketing no one ever considers?

A8: Marketing is an odds game. We start wide and we narrow focus. Marketing is about improving your odds of reaching the right people with your work.

Q9: What's the minimum number of books Kevin recommends authors have before they start marketing?

A9: Three.

Q10: What platform is great for building up a community around your work?

A10: Wattpad.

Q11: What's an example of a short-term gain?

A11: KDP Select and Kindle Unlimited.

THE SINGLE MOST POWERFUL (AND MOST OVERLOOKED) STRATEGY TO BECOME A #1 AMAZON BEST-SELLER (DAVE CHESSON)

WHO'S DAVE?

When he's not fighting dragons or chasing the bogey man out of his kids' closet the creator of Kindlepreneur likes using his previous Online Optimization skills to help other authors with the 'technical' stuff and get the right authors to the top of Amazon and any other eBook service out there. With a blog full of tips and tricks as well as tons of recommended resources, his site is great place to learn more about publishing for Kindle, marketing effectively, and growing your readership.
Connect with Dave at https://kindlepreneur.com.

THE GOLDMINE

Alinka:	Hey Dave, or should I say Kindlepreneur? You are the most qualified person to answer this question, and the question is: What is the most powerful and most overlooked strategy to become an Amazon best selling author?
Dave Chesson:	Well, it'd be making sure that there really is a market on Amazon for your book idea. When it comes to book sales, there's only two ways you

Make sure that there really is a market on Amazon for your book idea.

can do it. Either a) Amazon sends people to your book, and people buy it or b) you send people to your book and buy it. B is kind of hard, right? You've got to go out there. You've got to find the market. You've got to drag readers to your book and then get them to buy it. You need a big email list, mastering ad systems, all these things.

The other way, something that I think is really important, especially for new authors who really want to get that book out there and be discovered, is by getting Amazon to send people to your book. Once that's done, Amazon's doing the hard part. They're earning their commission. They're sending people who are searching for something to your book, and that will allow you to grow. Whether or not your objective is to make books or make money from your books or to get emails, whatever. Funneling traffic from Amazon can be an incredible thing for any author, new or super professional.

Alinka: How do you do that? How do you get Amazon to do the work for you?

Dave Chesson: Well, the key is making sure that there is an existing market on Amazon looking for that book idea. If you have this brand new idea that nobody's ever come up with, how does the market know how to find you? If you have come up with this new style of doing something, people aren't typing that style of thing, whatever it is, into Amazon. In this case, what any author should do is validate whether or not that book idea has a pre-existing market on Amazon. To do that, first start by going to Amazon and typing in your idea. Then, Amazon uses their search engine known as A9.

A9 will go through and look at all the books out there, and it will start to stack them. The number one at the top is the one they think is the most likely book you're looking for, and then, two, three, four and five. Having your book show up at the top for something that people are actually typing in, that is an incredible way to make sales organically. By organically, I mean day in and day out, whether or not you are writing your next book, going on vacation, Amazon's sending people to that book.

If you type in your idea in Amazon, and you look at the books that are showing up, and none of them are making sales, nobody's buying them, then that means there isn't a market on Amazon.

If you type in your idea in Amazon, and you look at the books that are showing up, and none of them are making sales, nobody's buying them, then that means there isn't a market on Amazon. People aren't going to Amazon looking for that topic. Immediately, when you have a book idea, validate that there are people buying that book on Amazon. If it comes back, and there's no sales being made on your book idea, it doesn't mean you can't make money, or it doesn't mean that your book won't sell. But it does mean that you can't rely on Amazon to do the work, and you've got to go to option B like we talked about, which is find the market and bring them to your book.

I think this is one of the most important steps for any author before they sit down, and they invest their time, money and energy into creating that book, is knowing full well if they can depend on Amazon to make the sale or not.

Alinka: Okay. What about the author who just has one book out and doesn't want to write the next book yet but wants to make the most of the book that they have out. What do you do now?

Dave Chesson: Well, it really comes down to what people are typing in to Amazon, and if those people are buying books. In this case, maybe you wrote a book about how to live a stress free life, and maybe you targeted stress free life as the thing that would show up, that if people type that in to Amazon, your book would show up. The truth is, is maybe a larger percentage of people are actually typing in how to lose stress or maybe you might even find out that it's how to lose stress as a parent. These things, if you were to target that and show up for those searches, you have a much better chance of getting more clicks and more sales.

Again, it comes down to researching and trying to figure out exactly what people are typing in to Amazon and then to make sure that it is something where people will buy books that show up for that search. Let me step back one thing, too. When we talked about book sales, I want to explain how you can figure out if a book is making sales or not.

You go to that book, and you scroll down. There's the Amazon best seller rank, and that's that first number that's right there. Use that number, because that is the only indication of how good a book is doing. In that number, if it's the #1, if the ABSR, and I'm just going to call it ABSR from now on, if that is one, then that's the best selling book in all of Amazon. If it's 4.7 million, then that's the worst selling book in all of Amazon, because that's how many Kindle books are out there right now.

Where's the sweet spot? We have a calculator on Kindlepreneur where you can just go to that and type in, just Google Kindle calculator, and it will show up. Just put that number in there, and that will convert that into books sold per day, so now you can go to any book there is, and you can look to see on overage how many books per day that book is selling and actually give you an indication of whether or not that is a profitable book idea or not so much.

Alinka: Okay, so where do we put those keywords in?

Dave Chesson: Well, once you've identified the right keywords, and again, the importance to those ... There's three importances to keywords. One is that there's people typing it in. Two, that those people actually buy books on that subject. Three, that it's not so competitive that you can't beat or at least show up for the first page. Then, by that point, it's really important to do two parts. One is to get Amazon to index it, and the second is to get Amazon to give you a much higher ranking, so that you show up at the top. Because books at the top get more clicks than books on the bottom.

Amazon is a search engine. It's an algorithm. It's a calculation.

Let's talk about indexing. Like we said, Amazon is a search engine. It's an algorithm. It's a calculation. It's not a person that reads a book and says, "Yes, this is a much better book than this one" or "Mmm, this one talks a little bit more about the subject." What it is is it's looking for the right words, so as to say, "Yeah, this book appears to be a part of this. We'll show up in the list somewhere." Could be on the first page, could be on the 70th page.

Those are where you stick the words to get indexed. That includes having this ... If you've identified the keyword, having it in the title definitely helps. Having it in the subtitle helps. Also, when you go to publish your book, you get to choose seven Kindle keywords. In KDP, they literally tell you to put that in there. Make that one of them. Those are ways that you can do it. Also, too, we've done a lot of experiments, and what we found is that words, if people use the keyword in their reviews, that too helps. That's a great indication, because if people are describing your book with that word, then Amazon's like, "It must be about it."

The way you do that is your title, right? People like to say the title of the book they're reviewing, so that's another clear indication that this book is about that. Another thing that we really enjoy is, we found that if you have the words in the book, and yes, Amazon does actually go through and look at your book, because they also test to make sure it's not copywritten or that there's not another copy of your book on the internet, like blog posts or stuff like that. They also index through that as well. That's how you can get your book to show up for search inquiry, so when people type it in, your book shows up.

The next part is making it so that you show up in a searchable way, that you show up at the top instead of on page three. That tactic is all about what makes Amazon more money. Use that as your core thing. If somebody types in how to lose stress, and say your book's at the top, but people are not clicking and buying your book. They're clicking the book that's below you, and they're buying that one. Well, Amazon realizes that more people are looking for that book, so let's put it at the top so it has more sales.

They're not caring whether or not ... Maybe your book is actually about stress free, but the book under you is about your dog's stress or something like that, I don't know, something crazy. If that's the one that keeps showing up, then it's going to sit at the top. At this point, it's all about conversions for that keyword. This is really important, and a lot of authors make this mistake, because ... Say, for example, you're a fiction author, and you write fantasy. You're like, "Oh, if i rank #1 for fantasy, I'll make lots of money." It's like, no you won't actually, because if you're at #1 for fantasy, somebody who types that in, they don't know what they want, so they may click all the way down. They may be looking for a certain type of fantasy.

Showing up for the right keyword helps with your conversions. Having a great cover that sticks out, that looks right for that keyword, having the right title that truly engages and a subtitle that hooks the person, that tells them the benefits or for a fiction author, reaffirms that this is truly a great, epic sci-fi military book, and your book description. All these things come in to prove that you should have the higher click to conversion rate. That is what brings you to the top.

Alinka: Yeah, so maybe for authors who are new to keywords, keyword is not actually just one word, right?

Dave Chesson: No, it can ... Matter of fact, I would highly recommend not targeting one word. If I'm writing that sci-fi book, sci-fi military is much better than just sci-fi. War zone space aliens is way better than just aliens. These words are what the algorithm is looking for. Again, I would much rather rank #1 for sci-fi military space war than #1 for just sci-fi.

Alinka: Yeah, okay, #1 in the category. Once you're #1 in a category, you are an Amazon #1 best selling author in that category.

Dave Chesson: No, what I'm saying is, for the keywords, I would much rather rank #1 for that keyword, so that if somebody types in sci-fi military, and my book shows up #1, I'm going to most likely get the sale. Now, yes, that actually is a category, science fiction military, but remember, category rank is completely dependent on how many sales you get compared to all the other books that are in that category. Categories, while it's great to have that #1 best seller mark, the truth is there's only two times that categories help me sell more books. That's one, if I am #1, and I get that nice little mark that says, "I'm #1."

There's only two times that categories help me sell more books.

1) *If I am #1, and I get that nice little mark that says, "I'm #1."*
2) *If you rank in the top 25 for a highly sought after category.*

That helps with conversions. Remember, we said how important conversions are? If you're the only book that come up in the results that has best seller, you stick out in people's minds, higher chance you're going to get the click. If you've got the good book description, you get the sale.

The second time that it is important, or it affects sales, is if you rank in the top 25 for a highly sought after category. The two ways people buy books is they either type in what they're looking for into the search bar, or they go to their favorite category and they look at the top 25 books, the books that show up on the first page of that category. I love epic sci-fi military, so I'll go to the sci-fi military category and see if there's anything new, and then I'll purchase based off of that.

Alinka: You have two categories, right? You have two categories you can choose, so you can aim for both of these strategies that you mentioned, right?

Dave Chesson: That's exactly it. When I look for my two categories, the first one is a category that, yes, my book fits in but is the easiest to become #1. To check that, again, you look at the #1 book, and you look at their ABSR like we talked about, and so long as your ABSR is better than theirs, you're #1.

Alinka: ABSR is author best seller-

Dave Chesson: Amazon Best Seller Rank.

Alinka: Yeah, okay.

Dave Chesson: Mm-hmm (affirmative), which we explained earlier before, that's that #1 you scroll down on the page.

Alinka: Just want to make sure that everybody's following.

Dave Chesson: Then, the second one is looking at categories that actually do get engagement, that there really are people going to. Sci-fi military's way better than sci-fi space opera military alien invasion, whatever that category is. Many people aren't clicking on that one. I like to hit them both, so as to maximize potential of sale, because that's really what I'm going for, is getting my book out there and read more.

Alinka: How would you test? Because obviously we should test everything. Would you test a set of seven keywords and where you put them in your KDP dashboard and then change maybe one at a time, or would you test first one set of seven and then another set of seven? How do you test keywords to see how they impact sales?

Dave Chesson: No, you actually just said the strategy right there. That's exactly it. You choose your seven and then at that point, you need to give it some time.

Alinka: How much time?

Dave Chesson: More importantly, give it at least two to three months, all right? Here's why. At first, because when you have a new book, when you first publish it, Amazon does what I call the honeymoon period, where they give your book extra love. They like to churn books. They like to bring the new ones up to the top. They'll promote you more. They might put you in the email. You get higher rankings in search results just because you're new, just to test you out. Depending on how competitive other books are around you, it's usually between one to three months, and then after that, it's like the honeymoon's gone. It's like, "Okay." People will see that ... "I was doing good. I was doing good, and then (dropping zoom noise), you know it drops."

I see a lot of people who will do this keyword testing, and they're like, "Oh, I changed it." They might have changed it right when the honeymoon's over, and they're like, "Everything dropped, and I can't ..." Give it until you see that drop. Give it until you see the honeymoon's over, and then start to look at one keyword at a time and make some changes. I would say majority of people who change a keyword will actually see an uptick in sales, and then it drops because they'll get re-indexed and will get put up there, but they didn't convert enough to keep it up there, so then it drops.

What other people will see is that they'll change it, and it turns out that was the good keyword, and then they drop. Immediately switch it back. You're fine. Again, just test one at a time. Don't change them all, and then be like, "Oh, I don't know what was successful or failed." It's important.

Alinka: Yeah, so, how can people assign these keywords? You can do it manually, or can you do it also in a faster, more intelligent way than manually?

Dave Chesson: Yeah. Well, manually, you can go ahead and if you go to Amazon, and this is the important part, you can get Amazon to tell you keywords they suggest. The way that they developed it is that, as you start typing in, they'll try to fill in the blank based off of what people have bought. To do that right, you need to go into Google Chrome and go incognito mode. Incognito mode basically makes you a non-existent person. The reason why that's important is because when you're logged in to your account in Amazon, Amazon knows [inaudible 00:17:15] you like looking for. They know that you tend to like sci-fi military books, so you may write romantic, and they're going to show you some sci-fi military books, romantic sci-fi military. They're trying to make more money.

Alinka: Yeah, it's their business, so-

Dave Chesson: Their suggestions will be more based off of what you've typed in the past. If I put in S, and I let it fill in the rest, it's probably going to say Star Wars, because as you can see, I'm a huge Star Wars nerd. I made a lot of purchases on Star Wars stuff. I can't help it. They're smart like that.

When you go incognito mode, it erases all that. They've got no history on you. They don't know who you are. There's no cookies, which are these things that they'll plug in to track you and make more ads. None of that. Then, when you type in that word, what they suggest is actually the legit, "We don't know who you are, but here's what people type in. Nothing pertaining to you, just people in general." That will give you a really good idea of what Amazon thinks is popular, and so you can start with those.

Another tactic that I like to use, too, is that I like to use Google. There's Google Keyword Planner, which is [inaudible 00:18:30]. You can get words there. Then, Google will give you a whole bunch of suggestions based off of what people are typing into Google, the other search engine. Remember, we called Amazon a search engine? Same with Google. That can give you some ideas, but again, you've got to remember there's a difference between Google market and Amazon market. Amazon is buyers. Google is searchers, but searchers can turn into buyers. That's when you've got to kind of look at that.

We actually just created a software that combines both worlds called KDP Rocket. It brings in all, everything we've talked about, it basically does all that. It goes through Amazon. It tells you what words people are using. It goes through Google and does the same thing, gives you a whole list. Most importantly, it tells you an estimated amount of people per month that type those words into Amazon, so you can know that 40 people a month are ... Excuse me, 200 people a month are typing in stress free, but 400 people a month are typing in how to lose stress. That's huge for a book marketer to understand, that people like these words more than these words, and that can help in so many ways, getting found on Amazon, creating your title and subtitle, increasing your conversions like we talked about.

Then, my favorite part is, we created a competition score, so now you can figure out, "Huh, that's a great term, but there's no way I'm going to beat those books and show up at the top." Like we said, three important parts to keywords. People actually type it in. People actually buy, which we see that, too, how much money people are making, and how competitive it is.

Alinka: Yeah, so we have to figure out where you're sitting between the demand and the competition.

Dave Chesson: Bingo.

Alinka: You're looking for high demand and low competition would be the perfect place to be. Do you think it's possible that there are keywords that will get you into this area?

Dave Chesson: Yeah, my whole business is based off of that. I've got nine best selling books, and every one of them is under a pen name, because I found keywords that are high demand and super low competition. Right now, I think I'm at a $116,000 made from those books.

Alinka: Awesome.

Dave Chesson: Yeah, my first book ... Again, this goes back to that organic traffic. My first book still brings in $1,400 every month, and it has for the past three and a half years. I've never done big promotion pushes. Matter of fact, I caught one family member actually reading my book, and they had no idea I wrote it.

Alinka: That's hilarious.

Dave Chesson: That was actually two Christmases ago, and I'm like, "Oh, this is kind of weird. I feel like I should give you your $10 back."

Alinka: Do you tweak these keywords on a regular basis? How often do you ... That book that you just mentioned, how often do you go in and test a new keyword or change it?

Dave Chesson: Well, I did, when I first wrote the book, it was probably a couple of months of just testing. I actually at the time didn't know anything about the Amazon honeymoon. I probably changed it prematurely. Over time, it was just kind of tweaking it until I got it to its groove, we'll say. I wasn't as motivated to change up those keywords considering that it wasn't doing bad. It wasn't like a dead book, and then I switched it up.

Here's one parting high, big recommendation I give authors. You'll find more success when you niche down. This isn't about rediscovering. This isn't about physicists trying to find that new quantum leap or anything like that. This is about finding something and applying it to a certain market. An example: back in the day, Evernote used to be the thing. There were a lot of people writing books about how to use Evernote. The truth is, is that with like thousands of books that got out there on how to use Evernote, the ones that were truly making the money were the ones that actually really niched down, and they wrote Evernote for Writers, Evernote for Engineers, Evernote for Teachers. You may say, "Yeah, but there's only a small percentage of people typing that in," let me tell you, if you're an engineer, and you type in Evernote, and you see that there's a book just for you, your conversion rate is through the roof.

Those people are going to buy that book over all the other ones, because you're speaking to them specifically. If you're the only book on Evernote for Engineers, well, then for the next couple of years, every engineer that types in Evernote, you're getting those sales. You're not competing against the others. You're always going to have those engineers buying your book. That is a prime example of where people can truly benefit, and knowing that there are engineers typing that term in is a big part of discovering that new market and having yourself that organic sales.

Alinka: This is incredible. No wonder you are the Kindlepreneur after all. This is what you specialize in. How can people connect with you to learn more about keywords and much, much more that you do?

Dave Chesson: Yeah, if you go to kindlepreneur.com, click on my contact page. We have over 100,000 readers per month on that website, but to this day, I don't miss an email. If somebody sends me that contact, if you've got a question out there, maybe I went over something way too fast, hit me up there, and I will personally respond.

Alinka: I know that's true. Dave, now before we go, we need you to assign us some homework. What's the one thing we need to go and do right now to make sure that we have the highest chance to hit that best selling author rank on Amazon?

Dave Chesson: Take your book idea, type it into Amazon's search bar, look at the top five books, look at their Amazon best seller rank and see whether or not they're making money. Again, you use that calculator on Kindlepreneur to convert that into books sold per day, and just track. If you see that those books are making sales, then you know that that idea can make money. That is a much better start than just writing a book and hoping you make money later.

Alinka: This is perfect. Thank you so much, Dave.

Dave Chesson: Yeah, no problem. Thank you for having me.

WERE YOU PAYING ATTENTION?

Q1: What's the first thing you should do before you launch?

Q2: When it comes to book sales, there are only two ways you can make them happen. What are they?

Q3: What is the perfect way to make sales organically?

Q4: What if books similar to yours don't pop up at the top of Amazon's search?

Q5: What is the only way to check if a book is selling on Amazon?

Q6: What are the three things to consider when choosing keywords?

Q7: What are the two things you want Amazon to do for your book?

Q8: What are the five places you should include your keywords?

Q9: What brings you to the top of the page in searches?

Q10: What are the two instances when categories help sell more books?

Q11: What are the two categories you should chose to sell most books?

Q12: How do you test your keywords?

Q13: In what "mode" do you let Amazon's search box fill out the blanks to suggest keywords?

Q14: What's the other place to look for good keywords?

Q15: What type of keywords sell most books?

Q16: What's Dave's big recommendation for authors?

CHALLENGE

Take your book idea, type it into Amazon's search bar, look at the top five books, look at their Amazon best seller rank and see whether or not they're making money.

Use the calculator on Kindlepreneur to convert that into books sold per day, and just track.

If you see that those books are making sales, then you know that that idea can make money.

That is a much better start than just writing a book and hoping you make money later.

THE GOLDEN NUGGETS

Q1: What's the first thing you should do before you launch?

A1: That there really is a market on Amazon for your book idea.

Q2: When it comes to book sales, there are only two ways you can make them happen. What are they?

A2:

a) Amazon sends people to your book and then people buy it
b) You send people to your book and they buy it.

Q3: What is the perfect way to make sales organically?

A3: Having your book show up at the top of Amazon's search engine, known as A9.

Q4: What if books similar to yours don't pop up at the top of Amazon's search?

A4: You won't be able to rely on Amazon to send you traffic. You will be responsible for sending traffic to your book.

Q5: What is the only way to check if a book is selling on Amazon?

A5: Check it's ABSR (Amazon Best-seller Ranking)

Q6: What are the three things to consider when choosing keywords?

A6:

1) That there are people who are typing them in the search box.
2) That those people actually buy those books.
3) That it's not so competitive that you can't beat or at least show up on the first page.

Q7: What are the two things you want Amazon to do for your book?

A7:

1) Index it.

2) Give you a much higher ranking so that you show up at the top (because books at the top get more clicks than books at the bottom).

Q8: What are the five places you should include your keywords?

A8:

1) Title
2) Subtitle
3) KDP dashboard
4) Reviews
5) Inside the book

Q9: What brings you to the top of the page in searches?

A9: The highest click to conversion rate.

Q10: What are the two instances when categories help sell more books?

A10:

1) When you get Amazon's #1 best-seller mark.
2) If you rank in the top 25 for a highly sought after category.

Q11: What are the two categories you should chose to sell most books?

A11:

1) A category your book fits in and is easiest to become #1
2) A category that gets a lot of engagement.

Q12: How do you test your keywords?

A12: You test a set of seven and change one keyword at a time (give it two or three months)

Q13: In what "mode" do you let Amazon's search box fill out the blanks to suggest keywords?

A13: In incognito mode.

Q14: What's the other place to look for good keywords?

A14: Google Keyword Planner

Q15: What type of keywords sell most books?

A15: High demand and low competition.

Q16: What's Dave's big recommendation for authors?

A16: Niche down.

WHAT NEVER TO PUT ON YOUR COVER. THE REASONS WHY READERS DON'T GIVE YOUR BOOK A SECOND GLANCE (DEREK MURPHY)

WHO'S DEREK?

Derek Murphy is an award-winning book designer and artist; now he's committed to writing YA fantasy novels of his own. He also just finished his PhD in Literature, and loves weaving mythology and history into his stories to make readers question the boundary between reality and possibility. Derek specializes in launching services and businesses, building websites, getting more traffic, and creating content that people like and share. In other words he has all the skills necessary to launch a book well. Derek rented a castle for NaNoWriMo 2016!
Connect with Derek at: http://www.creativindie.com.

THE GOLDMINE

Alinka:	Derek, I'm really excited to be able to pick your Creative Indie brain. This is what we want to learn from you, what never to put on our cover and the reasons why readers would never give a book a second glance. You're the go to guy on this subject, so we're all ears.

Derek Murphy: Two parts, so I'll talk about the first one first, which is what never to put on your cover. It's an idea rather than a specific thing. What most authors do wrong is that they try to put a scene together. I have friends who are USA Today, NY Times best selling authors, and they still have the same instinct. I think it's the common instinct for authors when they're starting to design their cover is they think, "I have a scene in mind. I have a picture," because authors are really visual people. They picture this scene that they want to represent their book.

What most authors do wrong is that they try to put a scene [on the cover].

For example, a romance cover where the guy is holding the girl and carrying her this way, and they have this kind of look on their face, and they're wearing these clothes, really specific details, which don't really come across through the cover anyway, because when someone first looks at the cover they've only got maybe a one second immediate emotional impact. For fiction especially you want to have that immediate emotional impact. The details are things that are not going to be noticed right away anyway. It's mostly going to be the color and the layout. The emotion comes from the color, and the contrast, and the layout, not the details.

The genre, which is the other really important part is communicating the subject of the genre on the book cover is going to be the text and the fonts that you've chosen, which are also really important. On the one hand you have the whole image, which should be the mood. You want to communicate the mood that you're promising to your readers through this reading experience, which is mostly colors and contrast. Then you have to communicate the genre, which is branding, and fonts, and text, and also [professionability 00:02:11], because you can see really quickly if something's badly Photoshopped or if the text hasn't been laid out professionally. Often in the cheaper covers it's kind of confusing, because you can get really nice art for two or three hundred dollars. You can get fantastic art by really talented graphic artists, but they aren't cover designers, so they don't know how to put the text on the cover.

I know this amazing artist from Spain who tries to put her pre-mades up on a pre-made cover site. Nobody buys them, because she charges too much, like two or three hundred dollars for a pre-made is kind of a lot, but also just because she doesn't really know how to put text on a cover for publishing. She has this great art, but the text isn't very good, so Indy authors will see it doesn't look very good, but they don't know how to fix it, because they're not designers. They won't spend two or three hundred dollars on a pre-made, because they know that it's like the art would be good if it had better text, which is an interesting thing. When you know what you're doing the text can be a really fast thing to do. I can add text in a couple minutes and choose some fonts, and that's the easiest part of a cover. At the same time, that's one of those things where knowledge really does come from experience.

Using bevel or drop shadow is a very common mistake to try to make your text pop out of the cover.

When I started doing covers 10 years ago I wasn't very good at text either, and I made a lot of the same common mistakes. Using bevel or drop shadow is a very common mistake to try to make your text pop out of the cover. Actually that just means if you had put the text a natural contrasting color against the background, so you have light text on dark or vice versa, and even if the text doesn't pop out, it really should look cohesive. Especially in 2016, bevels and drop shadow are really 1990s/2000s designs, so it really makes your cover look dated. In the last five years flat design has been a lot more common. In almost all covers you see the text kind of blending into the background, because it doesn't have shadow or bevel. You really need to find other ways to make the text pop out without using those kind of text effects.

I got off topic a little bit. Basically what I was saying is that Indie authors think in a scene, and they try to communicate to their artists that they want this scene to be made. Most of the time that scene's not necessary, and it won't have the same kind of emotional impact as something much similar. For fiction there are three layouts I always go to, which are ... I'll use my hand. You'll either have one picture with a landscape, probably with a humanizing element, like a shoe or a briefcase. If you don't have a person there, you need a little bit of something that suggests character, because stories are really character driven. You need to kind to hint at that, or you just have a person in the foreground of a background, or you have a big person in the foreground, or you have the face of a person up on top on the background, like their landscape on the bottom.

With those basic layouts you can do any genre, any fiction cover, and they're going to look pretty good. Those are mostly the matter of finding ... If you have a good cover designer, they can just put it together. Otherwise, if you're trying to do it cheaper, you can find the stock photos you want to use and just say, "I want this simple arrangement," and pay someone on fivver.com even to Photoshop them together and make them look decent. Then people ask about the special, cool effects are mostly contrast, and lighting, and colors, which you do to the photos afterwards. In Photoshop you're just doing layers. You just add layers of light and dark and stuff. The second part of the question, can you remind me?

Alinka: Oh, yeah. We sort of know now what we're supposed to do, but what are the biggest mistakes newly published authors make when creating a cover, either themselves, which is a no no when you're not a designer, or when you give somebody the job, somebody who's not necessarily a real pro? What makes readers go, "Ugh," when they see the cover?

Derek Murphy: It's mostly trying to do too much. It's mostly trying to do a scene with too many people and too many objects, especially the relationships between the characters and the looks on their faces. I've gotten some really bizarre descriptions about the internal temperament of the character on the cover. Almost always the character isn't really making a facial expression or you just see the character from the back. Where I like to cut off the characters is just below the eyes anyways, so you don't get the eye contact. I've tested a lot of cover designs. I still like faces on my cover, because I think they can make an immediate impact, but generally covers without eye contact tend to perform better in a lot of cases, so that's good to know if you're testing different things.

Covers without eye contact tend to perform better.

Basically trying to do too much and trying to do too much of a scene, especially because if you're working with a cheaper designer, they're going to try to do what you want. Often they can do exactly what you want really well and it'll still be the wrong thing, and it won't sell your book. That can be really frustrating, especially if you spend a lot of money on the designer, and you control the process, and you tell your designer what you want them to make. I'm in a weird place, because I charge more than most designers, so I'm going to make sure you get the best cover. I usually won't listen to my clients when they have this idea. I'll say, "That's kind of a mistake." I'll start off saying, "That's one option we can explore, but that probably isn't going to sell. I'll try to make you some other ones, because my reputation as a cover designer is to make covers that get results, that sell. I don't want people to have a cover that ..."

The first three or four years I tried to make covers that my clients wanted, and they were happy, and they got what they wanted, but then they didn't sell that much, which is why they had to keep coming back to me and asking questions about book marketing. That's how I learned so much about book marketing is I had to help all these authors to promote their books. It's really the simplest book marketing in the world is getting a really nice cover in the beginning, because otherwise everything is going to be so much hard just when you're trying to reach out to people, make relationships, try to get reviews. Everything is so much harder with a subpar cover, even a cover that's nicely designed, but just not the right cover for your genre, if it's not doing the job of attracting readers.

The mistake I think is over-controlling the process and also trying to think in a scene. You really need to keep it very simple and focus on an immediate emotional reaction. Focus more on the colors, but then also if you're doing it yourself or if you're trying to hire it cheap, getting the text wrong is a common mistake. That's why I've been trying to actually make templates to help Indie authors to be able to make better looking book cover designs. A lot of that is just text. I'll make like 100 templates with different text layouts. Even if they just try to put their pictures in and use my text or my font, it's going to look a lot better, just because the text is professionally laid out.

That's what I've been trying to work on for several years, but it's a side project, because a lot of authors, even if they're trying to do it themselves, I think if they watch the videos and they learn about book cover design, they learn all the stuff that I talk about, then they'll start making the right decisions. They'll start to notice what they're doing. A lot of it's training. If you don't know what you're doing and it's the first cover you ever designed, you're just going to go with your gut and do whatever you think looks good. Generally the first time you ever do anything is not going to be your best effort.

Generally authors finish their first cover, and they're really excited about it. They love it, because they made it. They go on Facebook and they're like, "What do you think of my new cover?", and they won't really listen to feedback, because they're happy with it, because they made it. That's another danger. I don't like to say that authors can't do things themselves, because I don't like to say that you can only publish if you have $5,000 of extra disposable income to spend on editors, and book cover designers, and everything, but if you can save up a little money to do your cover right, or if you can't save any money, at least if you focus on learning the principals of cover design, so that you make smart design choices, that's the first thing you have to do. It can be free. It's just education. You just have to take the time to learn how to do it.

Alinka: Yeah. You said a lot of super interesting things. I have a bunch of questions to follow up now. One of the things you mentioned are colors. Are there specific colors that attract readers? Do they depend on the genre? Can you go a little bit deeper on the color side?

Derek Murphy: Yeah. It depends on the genre. You can actually Google just psychological responses to color. If you're thinking about painting your room a certain color, if you're painting your room red, for example, you'll feel energized, but also possibly a little anxious, because red is a really activating color. If you're writing a thriller or a horror, then red can be a good color, but red doesn't really contrast well with anything else, so then you have to do black and white or gray. Also if you're doing romance, erotica, red can be kind of an activating color. I think for romance and erotica, generally for romance you use more pink and softer colors, and for erotica you use more right now bright colors, like hot green, or hot pink, bright yellow. Those seem to work really well for erotica.

Reds makes most people anxious I think, unless you're an Aries. If you know anything about astrology, I think Aries like red, but I think that depends on the personality. Every person's going to be attracted to different colors and feel comfortable with different colors, but also the colors have to communicate the genre. People are used to certain genres using certain colors. That's kind of an easy way. It's not exact, but if you look on Amazon, the top 20 best sellers of a specific genre, you'll start to notice some color that jump out. Even if you take a screenshot of those 20 colors, you'll see a palette. You want to kind of stay within that palette for that genre.

Alinka: You're very smart. That's very smart advice. You've helped a lot of authors create covers, you've designed these covers. I saw that you also redesign your own covers every now and then. Do you have some statistics or something you can share about the results after you've changed a cover?

Derek Murphy: Yeah, but it's been awhile. I did an experiment probably like three years ago where I just found I think 10 Indie authors whose covers weren't very good on Amazon, and I just offered to make them new ones to test the results. On average I think I doubled the sales on most of those authors after having the new cover, because there's a pass and fail with cover design. If it's working, if it's okay and it looks professionally designed, then getting a new cover may not have a huge impact, but if your cover isn't working and it isn't well designed, getting a decent cover can immediately boost sales quite a bit.

I've recommended against cover makeovers if someone's already selling well or if I don't think the cover is the problem. A lot of authors, if they're not selling well, they think, "I need a new cover," but if you're invisible on Amazon, if no one's seeing you because your rank is so low, your cover doesn't matter. If you're not reaching anybody, they're not seeing the cover anyway. That's not the reason they're not buying the book. You have to really figure it out first. You have to send some traffic. You do some Facebook advertising to send traffic to your Amazon page and see exactly where your funnel's falling apart and why people aren't buying.

You can do a test where you do Facebook ads with a cover, and then you do Facebook ads just with the description, the same description, but not the cover. Then you can do another test with just some pretty art or something that's attractive, but it's not the cover. If you can get people to click on your ads, that's great, because they're interested in your book. If they go to Amazon and they don't buy it with the same description basically, then it's the cover or a lack of reviews. If you have reviews, and you're getting clicks, and nobody's buying, then it's the cover's the problem.

If you figure out that that's your problem and you make a new one, that'll help a lot. You'll increase your conversions right away. You'll start to get a lot more sales. If you're already selling a lot ... I have another friend who is actually doing pretty well, but she wasn't happy with her sales. She wanted new covers. I was saying, "Your covers are really good already. You don't really need anything better. I don't think it's going to impact your sales a lot," but she managed to find a designer who made better covers than the ones she had. They were good before. They were professionally designed, but then she got the new style, especially in young adult and urban fantasy. It's like very bright, magical, a lot of lights, a lot of glow effects. She got a new cover that's really beautiful, very saturated with colors, just everything's a lot more emotionally gripping than her previous cover.

They are doing better now with the new covers. It's almost always a good idea. It's just that is you're going to spend five or six hundred dollars on a new cover, or more, you want to make sure that's your problem, and you want to make sure you're getting something that's going to work better, because often that might not be your problem. If you spend five or six hundred dollars and you don't see any results, it's not going to do the marketing for you. You still need to get the visibility to your book. Then if you already have that visibility, and you're already getting traffic, and your sales rank is staying pretty high, then it can work.

I do my covers every year, basically because I do all my covers in advance, and I usually start writing from my covers. I started publishing fiction this year. I have dozens and dozens of covers that I like that I've saved from art that I've found over the years. If I see a pre-made or if I see some digital art that I like, I'll just buy it right away. Then I'll write a story for it later. I get better as a designer the faster that I can write fiction. I published four books at the beginning of 2016, and I'm redoing all the covers now, because I'm a lot better designer now than I was a year ago.

I did a pretty good job. They were decent covers. Those books are doing okay, but now I want to focus on maximizing income basically, so that depends on using paid advertising to keep the rank really high. Conversion is really important, or else I won't be able to make a profit. I've been redoing my covers just to make them a little more classy and professional, because it can make a big difference.

Alinka: Yeah. Of course. Derek, what are the trends right now? You mentioned a lot of things, but you know, what has been the evolution of the cover? What did people come up with 10 years ago, and what's working now?

Derek Murphy: That's an interesting question. There's like five or six really good designers who are charging three or four hundred dollars, which I think is pretty cheap for their level or service, but they're all pretty new. Right now, especially in my circles, there's a lot of Indie authors who know who those artists are, so they're all getting covers that are kind of similar looking, because they are great covers and they are cheap. I think everyone's getting a good deal. I see a lot of trends. It's mostly for urban fantasy stuff. Like I said, it's a lot of glow. You know, a character with a lot of glow coming from behind and around her, a lot of magical fantasy stuff.

I see a lot of similarities in those covers, because they're being done by the same artist. I can usually recognize in my circles this one's from Rebecca Frank, this one's from Deranged Doctor Designs. I can recognize a Demonza cover. Demonza's a really good graphic designer. Bookfly is another one that I like a lot, who has really unique, interesting things. I can usually recognize covers that are from designers who are good designers, because I get to know their designs, but also because there's only ... Self-publishing and the publishing world, it's not a really huge community, so there's about six designers who are in my price range, which is like the above $600 price range. Then there's maybe six designers who are in the minus $500 range.

We get a lot of the work in self-publishing circles. Between like 10 or 15 designers I want to say we cover 50% of the market, but I think that's ridiculous. I think what's actually happening is just every self-publishing author I know in my community, in my circles, they're pretty savvy about book marketing and book cover design, so they're hiring these designers or these other designers that they've worked with, because it's kind of a small community and the recommendations float to the top.

At the other end of the spectrum there's tons of new authors who are signing up with AuthorHouse or even Amazon. CreateSpace used to have its own book cover design service inside of CreateSpace, and they don't have that anymore, which is pretty interesting that they decided to get rid of it. I saw a couple years ago they changed their pricing, because they used to have a really expensive pricing level, and then they tried to go cheaper. Now they just got rid of it. I guess it's not where they want to make their money.

If you're starting to figure out self-publishing, a lot of authors will just sign up with a big ... What do you call them? Authors services agency, or a small press, or a self-publishing service where they'll take care of everything for you, because it's easier. They don't know what they're doing, and it feels comfortable to just pay somebody to take care of everything. I recommend against that, because what often happens is those agencies are organizers, and they know how to put things together, and they know how to properly publish. They'll give you a lot of support, but they're going to outsource the cover work to somebody who's generally very competent, but not super, not amazing.

If you want to go that way, you'll get a decent cover that'll do the job, but you won't really get much marketing support. These days a decent cover isn't really good enough. It might be okay for a lot of nonfiction, but for fiction, just like having a mediocre or decent cover, it may not be enough for you to see the results you want. Covers are kind of getting louder to compete for attention, which is also a trend I think. I tend not to do it that way. I'm not that style I was saying, where there's a lot of color and a lot of glow. That's not really my style. I like it a lot. I think it works really well for fantasy. I'll probably hire some of those designers to make some of that stuff for me. My style's probably a little more understated, a little less flashy, but it looks really clean and professional. It also works pretty well. I think it depends on your genre and your audience.

Alinka: Totally. Lots of great value there. I do share your opinion on those organizers that you said. I have a fun question for you. I think you'll have a laugh. What do you think about this option that you have on KDP when you load your book that says,

	"Create your book cover now with our templates."?
Derek Murphy:	On CreateSpace?
Alinka:	On KDP.
Derek Murphy:	I don't know if I've seen that yet. Is that a very new feature?
Alinka:	[inaudible 00:23:31] Because you have your cover, so you don't even see it. When you upload your book you can create ...
Derek Murphy:	I should [inaudible 00:23:37].
Alinka:	... your own cover. They give you templates. Have you ever looked at it?
Derek Murphy:	I have never looked at the KDP side. I've looked at the CreateSpace one, and it's really bad, because their templates, they're beyond terrible, which I think is interesting. Before, it made a lot of sense, because they were selling cover design services, so it made sense that they had really ugly templates in their cover creator so that they could sell their services. That's smart business. Right now their business is in publishing. It would be so easy for them to make a better ... with their budget. I've been trying to build my own online graphic design/cover design software so I can make templates that people can use, and it's hard to make that kind of software. I've been using Google Slides, because with Google Slides there's actually a lot. I can set the size of the cover, and you can use all of the Google fonts. You can't really blend layers together, but you can do simple things and layout a simple cover. I've been doing it especially for marketing stuff, because I can make Facebook headers, or ads, or for book promotion and then share that Google Slide deck with authors. They can get in and edit and add their

pictures and everything. It's a really easy way to make graphic design templates online.

Amazon should totally be able to make a really good software with really good templates, which would make it so much easier for everybody who's self-publishing books on Amazon. That's something they really need to do, that maybe they haven't, especially because now they're not making any money from cover design. It is a huge market. Self-publishing is such a big market, and cover design is such an important piece of that puzzle. Like I said, if you're not going with one of the huge author services houses, if you Google like best cover designers for self-publishing authors, there's only 10 or 20 of us who's names keep coming up.

I don't know. I feel like it's a pretty small community. I don't know if I finished my thought earlier, but I was going to say I feel like 50% of the community is served by a handful of designers. However, there's actually probably 90% of the self-publishing market is coming in for the first time. They're not connected to these communities yet, and they don't know these designers yet. I kind of feel like I know all of these great designers who can do it for a low price, but a lot of authors are finding other websites that show up in Google, or they're clicking on paid advertising through author services. They just sign up for a publishing package or something. Generally that's the first step to publish the first book. After they failed for a year or two and they're ready to publish another book, that's when they start figuring out how to self-publish successfully and how to hire the right kind of help.

It's generally like people tend to find me when they're a little more experienced I think, which actually I just doubled my prices on my site. Before that I was pretty clear that I don't really like to work with first time authors, because they'll usually make my job really hard, because they'll be really passionate about getting this cover idea that they really want, that they think is going to work, and I have to educate them about using the right cover that's going to sell the book, because that's really their main focus. First time authors will get really distracted by the cover design, and they want to get in there and control the process. I think that's a big danger. I think most first time authors do that and end up with something that's not going to work very well for covers, regardless of how much money they're spending on a cover designer.

I probably lost a lot of business because I tell people, "I won't make what you want. I want you to be successful." I think a lot of authors hire someone who makes what they want. I lose business that way, but it also saves me a lot of time, because I don't want to struggle for the first five or more. Even now, even though I'm very clear on my website, I still struggle with authors. With every client it's a give and take between what I think will sell and what we want, and we end up with something in between, which isn't ideal. You always want the cover that's going to sell the most books.

It's personal frustrations. I'm always trying to help authors sell more books, and sometimes they choose cover designs that aren't really the best, like my best work. I always want to feel like I'm giving my best work if they're hiring me. Ultimately, if you're self-publishing, if you're the author, you're the client, and you're the boss, and you call all the shots ultimately. I can try to convince you, but I can't ... What's the word? Twist your arm. You won't be happy if I say, "You have to use this cover." I usually keep backups. I usually say, "Here's the one you wanted. I hope you'll use this one too to test it out. At least get feedback from your audience, because I'm sure this one will sell better," but that's the author's decision.

Alinka: Yeah. I remember the service you mention by CreateSpace, that they actually did covers. With my first book that I published in 2010 I used that service, and what they were doing was they were creating one book according to my specifications and another cover that they thought would work best.

Derek Murphy: Oh, really?

Alinka: Yeah. I remember that now that you mentioned it. I remember that they did that. That was actually a smart move. Now, I wonder what their statistic were on people's choices and then profound statistics on sales. What you really need to do is test. It's a really fun exercise to do, well fun for me. I think it's a fun exercise to test, like do Facebook ads maybe without yet an Amazon page, but just have two landing pages. You would do the same ad with cover A, let's say with a pre-made template that you made yourself, and you sent people to a landing page where they subscribed to your launch team or something, and they see that cover there. You run a separate ad with exactly the same elements, and you just change the cover that you get professionally done. You send them to the same replicated landing page with just a different cover, so that there's no discrepancy. You can't do it with Amazon and send somebody to a different cover than they saw.

You test that, and you see which one gets the biggest clicks and then the biggest sign ups. That's a way that you can test a cover before even launching it on Amazon. Then you have the clear winner. You have the numbers, and nobody can argue with numbers like that.

Derek Murphy: Right. As long as you're targeting well. I would do ads with the cover on Facebook, two sets of ads. I would also do I guess let's say one ad with no art and no cover, although it's kind of hard to get people to click on an advertisement for a book that has no image. You could just use a pretty background image or stock photo art or something. Then I go to a page where you have both covers and try to get the sign ups. It's good to test. I would say sometimes, like when you get Facebook feedback, oftentimes people will just post covers in book groups. That doesn't work so well, because you generally get a lot of other authors who also don't understand cover design. Especially with self-publishing authors, I think the bar is kind of low.

In some of the groups I'm in now everybody's getting the cover designs by these same designers. All the covers look amazing. In other groups where everybody's trying to do it themselves all the covers are pretty bad, and everybody's really supportive. They post a cover, and everybody says, "That's great. Good job. You made that yourself. That's amazing." In Indy author communities people are very supportive, and we try to help each other, but when you're trying to get feedback that can [crosstalk 00:32:22].

Alinka: You're looking for tough love.

Derek Murphy: Yeah. I have a Facebook group that's, "Does my book cover suck?", or, "Does my cover suck?", I think. I basically say if you put your cover in my group, I will tell you if it sucks or not. I can't really help. People ask for feedback, and I can give feedback on what's wrong with the cover, but I don't spend a lot of time on it, because I also know if they're doing it themselves, if I tell them, "You have to use a different font. You have to use different colors. You have to change this, and this, and this," even when they change all those things, it's still not going to look professional. It's still not going to look like a quality cover. Really they almost always need to start over with either use a template, or use something better, or learn Photoshop or something.

Often, I don't know, it can get a little better with enough feedback, but then at the same time, I could give 20 rounds of feedback and they keep coming back with the same cover with slight changes, which is a full time job for me. I don't have time for that either. I don't know. Right now I'm kind of in between. I still do a lot of commenting on Facebook covers, but especially in bigger groups, I don't comment, because almost everybody will say, "I love it." Then I'll say, "It's not good enough. It's not professional," and I'll be the jerk in the room. It's not a good way to make friends, especially people who don't know me.

If I'm in a group where people know who I am, they know I actually charge a lot for cover design, then they're more likely to listen to me. If I'm just in some Facebook group leaving a comment, people think I'm just an asshole who's not supportive. I don't spend that much time Facebook commenting on stuff like that anymore. It is important to get feedback. I think ads are a really good idea if you use Facebook targeting to target readers of your genre who like other books that are similar to your genre. You want to have a list of like your five top contenders, like your five best selling books in your genre that you want to share your audience with. That'll be your keywords and your categories. When you do targeting you'll use those authors. Then you do stuff like in your ad copy, if I'm targeting ...

For example, one of my fiction is kind of like Twilight with mermaids. It's a little bit like that. Another one is like Fallen and Percy Jackson, so I'll target specific books and say, "If you like Fallen Angels, and Greek Mythology, and Percy Jackson, then you might like this book." If you target that really well to people who like those books, it's a very matched audience, and the ad copy speaks directly to them. It's very likely that they would be interested in your book and click your ad. If they're not clicking your ad, it's your cover, because it's not good enough, and they're not interested. If you have a very targeted advertisement, and they're not clicking, it's a problem with your ad copy or probably your cover.

Alinka: Probably your cover, because there's also the description. There's social proof, which are the reviews, the title. If you've tested all those things, then you can easily test the cover. You can test one by one and see how your results change. Awesome. Well, Derek, this was such huge value for people who think they know about covers, but we don't really know so much. [inaudible 00:35:46] I didn't know all these things that you mentioned. I'm glad that I learned a lot, and I'm sure people did as well. I'm really glad that we managed to pick your Creative Indie brain. Talking about Creative Indie, where can people connect with you?

Derek Murphy: Yeah. Creative Indie is my main site, which it's a kind of personal blog about how creative people can make money with their genius. A lot of artists and authors are very creative and very intelligent, but they just can't make money with the things that they're trying to produce. That's the challenge I'm trying to tackle on my blog. For the last three or four years I'm mostly focused on publishing, because that's kind of my main focus and interest in writing fiction. Later it'll probably focus more on actually being more creative or starting businesses or whatever. That's my main, like my hub. I have lots of other sites focused on specific publishing things, like DIY covers, diybookcovers.com or diytemplates.com for book design type stuff. I think I'm pretty easy to find.

Alinka: Yeah. If you type Creative Indie on Google, you're the first [crosstalk 00:37:00].

Derek Murphy: Or Derek Murphy.

Alinka: I just checked that.

Derek Murphy: Yeah. I don't know if I'm first if you Google Derek Murphy. There's a few other Derek Murphys and we compete for the top spot in

Google. I might be pulling ahead now, but it's been awhile since I checked.

Alinka: Creative Indie then.

Derek Murphy: Yeah. Creative Indie works.

Alinka: Derek, well, this was fantastic, but our attendees are action takers, so we just want on last thing. In one short sentence what's the one thing that people can do right now to make sure that their covers convert?

Derek Murphy: I'd start doing the Facebook ads to test your cover right now, even if you already have the cover. You have to figure out if the cover's good enough. If you join some Facebook groups, I have a couple Facebook groups, like Gorilla Publishing, you can post your cover in there, and I'll give feedback, or the Facebook group, I think it's, "Does My Book Cover Suck," or, "Does My Cover Suck?" If you need quick feedback, you can post your cover there and get some feedback. I won't be very nice, but you'll probably get the hint if I don't think it's good enough and I think you need something better.

You can often pay $20 on fivver.com and get something better than what you made yourself. Although I like to help people do your own book covers and I try to support that as much as I can, it's often a lot easier and cheaper to just buy a nicer looking cover. I started recommending 99designs, just because 99designs is a pretty cheap option. It's like $300 for a cover that's decent. If you're not sure what to do, that tends to be a pretty easy solution.

Yeah. Figure out if the cover's the problem. If the cover's the problem, before you do any other marketing that's the problem you need to fix, because you're going to spend 10 times as much time and money basically throwing money away if you're doing advertising and marketing and people

	aren't buying, because the cover isn't professional enough. That's really going to kill you.
Alinka:	Perfect. Excellent advice, Derek. Thank you so much. We're all going to make sure now that we do everything we can to make our covers stand out and convert. Thank you so much for your time.
Derek Murphy:	[inaudible 00:39:17] having me on. Good luck.
Alinka:	Thank you, Derek.

WERE YOU PAYING ATTENTION?

Q1: What should you never put on the cover?

Q2: Where does emotion of the book come from on the cover?

Q3: How do you communicate the genre on the cover?

Q4: What according to Derek is the fastest but most difficult thing to do on the cover?

Q5: What would make your cover look dated?

Q6: What type of design has been more common in the last five years?

Q7: What are the three layouts Derek recommends for fiction authors?

Q8: What's the worst thing an author can put on the cover?

Q9: Do covers with eye contact sell better than covers without eye contact?

Q10: What do you need to focus on when creating a cover?

Q11: How do you find out what the best color for you cover is?

Q12: What does Derek recommend you do to find out if the cover is the problem?

Q13: What trends with covers does Derek mention?

Q14: What mistake do first time authors make with their cover?

Q15: How do you know if your cover will convert?

CHALLENGE

Test your cover right now even if you already have the cover.

THE GOLDEN NUGGETS

Q1: What should you never put on the cover?

A1: <u>An idea (scene) rather than a specific thing.</u>

Q2: Where does emotion of the book come from on the cover?

A2:

1) <u>The color.</u>
2) <u>The contrast.</u>
3) <u>The layout.</u>

Q3: How do you communicate the genre on the cover?

A3:

1) <u>Via the text.</u>
2) <u>Via the fonts.</u>
3) <u>Via the branding.</u>

Q4: What according to Derek is the fastest but most difficult thing to do on the cover?

A4: <u>Add the text with the correct layout and fonts.</u>

Q5: What would make your cover look dated?

A5:

1) Bevels
2) Drop shadows

Q6: What type of design has been more common in the last five years?

A6: Flat design.

Q7: What are the three layouts Derek recommends for fiction authors?

A7:

1) A picture of a landscape with a humanizing element.
2) A big person in the foreground.
3) The face of a person up on top on the background, landscape on the bottom.

Q8: What's the worst thing an author can put on the cover?

A8: A scene with too many people and too many objects. Trying to include the relationships between the characters and the looks on their faces.

Q9: Do covers with eye contact sell better than covers without eye contact?

A9: No. It's the opposite.

Q10: What do you need to focus on when creating a cover?

A10: Immediate emotional reaction.

Q11: How do you find out what the best color for you cover is?

A11:

1) Google "psychological responses to color".
2) Use the same color palette as the best-sellers in your genre.

Q12: What does Derek recommend you do to find out if the cover is the problem?

A12: Send some traffic to your Amazon page and test.

Q13: What trends with covers does Derek mention?

A13:

1) A lot of glow, especially in urban fantasy.
2) Covers are getting louder (a lot of color and glow).

Q14: What mistake do first time authors make with their covers?

A14: They insist that the designer creates a scene they have in mind even if it won't sell. They won't accept constructive criticism.

Q15: How do you know if your cover will convert?

A15: Test it.

HOW TO LEVERAGE THE POWER OF SOCIAL MEDIA TO BUILD A 5-FIGURE INCOME INSTEAD OF SUFFERING FROM TIME-SUCK AND OVERWHELM (KIRSTEN OLIPHANT)

WHO'S KIRSTEN?

Kirsten Oliphant wrote her first novel in third grade on the colored pages of a Hello Kitty notebook. After getting her MFA in Fiction from UNCG, she writes novels that she may finish sometime when her four small children go to college. In 2015 she founded Create if Writing, a site and podcast dedicated to writers and bloggers who want to build an online platform without being smarmy. She holds live workshops and has written books and courses about email lists and loves to talk social media. Connect with Kirsten at http://createifwriting.com.

THE GOLDMINE

Alinka: Kirsten, you live and breathe social media, so tell us, how can we leverage the power of social media to build a five figure income instead of suffering from time suck and overwhelm?

Kirsten: That's a huge question, and if we all could do it right then we'd all be making five figures in no time, right? Here's what I will say. I do love social media. I really enjoy spending time connecting with people. I love everybody seeing the numbers go up as you engage and start to see more followers, and when you see actual things happen from it, like when you see people interacting with your stuff and sharing your stuff and clicking though to something and buying something it's really exciting and such a good feeling, but it is a big time suck and so I don't know that there's necessarily a secret but I'm going to share with you guys some of the tips and the things that I've learned and maybe some advice that might surprise you, because as much as I love social media and think that it's an integral part ... We all know we can't escape it.

I think if we're not harnessing that power to do the right things, like giving people the right calls to action, it's not going to work for us. That's the mistake I see most people make, is that a lot of the authors and people, and I've made this mistake too and sometimes still do, we just promote our own stuff. We just share links and links and links and links to buy our stuff, to see our stuff, to read our stuff, instead of actual engagement and instead of driving people to our email list where we can connect on a deeper level.

Alinka: Yeah, plenty of answers in that. Let's sort of divide and conquer the subject. What's the rookie mistake that a new author makes?

Kirsten: The rookie mistake I think, and I see this most in Facebook because you notice it more. Twitter, I feel like everybody's just tossing stuff up, so if you're just up there promoting your stuff, that's just kind of normal. It's not really effective but normally you don't see it that much. Facebook however ... First I'll say every platform's different, so one mistake is that people treat them the same, and so the fact that I'm just making that distinction between Facebook and Twitter will tell you that every platform is not the same. Every platform has its own set of rules, set of expectations, and kind of a culture, and so you have to spend time on them to get that culture.

Twitter, it's not the best thing to just promote, promote, promote, but it's not going to hurt you the way it will on

Facebook, so if you're trying to do a Facebook page or even if you're trying to interact in Facebook groups, which there's tons of these author groups, the biggest mistake I see people making is only dropping those links to their stuff. "Here's my book, here's my book, here's my book, here's my blog post, here's my book, here's my website, here's my book." Because, no one cares. When you do that people just turn off because there's not a person behind it. There's no sense of urgency or reason to do that. There's no sense that you're actually trying to connect with anyone. You just want something from them.

On social media, it's called social for a reason. There is an expectation of interaction.

On social media, it's called social for a reason. There is an expectation of interaction and so if you're just going in to ... I joined a couple author promo groups on Facebook and after, like, a day or two I left because all it was was people going in and dropping a link, dropping a link, dropping a link, and nobody ever liked a post. Nobody shared. It was just authors hoping that this might result in one book sale or having their book really take off, but no one's going to interact with you or buy your book or anything if you just go drop links all over the place, and I run a Facebook group and I'll have authors jump in there, and the first thing they do within 30 seconds, they've got it obviously copied and pasted, because I approve them in the group and then 30 seconds later there's this giant post about their book, which I delete and then send them an email saying why that's not a good idea.

Often they'll just leave the group. They don't want to hear why. I've tried to have conversations like, "Hey, you know," really nicely, like, "Please don't do that." And it's not effective. It's not an effective strategy but people are like, "Okay, thanks." And then they just go keep doing that, so I think that's the biggest mistake, is not being social, dropping links everywhere, and really, it burns bridges and makes you look not super professional.

Alinka: Yeah, so what should people do instead?

Kirsten: Instead of that, and this takes more work but I'll kind of give you some tips in a second because if we're talking about avoiding the overwhelm, more work doesn't sound like it's really helpful for that, so I'll get to that in a second, but what you really want to do is you actually do want to dive in, and maybe you're just going to pick one platform and that's part of the tip I'll get to, but you need to find a group of people to actually talk to and find groups that you can actually talk to. If you're going on Facebook, if you have a Facebook page, there's debate about whether you should share other people's content or your own. I always share other people's content. I think that it only helps. It gives people a sense of ... I share content my readers would be interested in.

Whether that's mine or someone else's, I share that content because it lets them know who I am. It's kind of being a good curator of other people's content as well as your own that you create, so you're a creator and a curator, but even if you're just asking questions on your Facebook page, people love answering questions. Especially if it's easy ones. Things like, "Where do you live? Everybody hop on," or, "Share a picture of what you're doing right now." It's amazing, those kinds of things, and in a Facebook group as well. I don't do as much with my page. I do a lot with my Facebook group, and those kinds of posts, people love to post something.

They love to see each other's pictures and even things that are off-topic sometimes. Like, "Hey." I have kids. We don't talk about kids there much, but, "Share a picture of your kids." People love that. Or your cats or dogs. People really do [inaudible 00:05:52] that kind of thing, so anything that can get people talking, show that you're a human, so that there's some sense that you're not just trying to use them for what they can do for you, if that makes sense.

The hard thing is, like I said, that's a lot more work, but here's kind of the tip part for that, and I've done this a lot this year, which is that you might need to scale back. I do recommend at least getting a consistent handle, like your name, on social media platforms, but you can't, unless you have a ton of time and you really love it, you can't use them all well, and what works for another author might not work for you, for your personality, and you might not love a certain platform, so I would say scale down, pick one platform to start, and if you're trying to decide how to do that, think about what platform right now seems to be working for you, what you love.

Maybe one you hate and you're doing it but you really hate it. I'm sorry if the one you hate's the one working, so maybe you can learn to love it if it's working for you, but pick one that you love. Pick one that's working for you, and really dig deep. See what it takes. Try different things. Most social media platforms have some kind of analytics, so your Facebook page has analytics, your group often will just show you who's seeing things, and on mobile now I've seen something cool if you run a Facebook group. On mobile sometimes you'll get this little alert, like, "Hey, do you want to bump this into the notifications of people that didn't see it?" I think that's something they're testing because I don't see that all the time, but I always say, "Yes, of course. Tell them that they missed something."

Check your analytics. [...] What's working for you?

Twitter has analytics. Pinterest is the least social but Pinterest, I would say if you're an author who does a lot of blogging and creates a lot of content, Pinterest can be fantastic for you. It's not super social but it's a great traffic driver. Check the analytics. Instagram, that's the one I kind of jumped off of this year. I realized I can't do them all and I took a break from Instagram which felt really nice and it didn't hurt me at all, so sometimes you need to pull back. You can use Iconosquare to check your analytics there. Maybe just do a test. What's working for you, what do you love? And try to find that sweet spot where you can dig in and actually engage with people and be a person, where you can be social, so you're mixing up your promoted posts, your blog posts, your book posts, maybe with other kinds of content, articles they would like, and questions to actually engage conversation.

Alinka: All right. Perfect. Let's talk a little bit maybe about Facebook. What do you recommend that authors do? Get a Facebook page? Yes or no? Have a group? And what should they do? How should they engage? Instead of shouting, "Buy my book," how do you engage? What type of stuff do you share? You said real stuff, show that you're a human, but instead of posting about your cat all day what would you recommend authors post about?

Kirsten: This is always like the trick question, right? It comes in with email list as well or blog, like what in the world as an author do I share? And different authors do different things, so you may have to try out some things. I'll start with the first part of your question, the Facebook page versus group. I would say, maybe both, especially if Facebook is going to be your platform. Here's why. Here are the pros and cons of each. Facebook page, I would say even though they're really hard to grow, Facebook has just made that really difficult, so unless you're really, really posting a lot or posting good content or sharing viral things, memes and stuff like that, your Facebook page, it's hard to grow, but Facebook ads, I think most authors know, that's a really effective thing and a lot of authors are using this and doing trainings on this, so if you want to run Facebook ads you have to have a page.

I would say for no other reason, get a page so you have that, and do some minor stuff. You can schedule, even right within Facebook, where it says, "Post," there's a little drop down menu and you can schedule things, so you could go in one night a week, schedule a bunch of posts, like one thing a day, or try five things a day. Mix of questions or photos or links, and see what happens, because again, Facebook has insights on those pages and that can help you also see what is your audience even interested in. Sometimes if you're just getting off the ground, some of these other groups that may, like, "Hey, let's go like each other's pages." Sometimes you just need a couple likes on there and you need to do that, but if that's all you're getting is other authors liking your stuff, you need to find the readers, and that's where the Facebook ads can come in, because you can actually ... And there's tons of free trainings on those as well.

You can target certain kinds of readers. People who like this author's page if that author's like you, so that's really helpful to both build your page and also to maybe sell books. As for Facebook groups, this is where I'm really happy right now. I've mostly scaled back on almost everything except for Facebook groups right now, and Pinterest but again that's not super social, it just drives traffic to my site and it's not hard. I can click on Pinterest, you can go pin things, and disappear and it's not a big deal, whereas social media, most of it, you can't do that.

Facebook groups, they can be slow to grow as well, however, what this lets you do is really get to know the people in them. Some authors have kind of two parts, where they teach people how to write or talk about the writing process which might attract somebody different, and then the readers. If you're trying to attract just readers, that's a little bit harder and I think that's where so many people struggle, and I think it's really helpful to kind of peel back what you're thinking as an author and put on that lens as a reader, because most of us are readers, right? We all love reading which is why so many of us love writing, because we fell in love with reading, so think about some of your favorite authors. What, as a reader, would you want from them?

If you joined a Facebook group, and I'm going to use Stephen King, because I grew up reading Stephen King. If you were in a Facebook group with Stephen King, what would you want to be shared there and how would you want him to engage? What kind of content would be interesting to you? I would think ... I was actually really disappointed. I joined his mailing list and it was like there's no content at all, and I was kind of like, "I would be really curious as to what he would send out," but maybe you'd share trailers to scary movies. Maybe you would ask people what were their favorite scary stories growing up.

Those are the kinds of things I think of, and sometimes it's more helpful when we're looking at it that way from a distance, so maybe ask somebody else to do this for you. Like, "Okay, here's the kind of genre I write, you know me, what would you be interested in as a reader hearing from me?" Because I think the best thing we can tap into is curiosity. We are all so curious about other people, and I think the rise of reality television and celebrity gossip and all this stuff shows us, we want to know what's going on people's lives. We don't probably want cat videos all day.

However, people do like to see you're real to some degree. They like to see your writing life, too, like, "Here's my writing space." I have a friend who's building her author page and she's been sharing what her author space ... Like, "Hey, I'm renovating. Here's what it looked like before. Here's what it looks like after," and people are really engaging. "Here are my test covers, what do you guys think?" Asking for their opinions. Letting them have some ownership over what you're creating really helps us well, because it gets them engaged in a book before it's even out, but I know as an author it is frustrating.

It seems like so many people have a leg up if they're teaching you how to write, too, but then they're building a separate audience. I interviewed Joanna Penn who a lot of you guys may know, and she talked about how there's almost, she would guess, a 10% overlap of the people who follow the creative Penn and the people who buy her J.F. Penn novels, so non-fiction to fiction, there's not a ton of crossover, so consider that when you're posting, but it is a little bit easier to find people because if you're teaching people something it's just a little bit easier, so give yourself some grace if you're trying to build just an audience of readers that it can be hard, but we know books sell.

There are tons of readers out there. It's just a matter of trying to connect with them and then kind of really connecting with them and letting yourself be a little bit more vulnerable perhaps in the Facebook page or group.

Alinka: Excellent. You mentioned running Facebook ads. Do you usually run them towards your website or a landing page or your Amazon page? What do you do?

Kirsten: I am still really trying to figure Facebook ads out. I have mostly been running them not towards my books but towards growing my list, because my list is such a huge part of what I'm doing, but also I've done a little bit of promoting videos to kind of see what that does, because the other thing is, even if you're just testing and doing a five dollars a day for three days, you can kind of see how people are interacting. Like, "Okay, people love the video." I just recently ran one with a video. "They love the video, but nobody did anything," so the call to action was ineffective in the video, but it had a lot of watches, but it didn't actually bring me back anything.

Testing is the best way. You need to educate yourself,

So I think testing is the best way. You need to educate yourself, and I'm still trying to figure that out. I know a lot of stuff but I haven't seen a lot of things be super effective for me, yet, and that's what people say is that you need to learn how to do them and then test, but the nice thing is being able to choose a targeted audience, and actually the easy thing is to boost a post. They used to just say, "Boost," and it would boost it to your followers. Now if you boost a post, like click that, "Boost," button in the Facebook page, it gives you more of the ability to target, but not the full degree that if you go into the Facebook ads manager and the power editor, so that would be a tip.

You could boost posts more easily to kind of see what things do and choose some pages, but you might want to start by ... If you're getting started with Facebook ads, again, do a lot of research. I can't teach a whole ton on this, and people have whole courses, so it would be hard to do, but I would say, research, kind of make a list of who you think you could target, so similar authors ... Because Facebook, when you're doing ads and trying to target, they won't show you everybody's page, so you'll start typing it in, and it'll either come up with the name or not, so some authors, even if they have a big page, may not be on there, and no one understands this. It's a Facebook mystery, but trying to figure out groups to target.

Going on Amazon and looking for books that have a ton of reviews that are similar to your genre, then looking for that author, because people who liked, "This," are likely to like your book, right? I would say start by researching Facebook ads and then looking at that targeting, and don't be afraid to test and don't give up if it doesn't work at first, because that's what I'm finding is it's not bring in what it to bring in yet for me, so I'm just testing a lot of things. I think once you find, and if you talk to other authors who have found great success with this, once you find kind of the ... I hate to say formula, because anytime you find a formula it breaks right after you find it, but for you, maybe there's a perfect formula. Like, "Okay, this targeting works for these authors. This one it didn't. People liked videos or no, people only liked the image."

There's so many options within Facebook ads, there's a lot of testing to do, so I would just recommend learning about it, testing with a little bit of money, and if you see something taking off, pour more money into it, because you can start out by saying, like, "Five dollars a day," or even less than that a day, and then if you see it picking up steam and people really responding then amp that right up, because if it's working then let it keep on working for you.

Alinka: Excellent. There are certain ... A lot of courses out there, and also Facebook has their tutorials which are also valuable that we can follow. I did play with Facebook ads a couple years back, and I agree with you. Testing is a huge part of it. I would do like 10 different ads. I would test the copy, test the call to action button, test the image, target by one interest, and you really try to understand what's working and what's not, so it is ... And you said, you scale the winners and you kill the losers, and when you find something that works you incrementally pour more money into it, but you can't go from like five dollars to 500, you just go step by step, so yeah that can work.

I would recommend doing what you did, to direct people to a landing page, because once you've got them on your list, then you can tell them about your books and whatever, and if you just send them to Amazon, well, that's where they go, and the percentage of people who will end up on your mailing list will be much, much lower.

Kirsten: Absolutely.

Alinka: Yeah. Excellent. What's the trend in social media? What do you think will be happening right now?

Kirsten: It sounds really cliché, because I keep saying every year they've said this, but, video. I think especially live video because it's become so massive, whether it's on Facebook or Instagram is now doing that and people are on Snapchat doing these little bits. The nice thing about the trend being live is that for those of you who like me have kind of hesitated a lot at video because you need certain things to make it look polished, live video does not have to be polished, so you are free to do a live video with bad lighting. You want people to be able to hear you. You don't

Live video [has] become massive.

want it to be terrible, but people are not expecting a polished, professional video. They're just not.

Facebook, especially, that's a really great place to be using it. Even if you're an introvert out there and you're like, "No," I'm an introvert, okay? You can turn it on for a little bit of time and then hide in a closet or read for a couple hours to kind of debrief from it, but again for the engagement it's a great way to engage. Facebook, because it's newer, they reward it, and you want to do what Facebook rewards on its own, so Facebook is promoting live video, and that's just somewhere you really want to be.

Instagram just rolled out live video, and I think it was as we were recording this, like last week, so who knows how that will be. There's also Instagram Stories. There's a lot of options for video that are more entry level, so I feel like the barrier has been broken down, from the people who have these Youtube channels with these really get videos with the editing and all the lighting and everything great, you think, "Okay, I can't do video." Well, you can, because you can start at this place and do live video or do Snapchat or do Instagram, something that ... For the stories ... Instagram, the photos have to be really beautiful for it to really work over there, but for Instagram Stories, if you're doing video, it doesn't.

That's great for those of us who don't want to invest in camera equipment. No, polished videos may not be a part of our platform over all. We can dive in at this easy entry point, even though it's scary. It is. It's scary, but once you get used to it, the engagement really jumps up, and I started doing a live video. Last week I did a challenge in my Facebook group, and I showed up live every day. It was supposed to be at the same time, but because I have a baby it wasn't. We also have a puppy so it's nuts over here, but people still showed up and there was one day where only two people showed up and it was really disheartening, and I showed up the next day, I tried a different time, and like 15 people showed up and they were talking and asking questions and commenting and it was so much fun. I actually enjoyed it even though I do always get nervous before doing the videos.

You just have to kind of pretend. You have to jump over that hurdle, so I would recommend highly video whatever platform, but don't let the word video scare you, because live video makes it easy for you and for me who don't want to maybe have a polish. If you do have all the polish and you're like, "Oh, this is great news to me because I do video," great. Keep doing video. Bump it up. Mix in some live with the polished video, but they've been saying this is the year of video for like five years, but it continues to be the trend.

Alinka: All right, so everybody go do some videos. This question is important. What do we do to actually work on building our platform on social media rather than getting sucked into it and start playing all the games they push and losing most of our time on those sites?

Kirsten: Here's what I have been doing lately and this has really helped, is two things. One, I think it's really important to kind of develop almost like a workflow, and I read a post over at Jane Friedman's blog called, "How to Use Twitter in 15 Minutes a Day," and I kind of just talked through a workflow, and I don't always do it because, right now, again, I've scaled back almost everything but Facebook, just for the amount of time I don't have right now, but I made a workflow. Like, "Here's what I do. I check in. I see who's talked to me. I talk back to them and reply to them. I see who's shared my posts. I thank them. I look at content I want to share. I schedule that out, and then I get off."

Maybe you jump into the live stream a little bit of what's going just for a few minutes, and set a timer. The timer is really the key and that leads me into my second tip. I've started setting timers on my phone, so at noon a Pinterest timer goes off and reminds me to go to Pinterest. I don't have a timer that tells me to turn it off because typically I just don't have any time, so I don't need a timer. I have probably five to 10 minutes and then it's gone, so my Pinterest timer goes off, I open up the app on my phone and I go in and pin natively in Pinterest.

I have a Twitter alarm set at 11:40 PM. I stay up really late so it's also kind of a like, "Hey, you should probably think about going to bed some time soon," alarm. That reminds me to go into Twitter if I have time that day, because I've been, again, working on big projects in little spaces of time, so I don't always have time, but that alarm that goes off every single day reminds me that those two platforms, I need to spend some time. Facebook, I don't have to set a reminder because, again, that's been my focus is in my Facebook group especially, so I would say get a workflow going. Make a list, like, "Okay. I'm going to log into Twitter and do these four things and I'm going to do it for 10 minutes, and I'm going to set an alarm on my phone that tells me to start," and if you need it, "Tells me to stop," so you don't get sucked in.

For me, the danger's not getting sucked in because I don't have time to get sucked in, but if you do, then set the alarm to stop you also, so that has been really helpful for me to even just get on the platforms, say, "Hi," interact a little bit, if you don't have the time to spend a lot of time. Facebook, for me, I just kind of keep track. When notifications pop up I try to stay on top of them because as a group owner, that's something I really want to be present in my group to build that connection. So yeah, get a workflow and set a timer.

Alinka: Awesome. I think this is an excellent tip. Kirsten, do you have any other things, any other tips for authors regarding social media?

Kirsten: I would say, sometimes, I know it's not the same across the board, some people really enjoy social media, but I think overall, I see people kind of like groaning, because the idea of building your own platform is relatively new. We didn't used to, as authors, have to go out and find our audience. The way publishing looked when I dreamed about it as a girl, you get a publisher and they do that for you and you just kind of hang out, right? And write your books. That's the dream, although in talking to people that had that dream fulfilled, that's not actually how it worked back then either, but, social media has made it so that we have to do this, even if you're getting traditionally published.

If you're doing it on your own or if you're doing it through a publisher, you have to do it and so I think because we have to ... So much of the time the conversation, it just sounds really heavy. "Oh, social media." There's this ... I don't know, people don't like it. People don't want to do it and it sounds just like the last thing you want to do, so for me I would really encourage people to reframe that discussion. Instead of thinking about social media as this thing you have to do and you don't like it and you wish you were back in the good old days, think about the fact that we now have the ability to connect with our readers in ways we never did before.

I went to a book reading recently at a local bookstore and heard a guy who wrote books I read when I was in middle school. I took my nephew who was in middle school at the time, because he reads his books [inaudible 00:27:03] because he's still writing. He started writing when he was in high school. Gordon Korman, who's ... I don't know if he's from Canada. I think he's from Canada, but he has been writing since I was in middle school, so I read his books. My middle school nephew, we went to see him, we got to meet him and talk to him and that was so much fun, and I love meeting people live, but in the past, that was the only way to connect with your favorite authors.

Maybe you'd get to go to a book signing. Maybe you'd get to meet him. Maybe not. Now, you can connect. Authors are accessible. You can connect with your readers. Your readers can talk to you. They can say, "We love this part of your book. We're super fans." That was never really possible before. People could maybe write you letters or send them to your publisher back in the day, so there's no personal connections. I think if we can reframe the discussion of thinking of social media as this thing we have to do and think of, "Wow, what a privilege that we can actually talk to the people who have our books in their hands, or in their Kindles or in their iPhone. Wherever they're reading, we can actually connect with those readers. We can hear back from them, hear feedback from them."

That is kind of an honor. It's kind of a privilege, so that would be kind of my thing to leave people with, is if you're really struggling with social media, before we even get to the time suck factor, change your attitude. Think about the privilege that it is to be able to interact with your readers. To have them reach you, to reach them. That is just so cool, so if social media is bogging you down, realize what a gift and a privilege it is that we now have this really cool tool, and think of it that way instead of thinking of it as something that you have to do.

Alinka: That was awesome, Kirsten, and I would just like to let our audience know, because they don't know this yet, that you were able to conquer social media with five children.

Kirsten: Yes. Barely these days, it feels like, but yeah, there's seasons. Like, I'm in a season. I've got a seven, eight week old baby. I can't do as much and I have to realize that and maybe you hit a season where you can't do as much, and when that happens, that's when the rubber hits the road and you figure out, "Okay. I'm going to pull back on everything but this one particular thing. I can only do Facebook, only this much a day. I can only do this if I actually want to get my work done, my writing of my books done." You can do it, but maybe you want to take a break, if there's times I'm like, "Maybe I should have taken more time off," but I love what I do so it's hard, but you can. You can do it, but it does take a lot of, I think, planning, and there's where it's really key is the planning stuff.

Alinka: You're such an inspiration because if people want they can find a lot of excuses not do things but you can find ... If you want to, you find a way to get things done. Like you said, you have a limited number of small pockets of time, and you prioritize and you get things done, so way to go, Kirsten. This is incredible, yes, and if our listeners don't have five children ... Everybody has their own set of challenges of course but I just wanted to show that you can get it done. If Kirsten is able to prioritize and get things done ... Because with five kids you could just close the doors, never go out, never do anything. It's not required that you do anything at all, but you're going out there. You're active. You're doing what you love and it can be done, so this is amazing.

Kirsten: Well, good.

Alinka: Yeah. I only have two children, so-

Kirsten: There's no only, though. There's no only with kids. I feel like with one it was hard, with two it was hard, with three, so it just is hard all around. I'll point this out too, for me, I did have to let some dreams go. I do a lot. I love fiction, but for me, my head space, I can't write fiction with my kids. Until all of them are in school for a large block of time, because the way that my writing process is, I need hours, and when I get interrupted I get really mad, and so I don't want to ... For now, I'm doing a lot of training and podcasts and interviewing people because I'm curious, but fiction has kind of been shelved, so I don't want anyone to feel pressure. Like, yes, you can do stuff with five kids or whatever your situation, a full time job, whatever it is you're dealing with, but you may have to shelve something and that's okay.

I know it will be there for me. I wish I were writing it now, but I know I can't, and I've kind of released myself and given myself the freedom to do what I can, which is still a lot, but non-fiction or social media or training, all this I can jump in and out of easily, where fiction, I have to live there, so I just had to shelve it for a bit, so give yourself the freedom to do what you can, but you can do a lot. You just have to be smart about it.

Alinka: Perfect. I couldn't say it better. Kirsten, how can people connect with you?

Kirsten: The best way is to head over to my site which is creatifwriting, like creative, but creatifwriting.com I've got things on there, right on top there's a big sign up button, but if you want to actually subscribe, you can go to creatifwriting.com/subscribe which will get you onto my email list which is where all the good stuff is, and then I also have my Facebook community which is a really great place to be and that's just creatifwriting.com/community, so it's pretty easy to find me. My podcast, Creatifwriting is on iTunes so, Creatifwriting, if you Google that you'll find me all over the place.

Alinka: Awesome. One last thing. Our challenge participants are action takers, so what one thing should people be doing right now to make sure they use social media rather than getting used by social media on their way to a five figure income?

Kirsten: I would go back to what I mentioned about the timer, so right now pick one or however many platform, if you're doing a couple, pick those platforms, get your phone out, or if you use some other kind of device, whatever it is, an iPad, something with an alarm, set a reminder daily that will come up to remind you to do some kind of interaction, or maybe at the top of the hour, maybe every hour an alarm goes off and you spend five minutes on Facebook. Whatever it is for you, figure out an alarm that you can set, and maybe if you need it to pull you back out, the alarm to stop, but do that whether it's one time a day or a couple times a day so that you're actually spending the time, because sometimes we lose the social media.

We either dive in and get lost or we don't do it at all, so let's avoid the extremes, make a time, do what works for you in terms of that, but a couple times a day have an alarm, set it, go in there and then get out when you need to get out so that will get you in there, having you interact and actually do things, but avoid the getting lost forever.

Alinka: Perfect. That's what we're going to do right now. Thank you so much Kirsten.

Kirsten: You're welcome. Thanks so much for having me.

Alinka: Of course.

WERE YOU PAYING ATTENTION?

Q1: What's a crucial element of social media you need to get right?

Q2: What is the first mistake authors make on social media?

Q3: What's a rookie mistakes when it comes to social media?

Q4: Why shouldn't you be posting "here's my book"?

Q5: What's one piece of advice Kirsten gives authors on harnessing social media?

Q6: Which feature of social media should you be paying attention to?

Q7: What do you need if you want to run Facebook ads?

Q8: What Facebook feature really allows you to get to know people?

Q9: What type of contents should authors be sharing?

Q10: What's the key to success when running Facebook ads?

Q11: What's an easier way of running Facebook ads?

Q12: What's the trend in social media now?

Q13: How do you avoid social media time suck?

CHALLENGE

Pick a platform and set a daily alarm to remind you when to start and when to stop engaging on social media.

THE GOLDEN NUGGETS

Q1: What's a crucial element of social media you need to get right?

A1: The call to action.

Q2: What is the first mistake authors make on social media?

A2: Promote their own stuff.

Q3: What's a rookie mistakes when it comes to social media?

A3: Treating all platforms the same.

Q4: Why shouldn't you be posting "here's my book"?

A4: Because no one cares. That's not engagement.

Q5: What's one piece of advice Kirsten gives authors on harnessing social media?

A5: Pick just one platform and dive in.

Q6: Which feature of social media should you be paying attention to?

A6: Analytics.

Q7: What do you need if you want to run Facebook ads?

A7: A Facebook page.

Q8: What Facebook feature really allows you to get to know people?

A8: Facebook groups.

Q9: What type of contents should authors be sharing?

A9: Stuff they'd like their favorite authors to share with their readers.

Q10: What's the key to success when running Facebook ads?

A10: Testing.

Q11: What's an easier way of running Facebook ads?

A11: Boosting posts.

Q12: What's the trend in social media now?

A12: Video is huge.

Q13: How do you avoid social media time suck?

A13: Set a timer.

THE SHOCKING MISTAKES AUTHORS MAKE THAT KEEP THEM FROM GETTING TO 5 FIGURES (DEREK DOEPKER)

WHO'S DEREK?

Derek assists self published authors on how to successfully, write, publish, and market their books. After going through numerous trainings, reading books, and following the recommendations of gurus and still seeing stagnant sales he decided to do things his own way. His approach to book marketing led to hitting #1 bestseller in the highly competitive category of weight loss. He is committed to ensuring authors get the essential insights they need, which are often counter to what's commonly being promoted, to ensure any serious author can make a breakthrough in their own publishing and marketing efforts.
Connect with Derek at http://ebookbestsellersecrets.com/first1000.

THE GOLDMINE

Alinka:	Derek, as bestselling author of Why Authors Fail, we need to know what are the shocking mistakes that authors make that keep them from making a five-figure income.
Derek Doepker:	Alinka, first of all, thank you for having me on and I'll jump right into it. One of the biggest

The most successful authors [...] go, "What book will become a bestseller," and then they go write that book.

mistakes, this is the whole foundational mistake that I see authors make, is that is they take this approach of I'm going to write a book and then they ask themselves, "How do I make this book a bestseller?" If you're wondering, if you're thinking, "Okay, that's pretty normal. What's the flip side?" The most successful authors do something a little bit different. They go, "What book will become a bestseller," and then they go write that book. Here's what this looks like: I think with the end in mind, fiction or non-fiction or considering what's going to be the title, the hook that pulls people in, come up with that before even writing the book. Think about the description. Think about how this is going to stand out in the marketplace and really get a clear picture and plan on what that is and then go and create the book around that.

Now, the caveat I want to give to this is some people might hear that and they go, "Well, does this mean I can't be creative? Does this mean I have to just like sell out and do what the market wants?" My answer is this would fall into the other mistake of thinking that it's got to be one or the other. See, successful authors realize that you can have both. You can do what you want. You also need to cater innocence to the market. You're in a business that's about serving others, serving the readers, delivering what they want, so striking that balance between what I want to do as an author and making sure that aligns with what readers want and what readers are looking for because if it's only about what I want as an author, then I have a hobby and not a business.

Let's bring this into the realm of something really practical and actionable that you can take with that. One of the mistakes that authors make would be if they go with this seems like a good idea to me. That's it. That's what they base their decisions. That seems like a good idea and whether it's an author or market or, let's say, guess approach whereas I recommend an assess approach. I go, "This seems like a good idea." I'll go run a survey on it. Surveying book covers. Surveying book titles. Surveying what the opt-in offer I want to offer is. Coming up with a few ideas and constantly running surveys of that.

There's a few ways of doing this. Obviously, if you have your own following, then you can survey your audience. What if you're just starting out and you don't have a following? There's services like PickFu.com to run surveys. I heard about this from Rob Howard, using Amazon Mturk to run surveys. Going into a Facebook group take it with a grain of salt what you get. Going in there and engaging people for ideas. Going into a mastermind group with several other authors or even people who aren't authors and sharing hey, here are some ideas I have for a book title. Getting that outside feedback because what I found is no matter how much I've studied, no matter how much I've researched about my market or about book publishing, I could have an idea that I think is great and half the time, it's the idea that other people like the least. It's almost always something else comes up that's more captivating.

Learning to get my own perceptions out of the way, let go of any attachment that I have, and really being able to see how do I need to communicate with my audience, what are they looking for, and being able to strike the balance between doing that, and actually making sure it's something that I enjoy doing, and is fulfilling and fulfills that creative that side and really being able to find that balance.

Alinka: I love it, Derek. I love what you said about surveying and testing and I think authors listening to this will find it really interesting that the name of what you're participating in right now has been decided on via a split test. We're having a five-figure author challenge, but there were two other titles of this that we were discussing in our team. What I did was I did a split test with my email provider and I just sent the three titles to three different groups of people and the one that got most clicks won.

It wasn't necessarily the one that we would think would win, but you can't argue with the numbers especially if you have a statistically significant sample, which is, you know, a totally different story here. We're not saying 3 out of 5, but if you have 300 out of 500, that's already ... We're talking already hundreds of people that's starting to become statistically significant. That's awesome and that's the only way that you can have a valid answer is only your audience can answer and you can do that with the book title. If you already have some kind of following, you have three different titles in mind, you just send three different emails saying, "My upcoming book working title," and you say something to one group, something to another group and you see which ones gets the more clicks or the most opens and that's the title you should use.

That's something what you can do when you already have that email list and if you don't, I really like what suggested, all the different places where people can test their stuff. Obviously, there's a bit of awareness now that you should test, so that's why these places came up. I love it that people go into writing a book without having the market in mind so just hoping for the best. Hope is not a strategy. Then you mentioned testing. Another mistake people do is they don't survey, they don't test. What else? What other mistakes do authors do when they go into this book marketing world?

Derek Doepker: One thing that I'll share about that last point is it's a little bit of hope though too because if someone's like, "Oh, great. I'm already at the point. I got my book out and maybe I screwed this up or something." With my backstory just real quick, I've had multiple numbers on bestselling books, but my first books didn't sell that well. The good news is you don't have to knock it out of the park on the first book or even the first book launch. You can always do a relaunch. You can always upgrade the cover. You can always tweak the title. You can always change these things later and the great thing is we're in a day and age where that doesn't mean having thousands of books in a garage that are sitting there. We're in an age of eBooks and print-on-demand where a change can be made and in 24 hours, a book can be updated. If a book does need a bit of a reinvention or a recreation, it's really feasible and practical to do that in this day and age.

There is hope if an author decides that they want to change their title or their cover, their description, any of these different factors. It's important to do because, as I said, the next thing is, the mistake that they make is they don't understand the first most important step in marketing. They think it's about having just a great quality book and that's important. I'm all for a great quality book, but as we talk about marketing, it's not about how good the book is. We want that long-term for success and good reviews.

The marketing and sales comes from the perception of how good a book is. They don't know, no one knows how good it is until they actually have bought the book and have read it, so it's about presenting the perception and the first thing, think about getting perception, you think about vision, it's knowing the first step in marketing and that is how to grab a person's attention. It's the first most important thing. Struggling authors, a mistake they make, they don't know how to grab a person's attention. Their book looks like another me-too book. It just blends into the crowd. There's nothing that jumps out and that's attention-grabbing, especially in this day and age where there are so many competing books whether it's from other self-published authors or traditionally published books. You have to know how to grab attention and that means you do two seemingly contradictory things, but you need to do both.

The first step is you go, "How do I fit in? How do I fit into the marketplace so it's more of like what people want?" That's where the surveying comes in. That's where the market research comes in. Then you take that hat off of how do I fit in then I put on a totally different hat and I go, "Now, how do I stand apart from everyone else and not be just like everyone else?" If that makes your head spin a little bit, well, you know, life is a paradox. We're balancing these two things. We want to fit in enough that people go, "I get it. That looks more like of what I want," yet it's different. It's something like not exactly the same as what everyone else is doing. What makes this author unique? What makes their approach unique?

The empowering thing that I have learned coming from the world ... I do the world of personal development, health and fitness, that's my background, it's just as relevant in any genre because it's a business principle. Fiction, children's books, same concept. In my world, self-help, it's like there's so many other books out there like this. Who's going to want to buy my book? What can I possibly do differently? What I learned is that people aren't buying what you say. They're buying how you say it. They're buying your perspective. They're buying the way you tell the hero's journey because everyone else essentially uses the hero's journey and fiction. They're buying the way you package this information and put it together.

Grabbing attention, that's the first thing, and then making sure you pull people and then get them captivated by what makes you different with your background, with your story, with your style. That's going to be your unique selling point when it comes to your book, so make sure that's conveyed. If it's too vanilla, if it's too bland, if it's too just like everything everyone else is doing, that is not that going to have that X factor, so you're balancing these two worlds. Once again, it's not an either/or, it's a both and balancing things that seem to contradict one another but they really complement one another.

Alinka: I think I'll be speaking for a lot of people when I ask you this. What if somebody already has a book and it's their first book, just one, and it wasn't getting the attention that they thought it would? Now, they want to get it into the hands of readers and you said something about relaunching. How can you remake the book you've already got into something that people will actually buy?

Derek Doepker: This is a great question. This comes up to one of the biggest challenges that authors face and that is going okay, my book isn't selling but even before that, the question might be why. Why isn't it selling? Especially if it's an author's first book, they might not know. They might think, "Was it my title? Is it my cover? Is it just because I don't have enough traffic? There are so many different factors that go [involved 00:12:02] then it's like throwing darts in the dark is how one of my students described it before she went through my training. She says, "I was like throwing darts in the dark. You don't know what the issue is."

This is actually a segway into another mistake and then I'll answer the remake question. The next mistake is having these blind spots and not having outside guidance on what it is because a first time author simply isn't going to know what it could be that's going wrong, so they try to go in it alone or they try to get help from other authors who maybe are successful or aren't successful in that same genre.

The secret, the answer, if you look at the most successful people, is they get coaches. They get help. Imagine a person wanted to become a doctor or any sort of career and they never had teachers or mentors or someone to watch over their soldier and make sure they're doing a good job, it's so important for virtually any other career and yet somehow, I notice many struggling authors think they can just jump and just do it alone or maybe read some books and watch a video and think they'll figure it all out. It's so challenging, it's important to get this outside feedback. That's the first thing.

Then with outside feedback, you can really break it down into one or two things. Is it not selling because of conversions like people land on the book page but they don't click the buy button, there's people seeing it just not buying it, or is it not selling because no one's even seeing it or maybe it's both? That's the first thing to answer. If it's because it is getting people landing on the book page, it is getting quality traffic, which I'll talk about in a moment some of the best ways to get consistent traffic and be able to sell a book at full price, that's one strategy, but that won't work, getting all the traffic in the world won't work if people don't actually click the buy button. If they're not clicking the buy button, then it's time for this remake, this relaunch approach.

How do you go you about doing it? We start, first of all, with the end in mind. Who is my audience? Run the surveys. Figure out the title. Figure out what to do. Then we need to adopt a mentality. You'll notice I often come back to a mindset and then I give really practical action steps. The mindset here that many struggling authors have at this approach that might keep them from remaking a book or keep them from doing it well the first time is they see all the energy and effort and financial money involved as a cost rather than an investment. Before anything else, we need to get in this investment mentality.

Here's a little pop quiz for you listening to see where you're at. If I showed you two items and I said which one is more expensive, a $5 item or a

$500 item, which one's more expensive? You can just sit there and come up with your answer. Think which one feels more expensive. Now, let's put it in the world of book marketing. What's more expensive, a $5 book cover or a $500 book cover? Here's the thing, the answer is it depends. See, you can't answer which one is actually more expensive from a long-term perspective because if the $5 book cover results in no sales but the $500 book cover results in tens of thousands of dollars in sales, isn't the $500 book cover actually less expensive? Didn't it actually make you money? Taking this approach with everything that you invest in going, "What's the outcome this is going to give me," that's the important thing.

Then diving into the practical steps, you run the surveys, you invest the book cover, you invest in the surveys, you invest in the guide, and the mentor, and the people that can help you, take you through that process, and then it's essentially just a matter of making [inaudible 00:15:54] a great cover, a great title, and a great description, and then we get some reviews in place. Those are pretty much the main factors and then the first 10% of the book might be a factor. When you really break it down it's just a few pieces, but there can be a number of things that go wrong with each one of those pieces, which is why it's important to get help.

The cover, trust the graphic designer on that. That's another thing, if you're not a graphic designer, big mistake is they try to do it themselves. The graphic designer is going to handle it for you. The title you can get from surveys and feedback, and I've spent a lot of time coming up with a good title. If you look at the amount of time I invest, I put days, sometimes weeks into a title. It doesn't mean I'm sitting there every moment of everyday thinking of a title, but it might take that long to come up with a title. Description takes me maybe several hours worth of investment to do it.

The point is the initial factors of title, cover, description and getting reviews, I might put all in all weeks into doing all of those things just as much time or maybe a significant amount of time compared to even just writing the book because those are the things that are going to sell the book. That's the, in a nutshell, answer and really I could sit here and tell you like, "Try to use these fonts or different things like that," but my suggestion for most authors is go to the experts. Get help on this. There's experts. Bryan Cohen is great at helping you write book descriptions. He's got resources on that. Derek Murphy knows a lot about book covers and graphic design. Seek out the experts.

Alinka: We have both of them on this challenge.

Derek Doepker: Yes. You're in the right place. You have all the experts, you're going to be hearing their interviews here, that can help you with each one. My goal here is to simplify it for you and package it for you so you go, "Oh man," instead of there's a million things I got to do, it's, "Actually, there's just five things that we go through each one of these strategically and make sure they're on point."

Alinka: Awesome Derek. You mentioned two things that we need to analyze if the book is not selling. One you said is the traffic, traffic to our Amazon page, and the second one is conversion. Can we break it down and talk a little bit about the first and the second?

Derek Doepker: Sure thing. Traffic and conversion. The conversion, I covered a lot of that. That's your on-page factor. That's when someone looks at the book, do they go, "That looks like a book I want"? Here is the thing to understand: one of the mistakes authors make is they look at their book in isolation. They just look at their book page and go, "Yeah, that looks pretty good," but they don't realize that their book is going to be sitting next to maybe 20 other books on an Amazon page, maybe hundreds of other books on a bestseller's list imagine your book in a bookstore. Imagine it's sitting on a shelf with a number of other books surrounding it in the same genre. Will your book stand out as I covered before? That's the important thing.

Then going into traffic, a lot of conversion, it can get feedback and see does it convert and get some guidance. The traffic thing, I think, is where many authors go, "How do I get traffic?" This is like the sexy thing, the marketing, the-getting-readers-to-my-book-page. That's what I know so many students want. I covered conversions first because a lot of times when students come to me, I go, "Actually, you're not ready for traffic yet. That would be a waste of time and money. First, let's get these conversion factors." Once you feel confident about that, have tested it to be confident, now we want to get into traffic.

I would say the mistake here is an author is going to look at 101 ways to generate traffic or hear about 101 things or 1,001 things, get completely overwhelmed and go, "I'm not good at this marketing thing. I am not a marketer. I just want to write books," and I can relate to that. The solution to that is to keep it simple. Focus on a few of the most powerful ways to get traffic and really make sure you're effective with a couple of those things before trying to master all these different things. I don't want 101 way. I've been doing this for years. You give me 101 things to do to get traffic to my book and, instantly, I shut down. I'm like, "I don't want to deal with that. I don't want to sift and sort through that. Just give me the most effective thing."

If you're like that, then I'm here to give you the simplest, most effective thing starting with what I consider to be, hands down, the best way I've come across in the past several years to get consistent traffic, to be able to track conversions, to be able to get sales of full priced books, to make it [targeted 00:20:44] the people that want to get books.

Alinka: Tell us!

Derek Doepker: Here's what it is: Amazon Advertising. To go even bigger picture, advertising, in general, is probably going to be your best source of traffic. The key thing is making sure you know how to do it right otherwise, there's a potential to lose some money. With Amazon Advertising, in particular, their newest type of advertising, which I've been doing a lot of training on, had a lot of success by students in all kinds of genres from fiction to non-fiction to pretty much anything I've seen out there that they allow for advertising, it allows you to get targeted traffic on other people's book and on search terms that people are going for. This is absolutely something to explore and get educated on because this means we're now seeing more opportunities for targeted traffic to your book that you can track and that you can measure.

Now, if that's not an option for you or if that's one option, don't worry, I'm going to cover a few other things too that I've been working for years and it's how I built my business before Amazon Advertising became an option, but now that it is an option, it's the thing I'm most excited about, you might be able to tell. It is a new way that if you're willing to invest even just a dollar a day, you can go as little as a dollar a day, and you learn how to test it, you learn how to do it, then this is the solution to traffic and it's brutally honest with you.

I see student and they get a lot of traffic from really good books, when they convert well they're getting two times their money back, three times their money back, four or five times their money back in some cases from what they spend on ad to what they get in book sales, but if a book doesn't have that cover, that title, that description, you see all the traffic coming in whether it's from Amazon, whether it's from Facebook and it simply doesn't sell. That's the reality check that it's like it's not the ads that are the problem, it's not the traffic that is the problem. Clearly, now you have a conversion issue. This also helps you identify where the issue is or if some of these things need to be tweaked. Is it traffic or is it the conversion or is it maybe a little bit of both?

Alinka: It's great that we have an expert on Amazon Ads. I don't think we have the time to get into the nitty-gritty of Amazon Ads, but if you could just point people where they can get educated on Amazon Ads and then we can move onto the other channels.

Derek Doepker: Sure thing. I have a training for my students. One of the things I'm going to share with you here, which I'm sharing at the end, but I can mention it, is my website ebookbestellersecrets.com. If you sign up for the email newsletter or send me an email, info@ebookbestellersecrets.com, that's a great way or ebookbestellersecrets.com/kdsales. Either of those resources will get you pointed at the right direction.

I'll say that the way you get started specifically is AMS, stands for Amazon Marketing Services, .amazon.com. It's the sponsored product ads as opposed to the product display ads. That's the start and I would recommend getting educated because I spent thousands of dollars and months testing and trying things to really figure it out and I either lost money because I didn't know what I was doing or I made some sales but I was only making a few sales a month because I didn't know how to scale up. Even though it was profitable, it wasn't significant. I found how to actually get significant sales and make profit through a lot of testing and my students have found the same. That's the resource.

I'll also cover that regardless of where you're at ... Actually, I'll cover one more advertising thing that something that you think would be helpful, something else that's new coming out. That's going to be, what's in beta right now, BookBub Ads. I've just been doing some testing with BookBub Ads. I found that with the right approach, you can make them profitable. I'm really excited about BookBub Ads that are going to be opening up for pretty much, I believe, all of us here soon enough will get access to them. BookBub Ads, in my early experience, it'll take more time and testing to give good general recommendations. From my experience, they can sell some full-priced books, but it's a little bit more for discount books. That's what people on BookBub are looking for.

You have something like BookBub Ads that, to give some clarification, a BookBub Featured Deal needs approval. You got to get accepted. It's really challenging. BookBub Advertising is self-serve. What this means you can actually go in and create your own ad, run a marketing campaign for your book on BookBub and it doesn't need their approval process. Pretty much any author can do it. This is a great opportunity and the key once again is if there's more competition, there's actually more opportunity as long as you know how to make yourself stand out. That's going to be the key is being able to stand out. Typically, I found that discounted books get a good response on my testing on BookBub ads.

Now, in addition to advertising, all of these things whether it's getting sales on Amazon or these other eBook platforms or even your own website, we really come back to this idea of these are great resources, but what do I own as an author? What do I have if ... Amazon changes? What if some of these things don't work as well? There's all these X factors with that. What you have control of and if there's just one thing to focus on in terms of building up as an author, you probably hear this from a number of people, your email list is like your greatest source of being able to get sales on a launch, of getting ongoing sales, you have some other people on here about email list. I just want to emphasize that the email list is the [inaudible 00:26:51] things like Facebook advertising, that's where you can build up what I found [inaudible 00:26:58] just go to direct book sales.

Alinka: Awesome. I love it. I can see you're really excited about Amazon Ads and BookBub Ads and yeah, it's best, of course, when we run any type of advertising to our book that, as you said, it's already optimized and all the elements are in place, that we've tested the cover, the title, the description, and then we have that link to our opt-in page in the book. Ideally, we also tested our opt-in page in the funnel, et cetera.

We do cover this in another session, but thank you for emphasizing it because when we hear people sharing the same ideas, multiple successful authors emphasizing the same thing, then obviously, we pay more attention to it, so I think that's really important too. I have a question about Facebook Ads because I agree with what you said that when you do this type of advertising, you really save a lot when you do some type of program and follow somebody's best practices rather than trying to discover it by yourself from scratch. Have you done Facebook Ads?

Derek Doepker: Yes. I've done a little bit with Facebook Ad and what I found when I studied is that I have not seen as much conversion straight from Facebook Ads to a book sale, but I know those with, let's say, a fiction series and a [inaudible 00:28:27]. Out there I know Mark Dawson does quite a bit with Facebook Ad that they've had some success. I've just been going all in [inaudible 00:28:45] ROI on straight book sales and then I use Facebook Ads on occasion for some other areas of my business as well as building up an email list. It's great. This also brings me to [inaudible 00:29:00] on the subject is that authors think they got to do it [inaudible 00:29:08]. Successful authors go, "How can I reach those who can reach my followers [where 00:29:23] they get leverage?"

This is collaborating and instead of seeing other authors as competition, they see it as potential collaborators. Doing cross promotions. Building relationships with people, building relationships with influencers because if I connect with 10 influencers who can reach thousands of people, that's a much quicker shortcut to get to all those people I've been trying to find the all myself. Then I get to third party validation. There's a number of strategies I have for this, actually, something I give for free on my website.

This is the shortcut of how I got started was it wasn't just me trying to reach people. I connect with other people in my genre, other bloggers, people who already have built this following and then through the relationship, through going, "How can I serve them? What can I offer them?" There's a number of strategies for that even just starting out as a no-name author that now you get leverage. Now, you don't have to start from scratch, you can start by reaching other people. That's one of the most important mindsets to get is that who are my allies? Who are my collaborators? How can we do this? Who can I get to help me rather than what do I need to do?

Another insight on that is I don't go, "How do I just sell my book?" I go, "How do I get my readers to sell my book for me?" Just think about your own experience. Do you often buy a book just because an author you've never heard of says, "Buy my book. It's so great," or do you buy it more often because you hear someone recommend a book, you hear someone that you know, like and trust, a friend or someone that you follow, they recommend the book and then are you more likely to get it? You think, "How can I incentivize people that share my books?"

Of course, that does come back to something that's very important, which I mentioned was not the initial factor but it is important long-term, and that is having a great book. I love to say it only takes having a great book. I don't think that's the case. However, it does take having a great book because I don't think people are going to share a book if it isn't really great and if it isn't life-changing and impactful. Absolutely have that book that's so good that people can't help but to share it.

Here's the other tip: ask for the share. Be willing to make this bold request to say, "Hey, if you enjoyed it, would you be willing to post about it on social media? Would you share a review?" Whatever it is, be willing to make those requests. That's another mistake. Not enough authors actually ask for what they want. Then people aren't actually going to go, "This book was so good. Of course, I'm going to share it and tell other people about it."

Alinka: Awesome. I love it, Derek. Fantastic. We know how we can connect with you. The link is under this video. I know you shared plenty of tips and I think people have to listen to this twice to actually absorb everything, but authors listening to this are action-takers, so we want just one last thing that we can go and do right now to get closer to those five figures.

Derek Doepker: The one thing, if there's one thing that gets you everything else, in a sense, if you ever felt overwhelmed like, "Okay, there's so many things I can do," I feel pretty safe in making this one recommendation that regardless of where you're at in the journey, you follow this one piece of advice or expand upon this one piece of advice, it's going to do more to move you forward than anything else I could say and it's going to help you overcome all the overwhelm and really simplify things for you and that is this: get a coach or a mentor. I'm not going to say just hire me because

I might not be the best person for everyone. You have a lot of speakers here. You have a lot of people that you're seeing that are experts in book publishing.

World's most successful people [...] all have coaches.

I'd say as you go through this summit, you're seeing a number of people. Explore what they have to offer and I would take it one step further, you might get multiple coaches and mentors. You might have a coach or a mentor, someone that helps you with your book description. You might have a coach or a mentor that helps you with overall business. Then you might have someone that specializes in book marketing. What I've heard is three coaches, two mentors, and one mastermind as a formula for success. As you get this outside help, as you get these people who are experts, once again, the world's most successful people, the world's richest entrepreneurs, and highest earning CEOs, and top Olympic athletes, they all have coaches and they're masters at what they do.

It's funny, what makes someone think that as someone who's just starting out or has even had a little bit of success makes them think that somehow they don't need a coach or multiple coaches and mentors. It's crazy. If you don't already have a coach and even if you do, continue to go down that journey of getting that help, getting that coaching and that mentorship and you're in such a great opportunity because if you're like, "Where do I start? How do I begin," you're hearing so many different people that you hear them, you hear what they're knowledgeable about on this summit. You'll get a feeling of who do you resonate with and then you can pursue them and then see who offers coaching, who offers guidance, who has courses, who has something that they can use to help you. Ideally, something where they can offer you some type of more one-on-one help or at least group coaching where you get some more personal guidance and feedback.

Alinka: Awesome, Derek. I'm sure Napoleon Hill, who wrote Think and Grow Rich by interviewing thousands of successful entrepreneurs of his time, he had the same advice. This is a wisdom. Awesome. Thank you so much, Derek.

Derek Doepker: My pleasure. Thank you so much for having me, Alinka.

WERE YOU PAYING ATTENTION?

Q1: What is the average writer's strategy to writing and selling books?

Q2: What is the successful author's strategy to writing and selling books?

Q3: What's the difference between writing as a hobby and for business?

Q4: How does Derek recommend assessing whether your book idea is valid?

Q5: What are the three platforms Derek lists for running surveys?

Q6: No one knows how good a book is until…

Q7: What is the first mistake struggling authors make?

Q8: What are the two seemingly contradictory questions you must answer to have a successful book?

Q9: People aren't buying what you say. They're buying…

Q10: What's the most successful people's secret?

Q11: What are the two reasons a book might not be selling?

Q12: Which should you take care of first, traffic or conversion?

Q13: What does Derek recommend as the best way to get consistent traffic?

Q14: What other advertising channel does Derek recommend?

Q15: What "unconventional" type of promotion does Derek recommend?

Q16: Who is a great ally in selling your books?

CHALLENGE

Get a coach or a mentor (you meet many coaches during this challenge). You might get multiple coaches and mentors. Three coaches, two mentors and once mastermind is the formula to success.

THE GOLDEN NUGGETS

Q1: What is the average writer's strategy to writing and selling books?

A1: <u>They write the book first and they try to sell it later.</u>

Q2: What is the successful author's strategy to writing and selling books?

A2: <u>First they figure out what would become a best-seller and then they write that book.</u>

Q3: What's the difference between writing as a hobby and for business?

A3: <u>When you just write what you want – that's a hobby. When you write what the market wants – that's a business.</u>

Q4: How does Derek recommend assessing whether your book idea is valid?

A4: <u>By running surveys.</u>

Q5: What are the three platforms Derek lists for running surveys?

A5:

1) Pickfu.com
2) Mturk
3) Facebook

Q6: No one knows how good a book is until…

A6: They have bought it and read it.

Q7: What is the first mistake struggling authors make?

A7: They don't know how to grab a reader's attention.

Q8: What are the two seemingly contradictory questions you must answer to have a successful book?

A8:

1) How do I fit in?
2) How do I stand out?

Q9: People aren't buying what you say. They're buying…

A9: …how you say it.

Q10: What's the most successful people's secret?

A10: They've got coaches.

Q11: What are the two reasons a book might not be selling?

A11:

1) Conversion.

2) Traffic.

Q12: Which should you take care of first, traffic or conversion?

A12: Conversion.

Q13: What does Derek recommend as the best way to get consistent traffic?

A13: Amazon Advertising, Amazon Marketing Services (AMS)

Q14: What other advertising channel does Derek recommend?

A14: BookBub Ads.

Q15: What "unconventional" type of promotion does Derek recommend?

A15: Crosspromotion with other authors.

Q16: Who is a great ally in selling your books?

A16: Your readers!

PART 3: SELL TO YOUR TARGET AUDIENCE

WHAT YOU NEED TO STOP CALLING YOURSELF TO BECOME A 5-FIGURE AUTHOR (JIM KUKRAL)

WHO'S JIM?

Jim is the founder of Author Marketing Institute, where he teaches authors how to promote their books. He's a 20-year Internet marketing professional who was recently named by Dun & Bradstreet as one of "The Most Influential Small Business People on Twitter." Jim also serves as a Program Faculty Member for the University of San Francisco's Internet Marketing Program where he teaches classes to students around the globe on the topics of Internet marketing, entrepreneurship and social media. In addition, SmallBizTrends.com chose Jim as one of 100 top small business influencers online.
Connect with Jim at http://www.authormarketingclub.com.

THE GOLDMINE

Alinka: Jim, as founder of Author Marketing Club you obviously know authors very well and how they market and promote their books. What we would like you to do now is answer this super important question for us.

Jim Kukral: I'm ready, go.

Alinka: What do authors need to stop calling themselves in order to become five figure authors?

Jim Kukral: You know I thought about this a lot. I think the biggest problem I see with authors is they [inaudible 00:00:33] themselves. This is a business. If you're writing with that artistic mindset, you have a lot of trouble becoming a five figure author because you're not thinking like a business person. That's probably the biggest thing. The mindset that you need get yourself out of. People say, "I'm writing because I'm writing this craft." It's fine. If you are okay with the potential of never having success, or you're okay with being the proverbial starving artist, then you can stay in that mindset. The truth is that you have to be able to be an entrepreneur to be successful as a writer in today's world, especially selling e-books.

Alinka: What's the first step for a writer, somebody who has been calling themselves a writer, to become an entrepreneur?

Jim Kukral: The first step, obviously, is you have to have a great concept for a book. I've been talking a lot about this lately with authors is writing to market. I see a lot of authors who ... This kind of goes back to what I just said. A lot of authors who are writing in genres, or writing to places where the audience doesn't exist.

There are two reasons people use the internet: Number one, to have their problems solved. Number two is to be entertained.

I have 20 years experience in the internet business. I've been doing this a long time. One of the things I learned early on, this is way before books, is you can't build a product or a membership site, or anything, or content, for an audience that doesn't exist. I'll give one of the tips that internet marketers have done for a long time, they have actually gone out to a group of people. This is before social media. It's so easy now to get information on social media, but before that you didn't have that. They will actually go out to a group of people and say, "What are your biggest problems? What do you want to be entertained with?" There are two reasons people use the internet: Number one, to have their problems solved. Number two is to be entertained.

When you put those into books, you have problem solving, nonfiction, and entertainment fiction. Those are two reasons why people use the internet and they're the same two reasons why people buy books. You have to be able to figure out how to write for a market of something that people want. You're either solving their problems or entertaining them.

Let's talk about fiction for a second. I just did a big promotion on Author Marketing Club where we help people find reviewers for their books. I got thousands and thousands of emails from people, "Help me find reviewers for my horror books," Or my vampire books, or whatever. 90% of those people had categories and genres that made sense, but then a couple people who had emailed me like, "Jim I'm trying to find reviewers for my 20th century pirate Renaissance book," Or something, poetry book. I'm like, "It's wonderful that you wrote a book about this topic. However, nobody is really buying a book on that topic because it's not a big genre. It's something that people aren't interested in." They say, "What do you mean?" I said, "You can't write something or build something, or produce something, if the audience doesn't exist. You can, but you're not going to turn yourself into a five figure author."

A long winded answer to this is be writing to market. The artist mentality, you've got the artist over here and you've got the business person over here on your shoulder. The artist mentality in your head is saying, "I'm just going to write what I love and I don't care." The business person over here knows that you're going to have to write into a market that actually makes sense for you if you want to have success. Again, maybe you don't want to have success. If you're watching this presentation right now, I'm pretty positive that you're actually looking to have success. You need to start writing to a market that sells.

Alinka: That's what every business person should do. Find a hungry market and deliver what they're looking for. Let's say that we do this part right. We actually do the research and we understand what people are looking for, and we either entertain them the way that they want to be entertained or we solve their problems in the book. What's next? What does an authorpreneur do after that?

Jim Kukral: Let me explain to you my process. I write nonfiction books. What I do is once I figure out that there's a problem that needs to be solved, I will go to social media and I'll start exploring that within forums or Facebook, Twitter, whatever. I'll start asking people, "What do you think? Would you like the solution to this problem? Is this something that interests you?" Like I talked about, you're researching what people want ahead of time. That will help me shape and craft the message that I'm going to give to people, and also help me determine whether or not they even want that information. Why am I going to spend all this time and effort writing something unless I know that there's an audience for it.

Crowdsource the opportunity for your title before you even write the book.

That's the first step is finding that out. Then the next step for me is ... I'm a very linear thinker so I like to come up with a title for the book. One of the things I recommend for authors to do, if you're writing a fiction or a nonfiction book, is to crowdsource the opportunity for your title before you even write the book. I'll go on social media and I'll say, "I'm writing a book. I think I want to write this book, do you like the idea? Here's what I'm going to call the book, or what do you think it should be called?" Once I get that, I'll design a cover and I'll put that online. What do you think they're going to say, "I can't wait to read it or it looks stupid, or you should try this."

What I'm doing the whole time is I'm pre-selling. This audience of people, I'm saying to them, "I'm thinking about writing this book." I'm telling them, "I'm going to write this book." I'm giving them feedback and opinions into the book the whole time, so that when the book is done, whether it's six weeks or six days, I can say, "Here you go." I'm effectively using the business side to pre-sell the book and get people interested in the book. That way when it comes to the time of purchase, they don't have to be sold on a cold call. It's much easier to sell somebody on something they're already educated about. This is the number one rule of sales. That's why they call them cold calls, for sales people, because you're calling somebody ... That's an old term ... You're calling, emailing, getting opinions from somebody who doesn't know about your product or service, or your book. It's much harder to sell to somebody if they don't have that information ahead of time.

That's the first step. The second step is, of course, writing that great book. Getting the great edit done on that great book, which is really important, if you have a book that's not edited wonderfully you're going to be in big trouble. My big thing is before I launch the book, the biggest thing I that I think authors need to do is get those reviews on that book before you start spending money on marketing, and spending time to promote it.

Let's talk about social proof. Social proof is using the power of what other people are doing and have already done in your head to determine whether or not you think it's worth it or not. It's a psychological thing. The best example I can have for social proof is: Let's say you're in Berlin. Walking down the road and you've never been to Berlin before, and there's two restaurants. One is on one corner and one is on the other corner. You walk into the one, smells good, it looks good. Person says, "You can sit right now and eat." The menu looks good, but right before you walk into that restaurant A, you look across the street and restaurant B has 150 people walking out the door of that restaurant, waiting to get seated. What happens in your brain at that exact moment, subconsciously, is your brain says, "Why can I sit here right now when there are 150 people waiting in line over there?" Your brain says, "Boy, there must be something special about that restaurant." The power of other people have already proven to me instantly.

My point is this. When you go to Amazon or Barnes and Noble, or whereever it is, Smashwords, Kobo. When you go to look to purchase a book, you may not read all the reviews. You may not look at everything, but you look see if the social proof is there. You do not want to have your time wasted. In today's world we want other people to validate that it's okay. When I shop on Amazon, when I look for SciFi books ... I'm a big SciFi fan. I admit it, I look for the books that have tons of reviews. The social proof tells me that this is good and I don't have to waste my time or my money, or my effort, and I know it's probably going to be good.

The reviews are extremely important. If you do not have those, that switch goes off in that person's head and they say, "If other people haven't validated this, why should I take the chance?" You've got to have at least, in my opinion, 10-15 reviews on your book before you spend any money marketing or promoting that book.

Alinka: I wanted to ask you about the number and you just said it.

Jim Kukral: You want to have more, but I would never ever spend any money or time, or effort to promote a book if I didn't have at least 10 or 15 reviews. Obviously I want to have more. You could spend months or a month working on getting those reviews before you spend any because of those reasons I just said. We all know it's true. When you go to buy anything online, you're looking to see if those other people have validated your purchase. It's the way the world works now.

Alinka: As savvy authorpreneurs we want to make the best decisions. The decisions that have the best return on investment. You're right, it doesn't make much sense to invest in anything if we're promoting something that's not even been optimized, or doesn't have any social proof as you're saying.

I want to talk a little bit about once you've done your homework and prepared everything so that you're Amazon page looks good, and your book is awesome. What are the best marketing strategies that you recommend, that you've seen work?

Jim Kukral: Obviously I'm a big proponent of the email. One of the biggest strategies that authors do nowadays is having the lead into their email list on the inside of their book. Something that every author needs to be doing. If you're not doing this already, you're making a huge mistake. You're not building your email list up. I wrote a book called Go Direct a couple years ago. My premise of the entire book is you want to build up your own audience. You want to build up your audience of people that you can connect with. You don't want to have this middle man in the middle like Amazon or Barnes and Noble, or whatever. You've got to do everything you possibly can to get everyone onto your email list, so you can sell direct to them in the future.

That is probably the biggest tactic that I've seen. I believe Nick Stephenson calls them lead magnets. For fiction, it could be something as simple as, "Did you enjoy this book? How about I'll give you a free chapter or a free novella, or copy of another book, or an addition to the story if you go to my website and sign up." He builds an audience. It's a lead magnet. In nonfiction, I've done it very successfully with my first book. My only book I had traditionally published was called Attention: This Book Will Make You Money through Wiley and Sons about seven years ago. I put a lead for them in the back of that book. This is before anyone was calling them lead magnets or whatever. I put a page in the back of the book and it said, "If you enjoyed this book, go to this little link." There was a form on it, it said, "Schedule a no cost, no obligation, 15 minute consultation with me."

I got 90% of my business from that book for about five years. Simply from people reading the book. After they read the book, they were like, "Wow. I really liked what this guy said. I like his stories. I liked everything." They scheduled the appointment. People say, "Jim, didn't you do a lot of calls?" Yeah. I did like 15,000 15 minute consultations. There were days when I did 15, 20 of those or more. You know what? When I got somebody in front of me on camera or on a Skype call, or on a phone call, I was able to close business. It's a lead.

The whole point of this whole interview is you've got to start thinking about this as a business. You're generating leads. People pay big money for leads. When I owned a search engine marketing company, we had 150 person search engine marketing company ten years ago. We were spending anywhere from $50 to a $100 just for a lead. Not a sale, that's just for information about somebody to potentially sell them our services. It's much easier to do now with social media, we didn't have all that back then. You've got to start thinking about generating leads.

Alinka: For nonfiction anybody can emulate what you just said. What about fiction authors? What can they do?

Jim Kukral: I gave a brief example of that. Basically it's about offering additional content. That's why it's so important to have a back list or have a series. If you have multiple books, you want to have your first book, your second book, your third book. You need to start thinking about it as a business person, as a strategy. Maybe the first book, you write two or three books, and the first one is the lead gen. It's the free one. You constantly use as a perma-free or promotional KDP Select, or whatever, that leads into the second book, that leads into the third book.

That is the mindset you need to have. There are people ... I will tell you this, if I was writing fiction books, which I'm a horrible fiction writer. I tried it, I'm horrible. If I was writing fiction books, I would write two to three books and I would not release the first one. I would wait until I had all three of them. I would go for a strategy where I did the one, two, three, four, whatever. I would release them in that manner because I think it's a much more effective way of promoting the books. I see a lot of authors doing that right now. They're busting through three, four books and then releasing them together. Then they can do the box set, they can do the free strategy, they can do the lead magnet. It's important. If you just have one book, fine. Maybe you can run some free promotions for that book. You're definitely going to want to offer some content that can people can give away so that they'll get on your email list, or in your Facebook group.

I love Facebook groups. I think Facebook groups are absolutely one of the best potential things that you can do to get people interested. I'm big a fan of James Clavell who wrote the Shogun series of books. It's probably my favorite books of all time. Shogun, Gai-Jin, King Rat, all those books. James Clavell, I don't know if James Clavell is still alive, probably not. If he had a Facebook group or a group of people who wanted to talk about all things related to those books, I would be in that Facebook group because I would be talking about chapters of the book and characters, stuff like that. If he was the author in there answering questions, how cool would that be? Of course that only works if you're a big brand and you've taken time, but let's talk about this real quick.

The power of a thousand true fans. If you haven't read about this or learned about this, anyone who is watching this I want you to write down, "One thousand true fans." I want you to search for it on the Google. Go and look for the concept of a thousand true fans. The basics of a thousand true fans is if you have a thousand true fans, you can have an entire career. Whether you're a musician or an author, or speaker, whatever it is. A true fan is somebody who will buy anything you write, or buy anything you produce, travel three, four hours in a snow storm to come see you. That is the definition of a true fan. Here's the best part about a true fan, a true fan will evangelize for you. A true fan will tell everyone in the world why you're so awesome and what you wrote is so awesome. You don't even have to ask them. If you have a thousand people who are willing to evangelize for you and buy everything you have, you can grow your career.

That's why it's so important to have Facebook groups, email lists, and interact with people. You say, "Jim, I've only got five true fans." That's more than you used to have. You have ten people promoting for you. There's a lot of things you need to do to be successful in that regard.

Alinka: This is perfect. What about people who say that they're not salesy or they don't like marketing, they just want to write. What advice do you have for them?

Jim Kukral: You either learn how to get there or you're going to spend a lot of money hiring somebody to do it for you. In my experience, there is not a lot of qualified people out there who are worth the money to promote your books for you. Bottom line is this, you've got to do it yourself. Unless you're a self-made millionaire and you've got all this money to spend to have somebody else do it for you. It's just the bottom line.

The business has changed. It used to be the traditional business where the publisher would do the work. I wrote my only traditionally published book seven years ago. That was seven years ago and I realized back then very quickly that basically all they did, besides putting the book out, was send out a press release. A press release.

That was the genesis for my business Author Marketing Club. I realized that everybody needs to learn how to do this on their own. You've got to get rid of that mentality. If you want to be successful as an author today, you must learn how to market yourself and get rid of that thing that you are not a salesperson.

You bring up a good topic because people used to treat salespeople in a different way. There's people like ... They think about it, they're like, "If I'm selling, then I'm a jerk. Nobody wants to be sold to." It's different than it was back then. With social media and everything, you don't have to sell like you used to. You can create content that's problem solving or entertaining that helps people. Podcasts, videos, Facebook groups, articles, blog posts, webinars, shows like this. Create content in content marketing form that solves people's problems or entertains them, and it's not selling. It is technically, but it's not. It's not like you going, "Hey you got to buy these scissors. I want to sell you these scissors." The classic sell me this pen thing. You don't have to be so schmaltzy salesy anymore to have success.

Alinka: It's a process now. From the moment somebody gets your first free content, you're actually getting them ready for the sale that you're going to make eventually.

Jim Kukral: Yes. It goes back ... I have artist friends who I've ... I have comedians, musicians, people like that who are [inaudible 00:20:55]. I know a guy who is one of the funniest men I've ever met in my life. If he did a YouTube video show, and I told him this years ago, "If you did a daily YouTube video show, you would have 500 million subscribers like that PewDiePie, whatever that guy is. You would be making $100,000 a month." He has absolutely zero interest in being that personality online. I know another guy who is probably one of the best writers of dialogue, who could sitcoms, he could be in Hollywood writing shows. He has zero interest. There's a definite thing if you're an artist and you're just interested in having fun, and writing and doing whatever, you have to have this side of it too. You have to be able to say, "I'm going to take it to the next level." Some people have zero interest in doing that. That's totally fine.

Alinka: They have zero interest but they have a budget that they could spend. What would be the wisest way to pay somebody to do it for them?

Jim Kukral: I don't even recommend it because it's too expensive. If I had to recommend something, I would say if you're going to promote your book, I would say ... First of all spend most of your money getting the book edited. If you're going to spend money, spend most of the getting the book edited professionally to make sure that it's right. That's really the most important thing. You can get covers for cheap cost. You don't have to spend a ton of money.

In terms of the marketing of it, if you want to pay somebody to do it there are ways to get advertising. BookBub is obviously the biggest one. Go out there and spend money if you can get access to BookBub. If you could get accepted, AuthorAdNetwork.com. There are lots of places where you can directly buy advertising to promote your book. Of course Facebook advertising as well. If you wanted to do it right, you could spend hundreds of thousands of dollars. If you wanted to do it on the cheap, you're going to get away with spending ... I'm talking about just for the marketing part, you can spend anywhere from $500 to $50,000. The results are going to vary. There's no guarantee. There's no putting it out $5,000 in Facebook advertising does not guarantee you're making $5,000 back. There's not a system or a process that is foolproof, that guarantees your return on investment. It really doesn't. The biggest guarantee you can have for success is the hard work that you put in. If you don't want to do that work, you're taking a gamble.

Alinka: You're right. What about these great people that are called virtual assistants? Do you think authors can get any help from them?

Jim Kukral: Yes. As a matter of fact, are you kidding me? I've had a virtual assistant for six years now. Same person who works out of the Philippines. Never met him, never spoken to him. I've only texted through Skype and email for six, seven years now. I pay him every month and he does all of my design work and everything that I need him to do. It had changed my life. Absolutely changed my life and my business because it allowed me to do the things I needed to do instead of worrying about coding WordPress sites or designing covers. I have graphic design background but I'm not good at it. It's better to have somebody else do it.

Virtual assistants change your life.

Virtual assistants change your life. There is ... My Chris Ducker has a great business that helps people find virtual assistants. My co-partner on the Sell More Books Show, Bryan Cohen has an assistant that he hires that does all of the things for him that he needs to get done, promotions, all that stuff. People say, "Jim, I can't afford to have an assistant." That's the way I used to think. The minute that I actually found the right one and found the right things that I needed them to do for me, my business and life changed. You will say the same thing when you do, do it. They're not as expensive as you think they are. You can find somebody to do the things that you need to do.

What I suggest you do is you sit down and write all the things you're spending time doing that are wasting your time when you should be writing books. Say, "I'm spending ten hours a week trying to figure out where to market my site. I'm spending another ten hours a week trying to make this website." Think to yourself how much stuff you could get done if you just let somebody else do that for five, ten bucks an hour or even cheaper. It will change your career.

Alinka: I agree because I invested in my first virtual assistant over a year ago, and you're right. Perfect, Jim. This is fantastic. Of course it is because you're the founder of Author Marketing Club. This is the top advice we can get. Please tell people how can we connect with you?

Jim Kukral: Check out AuthorMarketingClub.com, also check out AuthorMarketingInstitute.com. We've got lots of great articles and Podcasts up there. Got a free course about how to sell the first thousand or hundred copies of your book, I forget. Check that out. Lots of great information out there.

I love that you do shows like this, people do shows like this. The reason I came on to do this show is because if you want to reach people who are interested in being successful, you don't have to spend money on clubs and memberships if you don't want to. If you want to be successful to the point you don't want to have to figure out how to do all the work, there are people who can help you out there. Leave you with this, there's a lot of people out there who are looking to take advantage of you, and there's a lot of people who are looking to actually help you out there.

My business was started because I care about authors. I don't promote junk. I don't promote systems and formulas, and things that are no work, make money, no work. You'll never hear me say that it's easy to have success selling e-books. You'll never hear me say if you follow this formula, you'll make this much money or sell this many books overnight. You know that that's not true. I'm not talking to you, I'm talking to the audience here. You'll never get that from me. If you're interested, check out AuthorMarketingClub.com and we have lots of great information there for you.

Alinka: I confirm because I'm part of it and it's awesome. Jim, one last thing, our attendees are action takers and I know you've provided a lot of value during the interview, if you could leave people with one thing that they can do immediately, right now, to make sure that they get to these five figures as soon as possible.

Jim Kukral: The most important thing? Work on getting those reviews. I want to go back to that. I really can't stress how important it is to work on getting those reviews. We have tool at Author Marketing Club that helps you find reviewers who reviewed similar books to yours. That is, in my opinion ... I'm a big. If you haven't read a book by Doctor Cialdini, The Persuasion Principles, I forget the ...

Alinka: Psychology… Influence.

Jim Kukral: Influence, yeah. Go read Doctor Cialdini's book. It's C-I-A-L-I-N-D-I. You have to understand why people purchase things if you're going to produce content or sell things online. Once you get inside the head of why people purchase something, you can become a business person and a marketer, and understand how you have to craft words and headlines. It all sounds so horrible, I know people are like, "I don't want to be that person." The truth is until you understand your customer, you're not going to have much success selling to that customer.

Another great book to check out is a book called Don't Make Me Think by Steve Krug, K-R-U-G. The book is, I think 15 years old or longer. It is still one of the best books ever written on the psychology of the internet. This guy ... It's 15 years old, you would think it'd be outdated. He has an updated version. The lessons in that book about how people don't read, they scan. About how people make purchases, it's so important. It sounds so geeky and it sounds so boring, but the truth is until you understand what people think and how they react to the internet and to content, you're not going to have much success selling anything.

Alinka: Excellent. Two pieces more, three pieces of excellent advice.

Jim Kukral: Bonus.

Alinka: Awesome bonus. Thank you so much Jim, this was fantastic.

Jim Kukral: Thank you for having me on. I think you're doing a wonderful thing. I hope that everybody watching these takes some action, and goes out and is successful. Real quick story, I got an email from a friend who said, "Jim, I've been following your stuff for years. I thought I could write romance books," This is a man, he said, "I tried it." He wrote, "Confession, I've since written 14 romance books under a pen name. I just quit my job. Turns out I'm really good at writing romance books." Anyone can do this if you're good at writing content that solves problems or entertains people. You can be successful, so go do it.

Alinka: Go do it.

WERE YOU PAYING ATTENTION?

Q1: What mindset gets you to 5 figures?

Q2: What's the first step for a writer to become an entrepreneur?

Q3: What are the two reasons people go online?

Q4: How do the two reasons above translate into books?

Q5: What does Jim recommend you do to choose the right title?

Q6: What type of strategy is asking people for their opinion on your upcoming title or book cover?

Q7: What's the biggest thing authors should do before they start spending money on promoting their book?

Q8: What is the #1 marketing strategy Jim recommends?

Q9: What should you include in your book?

Q10: What strategy does Jim recommend for fiction authors?

Q11: How many *true fans* do you need to have a successful career?

Q12: What advice does Jim give authors who don't want to market and just want to write?

Q13: What does Jim recommend you spend your money on?

Q14: Who can authors hire to get help with their marketing?

CHALLENGE

Work on those reviews.
Read Cialdini's book *Influence* and *Don't Make Me Think* by Steve Krug.

THE GOLDMINE

Q1: What mindset gets you to 5 figures?

A1: Start thinking like a business person.

Q2: What's the first step for a writer to become an entrepreneur?

A2: The first step is to have a great concept for a book. Write to market. You can't build a product for an audience that doesn't exist.

Q3: What are the two reasons people go online?

A3:

1) To get their problems solved.
2) To be entertained.

Q4: How do the two reasons above translate into books?

A4:

1) Problem solving is non-fiction.
2) Being entertained is fiction.

Q5: What does Jim recommend you do to choose the right title?

A5: Crowdsource it.

Q6: What type of strategy is asking people for their opinion on your upcoming title or book cover?

A6: It's preselling.

Q7: What's the biggest thing authors should do before they start spending money on promoting their book?

A7: Getting reviews.

Q8: What is the #1 marketing strategy Jim recommends?

A8: Email marketing.

Q9: What should you include in your book?

A9: A link to your website (landing page).

Q10: What strategy does Jim recommend for fiction authors?

A10: Release multiple books all together.

Q11: How many *true fans* do you need to have a successful career?

A11: A thousand.

Q12: What advice does Jim give authors who don't want to market and just want to write?

A12: You either have to learn to market or you'll spend a lot of money hiring somebody to do it for you.

Q13: What does Jim recommend you spend your money on?

A13:

1) Getting your book professionally edited.
2) BookBub and similar.
3) Facebook ads.

Q14: Who can authors hire to get help with their marketing?

A14: A Virtual Assistant.

THREE COMMON HURDLES THAT BLOCK YOUR WAY TO A 5-FIGURE AUTHOR CAREER AND HOW TO OVERCOME THEM (HONORÉE CORDER)

WHO'S H. CORDER?

Honorée is the author of 20 books, including "You Must Write a Book", "Vision to Reality", "Prosperity for Writers", "Business Dating", "The Successful Single Mom" book series, "If Divorce is a Game", "These are the Rules", and "The Divorced Phoenix". She is also Hal Elrod's business partner in The Miracle Morning book series. Honorée coaches business professionals, writers, and aspiring non-fiction authors who want to publish their books to bestseller status, create a platform, and develop multiple streams of income. She also does all sorts of other magical things, and her badassery is legendary.
Connect with Honorée at http://honoreecorder.com/writers/.

THE GOLDMINE

Alinka: Honorée. One of your many superpowers is arranging Prosperity for Writers, and what we'd like to learn from you today is what impacts most authors directly and these are three common hurdles that block people's way to a five-figure author career. So can you tell us about these three hurdles and how writers can overcome them?

Honorée Corder: Oh, absolutely. So the first one is they don't have belief in themselves. The very first thing that I suggest to someone when they ask me how to make a living as a writer, how to be a full-time writer, is do they have the belief that they can be a full-time writer? So it's obvious that there are lots of people out there who make a living as a writer, but sometimes it's easy to look at those people and think, "Oh they're different than I am. They have superpowers, I don't have superpowers, therefore I have to stay in the work that I'm doing or continue to struggle as a writer." So the very first thing is they have to develop a belief in themselves that they can make a living as a writer, that they can be a five-figure author and maybe even a six-figure author.

Develop a belief [...] that you can make a living as a writer, that you can be a five-figure author.

Alinka: Do you have some practical advice as how somebody can do that? Develop the belief.

Honorée Corder: Yeah, of course. So the first thing is to say, "I am a writer." So a long time ago before I wrote my first book, or even considered myself a writer, honestly I was coaching a woman who was an assistant at a magazine and her boss hired me to coach her and we went out for lunch and I remember making her stand outside the table at P. F. Changs and saying, "I am a writer." Because she wanted to be a food writer, she loved food and she wanted to be a food writer, and she was an assistant, and she said, "I just don't believe that I can be a writer." And I said, "Grace you have to stand outside of this table, stand up and say 'I am a writer.'" So I made her do it. I think she hated me in that moment, but today she is a full-time food writer and coauthor in a cookbook with me. So what was great about that was taking that belief that someone else would have and internalizing it.

So the very first thing is saying. "I am a writer." Then you take that sentence and you add to it, "I am a full-time writer and I make a living writing X." So thrillers, or magazine articles, or whatever it is that you want to make a writing as. Then you say that in the positive present tense, "So I'm already doing it." And you say that to yourself over and over and over again. You will then as you own that belief. What we can not do as humans, we cannot trick our brain. Our subconscious mind is our supercomputer and it's working on our behalf so you can't say something over and over and over again and not actually do it. You'll either stop saying it or you'll start doing it.

You can say, "I only make positive choices, I write every single day." Even if you don't write every single day. So you're like, "Well I'm kinda saying I write every day and I'm not writing every day." But eventually if you say, "I am a writer, I'm a full-time writer I write every single day and I make a living as a writer." At some point you're going to wake up and go. "Holly crap, I'm actually a writer! Look at this check I just got. I can make a living as a writer." It's that simple, it's not easy, but it is that simple.

Alinka: I'm really big on these affirmations and I agree at first it might seem strange, especially if you have like some really big dreams that are in your mind and you start affirming it saying, "I am a five-figure author." At first you might feel a little bit like you have this alien thought in your mind, but the more you repeat it and the more you believe it, it really does materialize. So, I agree. I'm a huge fan of this method.

Honorée Corder: Yeah.

Alinka: Awesome, so what's the second hurdle?

Honorée Corder: The second hurdle is they don't develop a writing habit. So, the thing is you can think about writing and you can even say, "I am a writer." At some point, you have to put your butt in the chair and you have to write or you have to download Dragon Dictate onto your phone and you have to speak the words. At some point the words have to go from up here, to out into the world. So the biggest disconnect I think people have is that they think that writing, especially writing a book, is this big huge thing, like it's done all in a compressed period of time. So what I like to do ... I work with a lot of new authors, business people who want to write books. When I'm working with a new person they're wondering how on earth they're going to write this big huge book, with all these words in it, and what I tell them to do is the very first thing is schedule 15 minutes every day, and write.

Develop a writing habit.

The goal is to write about 500 words and they say, "500 words, that's like a zillion words." And I say, well no actually the email you wrote, right before we got on the phone, probably had 100 or 200 words in it. So it's not that big of a deal if you chunk it down into, "Oh, I'm gonna write 500 words a day of a 50,000 word book." Is only going to take you 100 days? 200 days? Right, so it's not that ... I can't do math in my head, especially on the spot. Anyway it's not that long, 1,000 words a day over the course of a year is 365,000 words. So you think ... I myself I only write about 300 days a year, I write 300,000 words. Well those words come in handy because I'm writing multiple books and so people think and say to me, "You must be writing all day, all the time." I'm like no not so much actually, I write between 5:00 and 6:00 or 6:00 and 7:00 in the morning and then that's it. Sometimes I write more the rest of the day, but most of the time I don't. Most of the time I'm working on other activities.

Alinka: But it's a habit.

Honorée Corder: It's a habit.

Alinka: 300 days out of 360, it's like the weekends are off. Right?

Honorée Corder: The weekends are off. I take the holidays, I take 2 weeks off at Christmas, 2 - 2 1/2 weeks off at Christmas. I take some time off in the summer. I like to write every single day, but there are some days I wake up and I just, I just don't have it. I just don't wanna do it. Or I finished a project and it's time to go back through that project and edit. So that time that I've set aside is used for something else. Now the interesting thing about building a habit, there's one level past a habit.

So the first thing is I want to develop a habit. The second thing is I'm engaging in developing the habit. The third thing is it becomes part of who you are. When I say, "I am a writer." I don't think to myself, "Oh I have to write." It's just 6 o'clock in the morning, it's just time for me to write. It's like, it's 8 o'clock in the morning and it's time for me to eat breakfast. I don't think to myself, "Oh I have to have breakfast today." I just have breakfast because it's part of who I am. So if you do something long enough, you build that muscle and you're actually going to instinctively and on purpose take that action. Does that make sense?

Alinka: It does. So internalize, as you stop thinking about it it becomes automatic.

Honorée Corder: Yeah so it becomes automatic. Once you've gotten there, then you're not working against yourself. Then you're not thinking, "When am I gonna have time to do it, and am I gonna do it?" You just have to get through that phase. Which scientifically, we've heard it's anywhere between 21 and 60 days. So the willpower part is that initial piece, where you're making yourself do it. When your alarm's going off and you're thinking, "Oh I'd rather sleep in." Or, "I don't feel like writing to day." Or whatever, you have to get through that phase and once you get through that, it's actually not that tough.

Alinka: So the beginnings are challenging?

Honorée Corder: The beginnings are challenging, you have to go through that yucky I don't want to do it, it's not part of who I am. It's not quite a habit, maybe I don't want to do it. What do I have to say? Those types of things, but once you build that muscle, and that muscle is strong, there is no problem. You will automatically write, and that's the coolest part. I've not really heard anyone talk about that before, but that's what I observe in myself and other people.

Alinka: Perfect. So we have number one hurdle that people don't own it. So say to yourself you are a writer. Then we have the habit of writing. What's the third hurdle Honorée?

Honorée Corder: The third hurdle is that they don't act with intention and purpose, and then there's a little subtopic there. Which is they think they're writing is their baby. So I'm gonna address both of those because they go together. One is acting with intention and purpose. So I intentionally and purposely write every day so I do my writing habit, but I'm writing my next book that I'm working on, I'm writing the next project, I'm being intentional and purposeful. I'm not kind of going where the wind blows me. Then I don't think that my books are my babies, I think my books are income generating products and so I treat them as such. I give them good artwork, I give them good editing, I do good copywriting, I make them look amazing with a great book cover, and then I market them with intention and purpose. So there's the prelaunch phase and there's the part where I'm working with the advance reader team to make sure that I have it all ... That the book is tight and its good and the message is good, and then I do the release phase of the book, and then the long term marketing.

Act with intention and purpose.

So I think people could shift from being a five-figure author is just sitting down to write, and it's very like wonderful and lovely and running through a field of flowers to its actually a book business. You're in the book business and you have to treat your book business like a book business, and do the things with intention and purpose.

Alinka: Yeah I love it. I love what you're saying about treating it like a book business and how you linked it to intention and purpose. Can we go a little bit deeper in this, because I think once people have internalized the first two things ... They own it that they're a writer and they have a habit of writing, so now it all boils down to treating it as a business. So what are some specifics things that you do before you write a book, before you even decide what you're gonna write? How do you decide what book you're going to write?

Honorée Corder: Ugh, well its funny because there's the part of our brains that say I don't have enough ideas and then there's the other part where we kinds slip into people ... We come up with a lot of ideas and then people give us book ideas. So people call me all the time and go, "Honorée you should write a book about X." And I'm like are you kidding. But I actually plan out prior to every year, what are the books that are on my productions schedule and what are the dates of the production. And I break it down based on expected word count, how long I expect me to write those particular words, and then the editing process, the review process, the proofing process, the artwork, the formatting, interior design phase of the book, getting the copywriting done, the cover design is really important. So I actually have a production schedule and pretty much every day multiple things are happening. It's like being a decathlete.

Alinka: I love it. I love the term production schedule.

Honorée Corder: Yeah so I have like a decathlete. You know, I'm working on my hundred yard dash and all the other events at the same time. So there are multiple things that are happening on my calendar on any one day, and then I just work from that production schedule. I don't wake up and decide what I'm doing, I decide what I'm doing tomorrow before I go to bed. I actually have a Director of Operations and I always tell her ... She has access to my calendar and I say you can go in and find out what I'm doing at any time during the day. Which thing I'm working on and what I'm doing. I think that that's important because I work between X hour and X hour, and the rest of the time I'm not working. Which is the beauty of working for yourself.

Alinka: You're very organized. I love it.

Honorée Corder: Yes, I'm a nerd.

Alinka: It's awesome and helps incredibly. So you told us about your internal process of how you decide, well how you organize your production. But how do you decide what you're going to write? Do you follow the muse, do you do market research, is it a combination of both?

Honorée Corder: It's a combination of both. If anyone looks me up, they'll think I'm kinda schizophrenic in my different verticals that I write in. So I've written a book series for single moms, a couple on divorce, business books, now I'm in writing books. I started writing books for writers, specifically because I ... My first book was Prosperity for Writers and I wrote that book because I heard a lot of writers say, I can't make a living as a writer. Although people can do that but not me, there special but I'm not special. So I wrote Prosperity for Writers, that was a whim. That was definitely courting the muse. I went to a conference and I heard people talking about that and I thought that's just not true, I don't believe that, I don't live that myself and I'm not special. So if I can do it I believe they can do it. So I wrote Prosperity for Writers.

You Must Write a Book was inspired by the professionals that I work with that I believe must have a book. I think every single person should write a book, I especially think every single professional should write a book. So that book was born of my desire to, because I can't talk to everybody, give people the information that they needed so that they could coach themselves through the process of writing a book. That they could have the idea and then know what they don't know, when it comes to writing and producing a book. If that makes sense.

This year, I'm writing a lot of books for writers. I'm also writing a book for my daughter because as we were talking about of the air, I have a 17 year old daughter and boy there are sure a lot of things I wish I knew when I was 17 years old and so I'm really writing a book that's from my heart to her heart.

Alinka: That's amazing.

Honorée Corder: I may or may not make that book for sale, I haven't decided. Because I'm sharing a lot of personal information and private lessons in things that I've gone through. I'm not sure that I would like the whole world to know about those things, but I certainly did not have that myself and so I'm writing that book for her. That's definitely a heart book, I don't have a commercial desire to release that book but we'll see what happens.

Alinka: Yeah, I like it. How you ... I like your terminology, a heart book and a commercial book. So most authors, I think the majority of authors that are listening to us, they have written or they're in the process of writing a heart book and then you know the cold world of marketing appears and then we start shifting into producing commercial books.

Honorée Corder: Writing to market.

Alinka: Yeah, what's your take on this and what do you advise people to ... Like in Prosperity for Writers, what's your take on that and what are your golden nuggets?

Honorée Corder: Well so I did ... I'm a slow learner I say at times and I have done things a lot through intuition and they have turned out to work for me. I think finding the intersection between your heart and your wallet is a fine idea. I know there are some great books on writing to market and launching to market, and using data. The upcoming Prosperity for Writers Guide to Making More Money is about data and how do you see if your book has a commercial factor. A prolific writer can write books of the heart and put those out and see if they sale and they can also do some good old fashion market analysis, as not sexy as that sounds, and see if their book could be commercially viable. I think that there is a bit of will this sale and can this contribute to the bottom line of my book business, that has to go into any five-figure author's mindset. They have to do some market analysis, and those that do really do prosper.

And there is a path to freedom, which says I write books that sell so that I can write the books that I love and if they sell great and if they don't great. I now can write a book to my daughter that I may or may not sell, that is specifically and only for her and I will have a professional cover done, and I will have it edited, and I will have it formatted, and I may only ever get one copy of that book, because I can. But I started, where anyone who has a book that their working on that they don't make any money from their writing started which is zero. I started from zero, and I made a lot of mistakes that I didn't know were mistakes at the time. I thought I was putting a cheap cover on my book and editing, who does that? So I made every single mistake and I wish someone had said, you can start from zero, use very little, iterate and optimize, go back and put new covers on your books, get better editing done, all of those things when you're making money. But there is a business aspect in the world that does contribute to whether or not someone will buy your book. There are lots of things you can do, and that can be something we talk about next.

Alinka: You're writing a book to your 17 year old and that you wish you know would've been cool if you'd got it as a 17 year old. Now what would you say to authors who are in the same position that you were when you just started out? So what would you ... What is the valuable things that you would have liked to know that would have saved you a lot of time, energy, money?

Honorée Corder: All of the things. I would have liked to know all of the things. Gosh, I would have liked someone to have said, "If you can't afford a good cover, it's better to wait until you can afford a good cover. So save up and while you're saving up build your list." There were no lists back ... I started in 2004, no one was talking about an email list to me in 2004. That's for sure. I wish I had known to build my email list, to come up with my opt-in, my giveaway, my bonus, my whatever, to get people on my list so I could have a conversation with them. So that when I had a book launch, actually people would have bought it. How about that. Online and stuff, whoa. Kindle wasn't even around in 2004 - 2005, when I was publishing my first versions of my books.

So what I mean by that is I published the original Tall Order, so Tall Order 10th Anniversary edition was published in 2015, late 2015. But the first version of that was published in 2004 under a different title. So have a good title, have a good subtitle. Bad cover, because I had a Graphic Design friend who created a cover and was like how's this, and I thought okay its great what do I know. So I threw it up with no ... I threw it together and had a bunch printed at a printer and I had no idea how bad it was, there was no editing. Then I met someone who is a published author and he said I think the writing has some promise but this book, light this one fire, this is terrible.

So I wish I had known to slow down, to speed up. If you can't afford a great cover today that doesn't mean you can't save or create some value for someone in another way. Maybe you have editing skills that you can trade for graphic design skills, right. Sometimes you have to get creative, if you really want something you'll find a way and if you don't you'll find an excuse. So figure out a way to get a good cover, figure out a way to get great editing, figure out a way to get great copywriting, figure out a way to get every single piece of your book to be quality and if you have to wait it's okay, because you're probably going to be on this earth another hundred years anyway. So another 3 months - 6 months, is not a problem.

I wish I hadn't had my first book, that then I had a bonfire with. I seriously had a fire pit, had a bonfire with my ... I call that my stupid tax. So I wish I had known to really step back and take my time and to be okay and to be patient. I see this with people, is they get 90% of the way there and that last 10% feels like the last 50%. Because they're tired of it, they're like 9 1/2 months pregnant and ... No I don't really care if the kids fully baked or not, just get it out. Then there's regret because you wish that they had been in there a little bit longer, because you have no idea how little sleep you're gonna get after you have children.

So you understand right? It's like you get to the end and you feel like oh I just want to get it out. If you just take a breath, take a little bit of space. Continue to build you're list, build your platform, do some networking.

Alinka: I think you mentioned something really important and fundamental in your career. When your author friend told you that the writing was promising but the book, not so much. I think the way you handled that, was that like a milestone in your career? Something that changed a lot or was there another point that put you on the path to prosperity?

Honorée Corder: You know, I think if I were wired differently, that comment ... because he was much more harsh than the writing is promising and the book is not so good. He was much more harsh. He was nice with the praise, much harsher with the criticism. I think if I were wired differently, I would have just stopped right then and there and I think that's ... You're touching on something that is critically important. You have to turn down the criticism and turn up the praise. I didn't take his comments to mean I should just give up and not do it, I took his comments to mean that my writing had promise and my production, which could be improved. If you're a bad writer, that's kind of a bummer. You have to work harder. So if your writing shows promise, if people are saying, "Wow, you're funny." Or, "You really make me feel connected to your writing." Or, "Your stories move me." Then great go with that. Still improve your writing, I practice obviously almost every day to get better at my writing.

This morning I was pulling an exert out of one of my first books and thinking, "Oh dear lord in heaven. I hope this exert is edited very well." Because you do get better and look at those early writings and think, "Ew, I wish I had been better." But you have to just start where you are. If you love it, and if you're a writer then you love the writing, so you cannot give up. You owe it to yourself and to the people who would get enjoyment or benefit from reading your words. You owe them and yourself to continue.

Alinka: Oh, awesome. Honorée, this is so inspiring. I like when you said, when you want something you're going to find a way to get it or you're going to find excuses.

Honorée Corder: Excuses not to do it, for sure.

Alinka: That's right. So I think now we're all gonna find a way to get to those five-figures.

Honorée Corder: I hope so, yes.

Alinka: That was incredible Honorée, but no wonder after all you're a greatly accomplished author and the coauthor of the Miracle Morning series, which is a huge success. So we couldn't have expected anything less than amazing from you. So how can people connect with you and get some of the positive mindset and get pushed by you towards achieving their goals?

Honorée Corder: They'll probably wanna go to honoreecorder.com/writers and get on my list, my newsletter list and get a couple of free chapters of Prosperity for Writers and see if that resonates with them.

Alinka: Perfect. That link is under this video, and one last thing. Honorée, our challenge participants are action takers. So what one last thing can people do right now to make sure that they don't let anything stop them on their journey to being a five-figure author?

Honorée Corder: Well everything that we talked about in this video, starting with write down you're I Am statement. "I am a writer and I write dystopian fiction full-time and I make five-figures as an author." Write that down, say it. Say it over and over again, write it over and over again. Eventually, you're going to wake up one day and that will be you.

Alinka: Perfect. I love it. Thank you so much Honorée.

Honorée Corder: Thank you so much.

WERE YOU PAYING ATTENTION?

Q1: What is the first hurdle writers face?

Q2: What practical advice does Honorée give to develop the belief that you can be a writer?

Q3: What is the second hurdle?

Q4: What does Honorée recommend you do to develop a writing habit?

Q5: What is the third hurdle that blocks people on their way to success?

Q6: What mistake do authors make when thinking about their books?

Q7: What does Honorée recommend you have to keep you organized?

Q8: What two types of books does Honorée distinguish?

Q9: What would Honorée have liked to know when she was just starting out?

Q10: What should you figure out before you publish?

Q11: What's does Honorée recommend we do about criticism and praise?

CHALLENGE

Write down your "I am" statement. Say it over and over. Write it over and over.

THE GOLDEN NUGGETS

Q1: What is the first hurdle writers faee?

A1: <u>They don't believe they can make a living as a full-time writer.</u>

Q2: What practical advice does Honorée give to develop the belief that you can be a writer?

A2: <u>Repeat to yourself "I am a writer". Then add to it.</u>

Q3: What is the second hurdle?

A3: People don't develop a writing habit.

Q4: What does Honorée recommend you do to develop a writing habit?

A4: Schedule 15 min a day and write.

Q5: What is the third hurdle that blocks people on their way to success?

A5: People don't act with intention and purpose.

Q6: What mistake do authors make when thinking about their books?

A6: They think of them as babies rather than income generating products.

Q7: What does Honorée recommend you have to keep you organized?

A7: A production schedule.

Q8: What two types of books does Honorée distinguish?

A8:

a) A heart book.
b) A commercial book.

Q9: What would Honorée have liked to know when she was just starting out?

A9: You need a good cover, so save up and while you're saving up build an email list.

Q10: What should you figure out before you publish?

A10:

1) A way to get a good cover.
2) A way to get great editing.
3) A way to get great copywriting.

Q11: What's does Honorée recommend we do about criticism and praise?

A11:

1) Turn down the criticism.
2) Turn up the praise.

BETTER THAN BOOKBUB. THE THREE STEP PROCESS TO BUILDING A FOLLOWING ON STEROIDS (BUCK FLOGGING)

WHO'S BUCK?

Buck Flogging is the creator of several successful online enterprises including www.buckbooks.net, www.archangelink.com, www.quitn6.com, and several others. After exiting the workforce permanently in 2011 as his first online business became successful (finally), he's been itching to help others achieve the very same thing. Or perhaps he has a fungal infection. Either way, he itches. A lot.
Connect with Buck at www.quitn6.com.

THE GOLDMINE

Alinka: Buck Flogging. You are the creator of several successful online enterprises, including the famous buckbooks.net. Please tell us, what's the golden formula to have something better then Bookbub or something like it? Private Buck Books or Bookbub or in other words, what's the three steps to building a following on steroids?

Buck Flogging: You want to create your own Bookbub and you want to do it by creating your own email list. You don't have to use theirs, you don't have to borrow theirs, you don't have to ask permissions to use theirs. You can build your own. It's easier than most people think. And happens faster than most think as well.

Alinka: I know people get stuck at it. They start doing something and then they see one or two or three people signing up everyday and you've brought thousands and thousands of people to many of your enterprises. How do you do that?

Buck Flogging: You have to be pretty creative with that. I could go on a long tangent about all the things that I've done and the little idiosyncrasies and nuances of how I get that accomplished but I would say, surprisingly, this might sound surprising to many people listening to this, that I think the key is to have a great product for sale, a really great process that sells that product. Common internet business talk with ... Would call that a fun ... A sales funnel. Then have a really good, high [inaudible 00:01:53] page where you're giving something away for free that's of good value. That's about all it takes. If you can do that, what happens is that as those persons subscribes to your list, they go through your funnel. They get used to you they, they like you, they trust you, they buy your product.

You want to create your own Bookbub and you want to do it by creating your own email list.

Let's say for example a person I've worked with, he sells a $500 product. Okay? And 5% of the people that enter his funnel buy that $500 product. What that means is that the average subscriber is worth $25 to him. Now that $25 is an insanely amazing abundant amount of money with which to go and get more subscribers. He can now ... He can now encourage affiliates to promote and if affiliates can promote it he can give them a lot of money for sending him leads. He can do Facebook ads, he's got a huge budget, right? He just needs to get them for under $25 and he'll make a profit. That's what opens up the floodgates. That's how I've seen people build lists of 30, 40, 50, 60 thousand people on a year or less.

If you're trying to do it organically by putting some books out there and you put a little thing in the back of you book to go get a free book or something on your website, or sign-up for new releases, or whatever, that organic process is going to take a long time. It might take you a year to get a thousand emails subscribers.

I'm a big fan of having something that can ... That allows for you to basically finance your whole list-building process. I think that's really key. It's also key to sell a product because you can collect that money right away. Okay? If you're selling only on Amazon then what happens is if you get an email subscriber, and that email subscriber buys one or several of your books, it's going to take two to three months before you see that money. That long delay basically kills your ability to go out and pay somebody to try to ... As an assistant. To go out and try to drive traffic back to your website. Back to your opt-in page. It completely inhibits your [inaudible 00:04:25] campaign because you have to wait months as opposed to getting that money back in a week.

All that little stuff matters a lot. I'm a big fan of doing something beyond just writing books. That's for fiction or non-fiction. Being creative and figuring out what you can sell and sell effectively to help really assist your whole writing career. You need more then just books in many cases.

Alinka: Landing page, funnel and product. What types of products do you recommend authors to have apart from books?

Buck Flogging: It's hard to say. It's all unique. I work with a lot of people who create programs of some kind. Educational programs. More than just an e-course, it might be a 30-day program for accomplishing something, right? Finding whatever your non-fiction niche may be.

If you're a fiction author it becomes a little but more challenging but you have the ability to think of ways to bundle some stuff together to make it work. When I think back to my original blog that I became successful with and the products that I sold, I had several books, I bundled them together and then I thought of an audio program I could put together to talk about another topic. Then I created some videos. Then I had audio [inaudible 00:05:55] package that I was able to charge $99 for and actually get $99 for. That was ... That's huge.

As a novelist you might want to think about maybe putting together a series of videos where you're actually narrating the book yourself. It's kind of overly artsy but that could be something that the uber-fans of yours are willing to shell out maybe 20 or $30 for when bundled with a couple of your books. Maybe you could have a signed copy of your .... Your [inaudible 00:06:34]. Maybe you could have some exclusive books that aren't published anywhere else. Maybe you could have some kind of fan loot such as t-shirts or something that you could bundle with that.

Then some of that authors in the fiction round that have been really successful have been ones who have decided to teach courses on how to ... How to write and publish and market fiction. Right?

Alinka: Yeah.

Buck Flogging: Think about people like Joanna Penn and Katie Weiland and some others who have done that. Becoming an educator in this space is just one option but there's ... You have to be creative but you have to come up with something. It's such a big advantage to be able to take a reader and a fan, collect some quick money, and then use that to then go and build a following quickly and many different fashions.

Ultimately it comes down to having to open up the flood gates somehow so that you, with money, because money ultimate is going to be what helps you build your following somehow, and without it your at a huge disadvantage and you're going to get out-competed by other authors. [inaudible 00:07:46] tools, more weapons available to them to got to be successful and competitive in the market.

Alinka: Right. We've got the product covered. The three steps, we have landing page, funnel, and product. Obviously first you have the product and then you create your way towards ... Towards it. To get to the product we have the funnel. What ... How should that ... What should that funnel look like to be affective?

Buck Flogging: To back up a little bit. What most people are doing is doing it backwards. Right? They go out and do a bunch of marketing in the form of blogging or they release free books or they're spending a lot of time on social media. They're trying to develop a big following and then they go out and try to create products. Publish more books or whatever it is, once they have that following. That's an okay method but what's the problem is that it's hard to get started in the first place when you're starting at zero. When you don't have anything for sale. You're going to have to do all that work and all that marketing and all that ... All that grunt work for six months, a year, maybe longer before you've built a significant following.

So yeah I like to work backwards. Where backwards [inaudible 00:09:12]. Start with the product, the end destination and you sort of work your way backward through that.

Alinka: Yeah. You like to work backwards. I lost you for a second. Yeah. Backwards. Product first to make sure that you can finance all that traffic that you're going to drive, right?

Buck Flogging: Right. Right. If you get that set up then you can go focus on writing books because you already have a mechanism that can be run in a more automated way. Like I said, you can set up those ad campaigns. You can hire assistants. You can ... Everything that you do you're going to get a positive return on. That's what allows you to actually grow substantially and not be stuck forever publishing books and only making $100 a month on those books. Or less.

Alinka: Yeah. A lot of authors ask me, what should they write to their readers? In that funnel, can we talk a little bit about the emails that people should set as their auto-responders. Do you have a golden formula for those emails? What's your advice on that?

Buck Flogging: I don't believe in formulas at all. I'm ... I believe most ... First and foremost in authenticity. Now a lot of people will tell you that video is the best. That you should do videos because somebody actually sees you and hears your voice, looks in your eyes as you're speaking. They're going to develop more of a bond and going to develop more trust. But that's not ...

Alinka: Right and we're ... We're not doing video right now. I think we should explain why not.

Buck Flogging: For me personally, that's not true at all. My writing is my best skill. I'm really good at conveying my honesty and authenticity and genuineness in my writing. So I can create a funnel [inaudible 00:11:21] a bunch of written emails that are very sincere. They have a little but of humor in them. They're not this uptight, sales-pitch kind of sounding thing. I usually really always accommodating to people who have a lower budget. For example, my Quit in 6 books is a choose your own price kind of experience. Just things, more [inaudible 00:11:46] without. Beyond a shadow of a doubt that I don't really care about the money so much. What I want is that I want to help people be successful. That's what you need to be able to do.

The product has got to be great and you have to believe in it. You can't fake authenticity.

If your product is going to help somebody with something, first of all the product has got to be great and you have to believe in it. You can't fake authenticity. You have to put your everything into creating the best product you can possibly create. Something that you can stand behind and know and feel confident that it's going to change people's lives when they purchase it. If you've achieved that then it's really easy to communicate. You can deal with audio, video or in written form. It's going to be really easy to communicate all the reasons why somebody should take the leap and buy your product.

I repeatedly find again and again that the people with the best product are the ones who are able to sell it the best because it's, in the year 2017, people don't buy cheesy, sleazy, marketing stuff anymore. It gets less and less effective every year because we've been expose to more and more of it. You have to go above and beyond that. The only way to do that is to be authentic. There's no formula for that. You have to look within, it sounds kind of cheesy, but you have to really look within your own heart and what you want to do and how you want to help people. Take money off the table and be really genuine and make an impression on someone.

There's no formula for that. Nobody can teach you how to do that. You have to really actually genuinely feel it. Then it has to flow out of you because you feel so strongly about what you've done, what you're doing, and the people that you want to help.

Alinka: Yeah. It's a question of mindset when you put your reader or your customer first, then your whole business or your whole author business shifts. It's true. It starts from within you and then it goes without into your business. People can feel it. They can feel if you're out there to serve them and to help them or if you're out there to make a quick buck.

Buck Flogging: Yes. It is so easy to detect. There is no way you can fake it. You said the word mindset. I think when people hear the word mindset, they think that that's something that they can go and work on. Like they can flip a switch in their brain and all of a sudden they can have a better mindset. To me, you have to earn that [inaudible 00:14:39]. Very competent in something with inside knowledge that can help people.

You have to earn that by studying it, by working with people, by doing whatever you can to become and actual expert. Then you have to ... Or just be a fabulous writer and be very confident in your abilities. Right? Because you've practiced it for a long time, you've been writing for years, you know the story you've created is amazing and is better than a lot of the stuff that's out there. You got to feel that way. The only way you can do that is to actually do your best work and to earn it. That part is hard. That's what takes years to cultivate and you have to do that in order to have the ability to go out there, I think, and have a long-term sustainable, successful business that is fun to operate and that people respond really well to et cetera et et cetera.

Alinka: Absolutely. You mentioned that it's a really good idea to do videos because when people can look into our eyes you establish a different type of connection. I think we owe an explanation to our challenge at [inaudible 00:15:58]. Why we're not doing video. Yeah. That's up to you.

Buck Flogging: Yeah. I ... It's kind of a long story but the short and dirty of it is is that I have ... I have a health and fitness business, that was my original business

	that I started, and my real name is [inaudible 00:16:20]. I maintain these two personas online at any given time. I've kind of retired from the health and fitness aspect somewhat ...
Alinka:	What's your real name? I lost you for a second. The big reveal.
Buck Flogging:	Sorry. My real ... My ... Maybe it's not meant to be revealed. Just kidding.
Alinka:	Maybe not.
Buck Flogging:	My real name is Matt Stone. Not the Matt Stone from South Park. I'm the other Matt Stone. That's why I don't do video. I don't want to confuse people. I used a different picture for Buck [inaudible 00:16:54].
Alinka:	A different picture for Buck Flogging and a different one for Matt Stone.
Buck Flogging:	That's right. I'm a ...
Alinka:	You don't have two heads.
Buck Flogging:	Yeah. It's funny that I can ... That I [inaudible 00:17:06] using a completely made-up name and face and being open and honest about that and having fun with it. It's silly but it goes to show how much you can do when you're really being honest. You really care about people. You really want to help people. Entertain them, inspire them in someway. If you've got, you've got it and you can connect with people if you do. If you don't it's always going to be a struggle.
Alinka:	This ... This Buck Flogging was a pen name for an ... Author's use pen names. Is that this sort of thing?
Buck Flogging:	Yeah. It started out as a pen name because I have a health and fitness-related business. That's how I made my livelihood. I was starting to write about

my insights for internet business and self-publishing and I didn't feel comfortable walking off on my health and fitness-related business that I had spent seven years building, to pursue this new venture. So I started out doing it discreetly under a different name. Turns out people like Buck better than ... Better than Matt.

Alinka: Oh.

Buck Flogging: Yeah. I've had a lot of fun with the old Buck-ster.

Alinka: Awesome. That's really an interesting insight. Going back to our three-step process. We discussed product, we talked about the funnel, and let's talk a little bit about landing pages. You're like the ultimate landing page expert. You've created so many of them and you know what works. What can you recommend that authors do when they set up a landing page? What mistakes do you see most often?

Buck Flogging: The biggest mistake I see is people try to over deliver. I wouldn't say that's the biggest ... Let's say that's one. You don't have to give away everything. Anything and everything to get somebody to subscribe. In fact if you make it sound like it's a huge ordeal, like a giant e-course or some 400 page book that you're giving away for free, that's often too daunting for people to opt in for. You want to keep it very simple. It doesn't have to be anything special. I still find, even after all these years, that giving away just a simple free book gets the highest conversion rate. I've [inaudible 00:19:48] books and a bunch of e-courses and the opt-in rate wasn't any higher than just giving away a simple ... One simple book. You don't have to over deliver. That's a big one.

The second biggest mistake, or just another big mistake I see, is people try to give more then one option. Right? When somebody gets to a webpage, if they have something else that they can do on that page other then submit their email address, then they will not submit their email address. Right? You've been to a site. You've seen something over in the sidebar, you don't run over there and enter your email. Nobody does that. It's only when you can no long continue any further, without entering your email, that you actually enter your email.

People don't ... People will enter their email to a million things. They're used to getting a big sales pitch as soon as they do. They're jaded about that process so it's seems a little bit ... It seems a little bit underhanded to force them to give them you're email ... Or force them to give you their email address but that's you're opportunity to wow them. Show them immediately that you're not like everybody else. If you want to see an example of that I would highly recommend people go to my website quitn6. Which is quit, the letter n, and the number six dot com. Just read the first few emails that you receive after your subscribe and you'll see immediately that it's not the same old same old that you're used to getting.

Alinka: Awesome.

Buck Flogging: That has a huge impact.

Alinka: Yeah. Let's check out quitn6. Now that we have the three step process down, the landing page, the funnel and the product, we still have to drive traffic to it.

Buck Flogging: Yeah. Yes.

Alinka: How should authors drive traffic?

Buck Flogging: One of the first ways is through your books. That's a no-brainer. You want to put something at the end of every book. You want to drive people back there. If you don't have a list yet at all, I would consider launching a book or two or maybe more, completely free just to start accumulating an email list. You can also run ads on Facebook and places like that to get some email subscribers. You can run giveaways. Giveaways are a good way to get subscribers. They're not always the highest quality subscribers but it's really easy to pickup thousand, two thousand, three thousand subscribers with a giveaway. There's dozens of sites that will promote your giveaway. So that's great. Some kind of event which I've done many events. The biggest over night email list that I've ever seen built [inaudible 00:22:48] pull together and those are really complicated and they're hard to execute ...

Alinka: What was it? What was the biggest ... What was the biggest website you've seen built? What event was that?

Buck Flogging: The biggest was these people call, I believe it's The Truth About Cancer. They got a million email subscribers in week.

Alinka: Wow. Crazy.

Buck Flogging: Promoted by ... It was promoted by some of the biggest people ... Some of the biggest names on the internet were all working hard to promote that event and they were getting paid when they sold a product on the back end. That's how ... And obviously those people really believed in the power of that product.

Again, that's getting back into the whole philosophy that [inaudible 00:23:34] product and that product sells well because you created a great promise to sell that product. Then other people, they'll be all about promoting that and making money themselves. Okay? I think affiliates, for me, affiliates driving traffic has always been the best way to get you traffic. It's always been the fastest way to get traffic because those people have spent five years, ten years building a following and they send all their [inaudible 00:24:06] they can all at one time. All on one day often [inaudible

00:24:10]. That's a great way to build a big following in a short period of time.

That's a hard [inaudible 00:24:16]. You can't explain it. [inaudible 00:24:18] is to talk about how to execute all that properly. Definitely to those of you listening to this, think about that in the back of your mind that, okay I need to create a product that other people would love to promote. Again, it's got to be a great product. It's got to be something that other people can stand behind and believe in.

I'm just ... Quality is huge. I've done so much [inaudible 00:24:44] internet that wasn't very good quality and I would give anything to be able to go back in time and do a much better job on the products that I've created. Including the books that I've published.

Alinka: Perfect. Then we have the complete system here. We did it backwards, well, not really backwards. We did it the way it's created but the way the consumer sees it would be, first you're driven to the landing page then they get into the funnel and then they're offered the product. That's how it's done.

Buck Flogging: Then you got a list that not only you didn't have to pay for but that actually you're going to have a list and money. Then when you go to publish a book or two or three or whatever your plans are as an author with your ... Writing career, you get to have a complete field day with this list that you've created. And make far more money then you would have just from the sales of your books alone.

Alinka: Perfect. I have one question. What do you have to say to authors who are ... Who don't bother with building any mail list?

Buck Flogging: It's still possible. I would say especially in the fiction realm, to just focus on your craft and focus on writing the best books that you can possibly write. Get them edited absolutely by the best editors that you can find. Pay big money to have the cover look spectacular. Make the best quality product that you can. It's possible to just go on Amazon and sell that book and be an author. It's fun to have a list. It's a huge advantage if you have a list but it can also be a hindrance if it detracts from your focus and dedication on creating awesome products. There's so much in this industry that is taking people's attention away from quality and putting it on quantity and focusing on marketing and ... There's reasons for all those things.

There's an argument to support all those things but I think, especially in the fiction realm, man, it's very possible to go to to there and focus solely on your writing and hope that the quality will carry it for you. It is possible. That can happen if you write [inaudible 00:27:15] the book will market itself and you as an author, it will market itself. But it takes somebody who's really special and really spectacularly talented to do that. The rest of us mere mortals have to build a list.

Alinka: Yeah. Man, especially non-fictional. For non-fiction authors it's pretty much a no-brainer because it's so logical that they would have a product related to the non-fiction book that they've written, right?

Buck Flogging: Exactly. People are paying three to $10 for a Kindle book, typically. And they're paying sometimes hundreds and even over a thousand dollars for very similar information that's delivered in an e-course. As a non-fiction author, only selling books is yeah, no-brainer as in you must have no brain if you're only selling books and you're not building a list. Exactly. Exactly.

It's different when you're an artist and you really have a craft like writing stories. Sometimes the scenario is different and ... There's some of you out there whose talent alone is enough to carry you and up-marketing is truly a waste of your time but it's probably just a few percent of you so don't go thinking ... Don't go thinking you're too good for marketing just yet. I do want to say that yes, absolutely there some people who should just focus on creating masterful prose.

Alinka: This was so inspirational Buck/Matt.

Buck Flogging: That's what I do. It's what I do. I'm so inspirational.

Alinka: Awesome. Obviously you are. You've created so many businesses. You're a serial entrepreneur, is that how I can call you?

Buck Flogging: I'm trying ... I'm trying to mend my ways. I'm trying to cut back on my serial entrepreneurship. Simplify things. I've started too many websites, I've done too many things. I think that's one of the reasons I'm talking about quality today because there's product diarrhea out there and everyone's like, "Must create more products. Must write more books." And I just don't ... I think that strategy is doomed to failure long-term. I think quality's been forgotten in a lot of this. I'm going back to simplicity and quality. I hope ...I hope you guys listening are going to come with me. I think that's where it's at and where it's been all along.

Alinka: How can people come with you?

Buck Flogging: I think ... I really like people to go and take my course. Obviously I worked really hard on it. This talk has been like a half an hour, there's very little that I can say. I felt at points during our discussion, I felt stupid even saying it, because without explaining how it's done and all those kinds of things, it just is ... It just goes right over people's heads. I've created that course. It's called the Quit Your Job in 6 Months course at quitn6.com. It's very conducive to people who want to be ... To have a career as an author. It's relevant to people who maybe even don't want to write books even I ... I encourage people to always write books in additions to everything that they're doing whenever they can.

That's a good course. It's choose your own price. It's a great educational experience. It allows me to talk about all these things in very, very close detail in the right sequence in a way that probably won't have you feeling like deer in the headlights. I answer every comment that people live on every module of the course as well. I'm there to help.

Alinka: Perfect. Quitn6.com Now one last thing. Our challenge participants are action takers. What one thing should people do right now to make sure that they the build a following on steroids like you have?

Buck Flogging: If I had one thing that I would say is my secret weapon, right? I would [inaudible 00:31:28] I am addicted to it. Obsessed with it.

Alinka: I lost you there. What's the secret weapon? I have to know.

Buck Flogging: All of my big secrets I'm trying to share and they keep cutting out. I would say that the biggest secret for me, the key to my success, [inaudible 00:31:49] that I'm interested in. I naturally just do it obsessively. I love it. I do it all day long and I have to peel myself away from quote unquote work. I think there's a lot of people trying to do something because they feel like they should or because somebody else did it and it seemed so glamorous but it's not really authentic to who they are and what they like. So for me the great secret is, once you've picked something in an area that you really love, you'll spend all day being productive and you'll never have to quote unquote work another day again. It's fun, it's exhilarating. Productivity is just a natural result of choosing the right ... That right activity to be focused on.

The great secret is, once you've picked something in an area that you really love, you'll spend all day being productive and you'll never have to "work" another day again.

Alinka: Following your passion. When you're following your passion you're never going to have to work another day of your life because it's not work, it's fun.

Buck Flogging: Yeah. I wouldn't even say it's fun. It's just ... It just is ... I get ... It's like it becomes an obsession because it's interesting. I wouldn't think of it like, wee fun, because fun to me is kite surfing or something that's pure pleasure, pure leisure. This is more of like playing video games and constantly wanting to get a higher score. Constantly being compelled to go further and see how much farther you can get and how much more that you can do.

I think if you catch that wave by picking something that really is something that you like, that you've always liked, that you like doing, not necessarily a cause that you're all about but something that you [inaudible 00:33:29]. Finding whatever it may be. If you pick the right thing than you will take off and be productive. You can't ... It's not fun to do anything else but work when you've really found that thing that feels like it just sets your soul on fire. To sound really, really, cheesy. Anyway, that's ... I'm done serving up cheese I think. I hope you guys get the point of what I'm saying and find a way to arrive at that destination.

Alinka: Perfect. That was awesome. We managed to cover the three steps to Building a Following on Steroids in just 30 minutes and get your big takeaway, your secret sauce to how you do it so successfully. I say I'm really happy with our interview Matt. Matt/Buck.

Buck Flogging: Matt/Buck. Yes. Beyond [inaudible 00:34:26] Was fun. Glad to finally speak with you. Thanks for putting this great even together for authors out there.

Alinka: Awesome. Thank you so much.

Buck Flogging: Love you guys. Write on.

WERE YOU PAYING ATTENTION?

Q1: How do you create your own BookBub?

Q2: What's the three-step process to bringing thousands of subscribers on your list?

Q3: What are the ways you can promote your product?

Q4: What type of products can authors sell apart from books?

Q5: What should you put emphasis on when creating your funnel?

Q6: What freebie gets the highest conversion rate on a landing page?

Q7: What mistake do authors make on their landing pages?

Q8: How should authors drive traffic to their landing pages?

Q9: What does Buck recommend we focus on in our endeavors?

CHALLENGE

Follow your passion. Be obsessive about it.

THE GOLDEN NUGGETS

Q1: How do you create your own BookBub?

A1: You build your own email list.

Q2: What's the three-step process to bringing thousands of subscribers on your list?

A2:

1) A great product to sell.
2) A sales funnel.
3) A highly converting landing page where you're giving away something that's of good value.

Q3: What are the ways you can promote your product?

A3:

1) Via affiliates.
2) Via Facebook ads.
3) A link to your landing page in your book.

Q4: What type of products can authors sell apart from books?

A4:

1) Educational programs.
2) E-course.
3) Bundle up ebooks, audio, video.
4) A video of you narrating your book.
5) Exclusive books not published anywhere.
6) Swag.

Q5: What should you put emphasis on when creating your funnel?

A5: Authenticity.

Q6: What freebie gets the highest conversion rate on a landing page?

A6: An ebook.

Q7: What mistake do authors make on their landing pages?

A7: They give multiple options.

Q8: How should authors drive traffic to their landing pages?

A8:

1) Through their books.
2) Via giveaways.
3) Via affiliates.

Q9: What does Buck recommend we focus on in our endeavors?

A9: Quality.

THREE, OFTEN OVERLOOKED, 5-FIGURE BOOK LAUNCH STRATEGIES YOU CAN IMPLEMENT NOW (BRYAN COHEN)

WHO'S BRYAN?

Bryan Cohen is the co-host of The Sell More Books Show with Jim Kukral. He's an actor, comedian, freelance writer, author and an occasional game show contestant. He wrote the Ted Saves the World YA sci-fi/fantasy series, and a collection of creative writing prompts books. His books have been downloaded over 400,000 times.
Connect with Bryan at https://www.sellingforauthors.com.

THE GOLDMINE

Alinka: Bryan, you are the co-host of Sell More Books Show. I think we could pick your brain about pretty much anything, but our participants decided to ask you about book launches. Our session is called, "Three often overlooked five figure book launch strategies you can implement right now." Bryan, you've done plenty of book launches, what are the strategies that work?

Bryan: I think there ... First of all, thanks for having me Alinka. I really appreciate it. I think there are so many strategies that can be used. There's no limit. There's so many things that you can start years before the process, months leading up to it. There are things you can do well after it to rejuvenate a book, almost like a second kind of launch. There's so much you can do.

First and foremost, there's not only three, but these are the three things that I think are the most time tested, the most likely to help you have a book not only be successful during a launch ... Fortunately we keep making money on these books after they're launched. These are the three things I think can last the longest and are actually, when it comes down to it, the least expensive. I know that we're all worried that only the people who have tens of thousands of dollars to throw into ads or something are the ones who are going to be the most successful. In some cases that's true, but it doesn't just have to be throwing money at the problem. Sometimes if we focus on these three key areas, we can be just as successful.

The three parts of the selling trilogy are: Copy, funnel, and network.

The three areas I want to cover today are something I like to call, "The selling trilogy." It's basically one of the best trilogies of all time. It's up there with Star Wars, it's up there with Lord of the Rings. It's very good. The three parts of the selling trilogy are: Copy, funnel, and network. Those three things ... If you have those working for you, you're going to have a successful launch every single time. I'm happy to go into all of those, but I've been talking for awhile. What do you think about all that, Alinka? Do you agree with me?

Alinka: I love it. I love the three parts that you chose because you're the first one on the challenge that's actually talking about copy. I know how extremely that is. You're a professional copywriter. I'm really into copy, so I would love to talk about that. That's the first part you mentioned. What is this copy thing anyway?

Bryan: What is this copy thing? You've got the words you write in your book. You've got your prose ... Some of us have our poetry, but we all know that is a tough sell. We've got our prose. We've got our words in our fiction or non-fiction books. Those words are very important, obviously. The better they are, the more captivating they are, the more likely someone who starts the book is going to read all the way through. How do we get them to start the book? In a lot of cases, it has to do with the words you write outside of your book.

It's the words you write that get people excited when they're reading your book description. It's the words you write when you get people into your email lists and you get them excited about your launch from the words you write. It's the words you write in an advertisement. These words are usually not nearly as many because if you're writing 60 to 80 thousand words, it feels silly to say, "These 250 words are hard," Or "These 20 words are hard." That's true. That smaller amount of words may do more to get people to read your 60 to 80 thousand words than any thing you write between the front cover and the back cover.

Alinka: Of course because those are the ones that the potential readers are going to read, and they're going to help decide if they're even going to click on that preview thing and read the first pages.

Do you have some ... The subject of copy is so vast that [inaudible 00:04:38]. Let's try to give people some practical advice. I know you have a whole ... You could call it formula or framework that can be used to create a description. Can we give people some pointers? We're not going to go into depth, but at least something that they can hang onto when creating a description.

Bryan: To keep things simply, I want to focus on the first line of your book description. If you've read anything on copywriting ...I'm always reading new books on copywriting. I'm reading Ogilvy on Advertising right now, an old classic with big black letters on white page. One thing he says that I've heard millions of times over and over again is that, "If you don't get people in your first line, you are not going to get them the rest of the time." I've seen it as 80% of people will stop reading after your first line. If you don't have a strong first line, you're in trouble.

If you don't get people in your first line, you are not going to get them the rest of the time.

I've heard the first line of a book description referred to as the headline or the hook. Doesn't matter what your terminology is, it needs to do the same key things. First and foremost, it needs to be interesting, captivating. It needs to draw people's attention and the people's attention you're trying to draw is readers from that genre. If you're a thriller writer you're not emphasizing the romance in the book, you're emphasizing the explosions or the race against time. If you are writing the romance, you're not talking so much about the action. You're talking about this guy, this girl, are they going to get together? It needs to make sense. That first line ... If it's just about one character in a romance some people may think, "This isn't really about people getting together." Even though three lines later you mentioned the other person. They didn't get to that point. You have to get them right away.

Another thing, it needs to make sense. I've seen people try to write headlines and try to condense it down to that movie poster length, and it doesn't make sense. It makes sense in their head, but they've never shared it with anybody else so it doesn't make sense to those other people. Lastly I'll say it needs to be really short. It needs to be probably 12 words or less. Get to the essence of what that book is about. I'm going to throw in one more thing. It needs to evoke emotions from your reader. That's fiction or non-fiction. You may think, "Non-fiction, why would that need to be emotional?" If someone's trying to solve a problem, they're certainly experiencing emotions about it. You need to tap into that in that very short first line.

Alinka: This is perfect. What about some examples? Do you have some from the top of your head? Some examples of a really good first line?

Bryan: Sure, I'm going to steal one. This is going to be good. I'm going to steal one from my friend Adam Croft who is a very successful thriller author who last year earned over six figures from one headline. Not necessarily from one headline, but from one book, but that one headline really made the difference. It was, "Would you murder your wife to save your daughter?" It's insane how good that headline is.

Alinka: It's excellent because he's talking to the reader. He's saying, "You."

Bryan: Got the word, "You." It's this almost impossible choice between the things. It's got the great words in general. It's a question which gets the mind going. It's an impossible choice between two terrible things. It works so well in the genre.

It's doing so much in so few words. Authors may think, "He's obviously just a headline genius." I'm guessing that he went through a lot of iterations of that headline to get it to work. We're so used to as authors saying, "I'm going to write it once and then revise it." That's not how copywriting really works. You put a lot of effort into a lot of different ideas, play around. Eventually if you get something that's so good, you can then use that everywhere. Book descriptions, ads, when you're submitting to PR people like newspapers. You can use it anywhere so spending time on that one line is so important.

Alinka: Totally. Correct me if I'm wrong, but I think Joe Sugarman said that you have to get your reader on that slippery slide so the first line has to make your reader ... First of all, they have to read the first line. Its purpose is to make them read the second line. The purpose of the second line is to make them read the third line. That's how you write the book description that people read.

Bryan: It's so completely true. That's definitely ... I don't know if that's Sugarman that said it, it probably is. What that quote says is perfectly true.

Alinka: Awesome. We could talk about copy for hours.

Bryan: We could.

Alinka: Let's move to funnel though. What is this funnel you speak of?

Bryan: A funnel, for those watching the video, you may know that a funnel looks like this.

Alinka: I think we have one in the kitchen.

Bryan: Do you have one? Nice. Wide at the top and it narrows as it goes down. The funnel for authors is that you are bringing as many people as possible into finding out that you exist, first and foremost. The widest end of the funnel is people finding out that you exist. There are lots of different ways that people can find out you exist and we'll go into that a little more when we get to the third part of the selling trilogy.

First and foremost, you need people to know you exist because if they don't know you exist they're not going to buy your books. That's for sure. As you bring those people in and you bring them into a mailing list, an email list, they will find out more about you. They will decide, "I'm going to open this person's emails or not." The funnel gets a little narrower because you're never going to get 100% of people open those emails. Then the funnel gets a little narrower when people say, "This guy sounds okay but I'm not going to buy his books." It narrows eventually to you got the people who are buying your books, who are really interested in the stuff you got going on and who say, "I like this person enough to buy all their books forever. To become that true fan that we're all craving."

Getting people through the funnel in a successful way is difficult. A lot of authors vaguely know how to do this but they don't always do a great job of deciding, "I'm going to send a few emails to these readers, what are those emails going to say and what are my objectives during those emails?" Some authors are just like, "Here's an email. Go!" As a result, they don't get the results that they're hoping for.

Alinka: You said that's the mistake that authors make, but what is your advice on people's objectives? Maybe you've tested and you put this to mind, so how many emails before you start selling something?

Bryan: Sure. First and foremost I'll say you don't sell right away. You're smart to say, "How many emails before you start selling," because you do not ... In the first email that you send to readers who just entered into your funnel, you don't pitch them because then they're going to think, "This person's just going to pitch me all the time." You start off by usually giving something away for free. Doesn't have to be a full novel, but it can be. Non-fiction usually has it easier, you can usually put together a one page cheat sheet and you'll be fine.

As you are giving your thing away for free, you're starting to introduce yourself. You're almost starting to tell your story. I like in that first email ... In all of these emails, I'm telling a little about myself. I like to delivery the freebie, the email that goes out right away, I delivery the freebie. Second email? Actually check in and make sure they downloaded the free thing. If they don't download the free thing, they're probably never going to buy the paid thing. It's good to have a second opportunity there. In the third email, I start asking to see if they want to connect in other places. Maybe a Facebook group so I can have more ... I like to call it connecting with them on the shareable platforms. Where people can share your books and people can spread the word. Where people can talk about you and you can respond easily. Social media is good for that so that's kind of what I do in the third email.

In the fourth email, I finally say, "You know a little more about me, would you be interested in buying my book?" Often that is tied with a story about writing that book, about how much that book means to me, about what they can expect to get out of it. It's not really until the fourth email, but I've tried to lay the foundation before making any kind of pitch. It's usually a couple of weeks before I even say, "I have books. You could potentially buy them."

Alinka: Smart people say that, "Marketing is salesmanship multiplied." Is that right or did I get it wrong?

Bryan: I think that works. It's definitely ... Authors don't like to think of themselves as salesmen or salespeople but they are. You need to ... Each email builds on the last. It's a lot about momentum, just like the copywriting. The first sentence is that momentum that leads to the second sentence. The objective is to get them to move on. Your objective is to get them to read the next email, focus on you, and enjoy you. The next email is to do the same. The funnel starts wide, but you don't want it to narrow to like one person at the end. You want it decently wide, narrows down, maybe you bring in 500 people and you want still a couple hundred people to be reading your emails when they get to the fourth one. As opposed to people feel spammed or something and they stop reading entirely.

Alinka: Basically, the first three emails that's marketing because you're not selling anything. The last email when you pitch is the sales email, but that sales email really works because of the marketing emails that you sent before. Sending out that first email where you're giving away the freebie, you're already getting people ready to buy that book. It's all this necessary process of courting.

Bryan: I love looking at it as a dating thing. For sure.

Alinka: It's like a dating thing. Dating your reader.

Bryan: I will say the biggest thing that authors tend to mess up with this is they don't give their emails as much care as they do their books. I have seen broken links, links that just go to nowhere. I have seen ... Typos stink, but it's not going to derail everything completely. I've seen typos. I've seen emails that are just really ugly. I like simple text, personally. I'm a simple text guy. I think that authors think of an autoresponder sequence, which is what this is often called in that funnel of emails ... They often think of it as just another thing to do.

I'm going to tell you, it's probably one of the three most important things to do. It may even be more important than writing the book. People think of the funnel after book three. If you had it set up after book one, you might actually have people to pitch book three to once you get to it.

Alinka: This is also where copy, that you're expert at, is so important. If you know how to write those emails, you're able to engage with your readers. They're going to know, like, and trust you. Eventually if they know, like, and trust you they're going to buy from you.

Bryan: Exactly, 100%.

Alinka: Do you have any fun examples of well converting emails in the autoresponder sequence?

Bryan: I think it's so easy to try to use a template or a swipe, but I'm not a big fan of those. I'm a big fan of from the heart stuff. I'm a big fan of figuring out that first story you like to tell. I'm married now and so I don't have first dates anymore, but I like to think about what's the story I would tell on a first date. What's thing that I would really ... If people are trying to find out more about me, or even if they're trying to find out more about me as an author ... I like to think about what would I tell that person. That should be your inspiration for writing this email.

It should be short. If you think about connecting with a new person, you don't have a four hour phone conversation. You don't have a six hour date more than likely. You probably have a short, sweet thing and that's what your first email needs to be. Then I recommend having a link to the freebie in the email. I'm a big fan of using BookFunnel. You just put in a MOBI file, the Kindle download file, an EPUB, the download file from everywhere else. It generates the link for you and you put that link in there. I like to have that link two to three times in that email just because people are lazy.

Alinka: Just like with dating, the easiest way to failure is to be all about me and not ask anything about your partner on the other side. I see a lot successful emails are about you. It's all about the reader. Of course you need to build authority and tell people something about yourself. We are very ego-centered humans, so we think a lot about ourselves. When you're able to connect, we understand that and you're able to connect with that. That's how you can really start engaging with people.

Bryan: You're bringing up a good point about not making it all about you. The end of every email I send, I like to ask a question. Usually that question is related to the offer that I have in that email. Could be about the freebie, but it could be a getting to know you kind of question. For my pen name, my fairytale pen name Casey Lane, I like to ask a question about, "Who's your favorite hero or heroine?" It's so awesome to get all of these responses. I must have gotten hundreds of responses from people. Those people now, they remember me a little better because I asked them something instead of just telling them about myself.

Alinka: Very smart.

Bryan: Thanks. I think I got it from someone else.

Alinka: You applied it.

Bryan: That's true.

Alinka: Guys, apply what you're hearing here.

Let's move to traffic. What is this traffic?

Bryan: Traffic is a tricky business because you've got a lot of different ways to generate it. You've got a lot of different ways to pay for it. You've got a lot of different ways to try to get it off of Google or get it off of Amazon. Maybe you've got a free book and you're trying to bring it back. I think all of those ways are too complicated. My favorite way to get traffic is to actually connect with other authors. I'm a big of fan of building up your network to bring new traffic. I think too many authors try to do it all themselves or they do it themselves with maybe a course or a book that they're reading, and they try to do it. They try to make it all self study, but it's crazy. You and I, we've worked on this together because this is something that the internet marketing world does a lot better than the author world in a way. The non-fiction author world does a lot better than the fiction world.

We've been both worked together. We've promoted each other's stuff. As a result, we've both been able to build our followings based on people liking me who then like you. People like you who then like me. This is a good thing. This is good for everybody involved. Nobody feels like it's a bad thing when you talk about me or I talk about you. That's just how it goes.

Alinka: It's a win-win-win because our audience wins as well.

Bryan: It is. Everybody wins. In fiction, and in some circles in non-fiction, authors think that they're in some kind of competition. They're not. This year has been the year of the joint promotion, the year of the group promotion with certain sites like instaFreebie with box sets and whatnot. I love when I see that sort of thing happen because it shows that authors are thinking outside the box and it shows, just equation-wise ... If I'm an author with 500 readers and I organize something with a bunch of other authors that have 10,000 or so readers amongst them, then those 10,000 readers some of them will come over to me and now I will have more than 500 readers.

If you work with other people who have more readers than you in your genre, often that's in the way of helping them, doing something for them, working together with them, you doing all the organizational kind of stuff. They have readers who may like your stuff too. You often just have to put in the work, you don't necessarily have to put in a whole lot of money to get those new readers.

Alinka: You've done a lot of these events, multiple types. Can you share your secret? Which one did you find was the most effective?

Bryan: Right now for non-fiction I'm still a big fan of those multi-author events like the multi-author Facebook events I ran for non-fiction authors. I think any category of non-fiction can do this and have success. You connect with six other financial bloggers or ten other people who do scrap booking. It really could be anything because Facebook works really well for having those communication threads where people are answering questions, people are doing give aways. I think those work really well for non-fiction.

Fiction people don't ask necessarily as many questions. They won't necessarily jump on to buy another person's book after finding out about them in the same way they do about non-fiction. Non-fiction readers, they want to buy every book on a subject. Fiction readers don't necessarily want to buy every book in that genre without getting to know their authors first. Those events can work well for one book if there's a multi-author box set or something. I think box sets and those big instaFreebie promotions are best the bet for fiction right now because everyone's pulling together their resources but you're not trying to force people to buy anything. You're trading those mailing lists, subscribers, for instaFreebie or for box sets. You're giving everyone a little taste of multiple authors in the genre so they get to know you a little better.

I don't know if I have any secrets, but I will tell you that those non-fiction events have lead to thousands of book sales. The multi-author anthology that I ran a little bit toward the end of last year has already earned over $15,000 and it's just short stories. Everyone just wrote 10,000 word short story and it leads to over $15,000 in sales. I think those are your best bets if you're trying to organize joint promotions for non-fiction or fiction.

Alinka: I love it. We have the whole thing down now. You said copy, funnel, and traffic. It's a great framework to make sure that your next launch is a huge success.

Bryan, that was incredible. I knew it would be because you're the co-host of Sell More Books Show along with Jim Kukral, who is also on the challenge. You've been running the show for so many years and you know everything that's happening in the [inaudible 00:28:13]. I'm really excited about all the input we just got from you.

Bryan: Thank you. I really appreciate you having me here. It's always fun to share what we learn on the show and what I've learned from my own dabblings in the author world.

Alinka: Bryan, how can people connect with you?

Bryan: I think the best place is to go to SellingForAuthors.com. You're going to get a little cheat sheet based on some of the concepts we talked about here today. You will also get to check out some videos on how to use the selling trilogy as a effectively as possible to make your career a success.

Alinka: One last thing. Our challenge participants are action takers, so what's the one thing that they should do right now to make sure that their next book is a smashing success?

Bryan: I'm going to keep it simple. I won't go into the whole trilogy here. We'll keep with the copy since you said no one had talked about copy thus far. I'm going to say write 20 versions of a headline for your best selling book, or the book you want to be your best selling book. Write 20 versions and then pick the best few, maybe go poll them out in a Facebook group or something. If you write more than a few, you're going to eventually get deeper in there and find the best possible idea for what's going to work well for your book. Write 20 different versions, pick a couple, figure out which one is the best, and then use that on your book.

Alinka: Perfect. I love it and I'm going to do that too.

Bryan: Good. Share them with me, I'd love to look at them.

Alinka: Thank you so much, Bryan. This has been incredible.

Bryan: Thank you, Alinka. I really appreciate it. I hope everyone enjoys the rest of the challenge.

WERE YOU PAYING ATTENTION?

Q1: What does the selling trilogy consist of?

Q2: What's going to get readers excited about reading your book and onto your mailing list?

Q3: What's the most important part of your book description?

Q4: What four things does the first line of your book description need to achieve?

Q5: What is a funnel for authors?

Q6: What are the four emails Bryan recommends you send?

Q7: What do authors mess up with the emails they send?

Q8: Who should your emails focus on?

Q9: What is Bryan's favorite way to build traffic?

Q10: What type of events does Bryan recommend to do to grow your network?

CHALLENGE

Write 20 versions of a headline for your best-selling book or the book you want to be your best-selling book. Then poll them out (on Fb for example).

THE GOLDEN NUGGETS

Q1: What does the selling trilogy consist of?

A1:

1) Copy.
2) Funnel.
3) Network.

Q2: What's going to get readers excited about reading your book and onto your mailing list?

A2: Your copy (like your book description or ads).

Q3: What's the most important part of your book description?

A3: The first line.

Q4: What four things does the first line of your book description need to achieve?

A4:

1) Be captivating.
2) Make sense.
3) Be short.
4) Evoke emotions from your reader.

Q5: What is a funnel for authors?

A5: A process in which you capture new readers, you bring them onto your mailing list. Then the funnel gets narrower because not everybody will open all your emails. Then it gets narrower because not everybody will buy your books. Eventually it narrows down to your true fans.

Q6: What are the four emails Bryan recommends you send?

A6:

1) Email 1: Giveaway freebie, introduce yourself.
2) Email 2: Check in to make sure they downloaded the freebie.
3) Email 3: Connect in other places.
4) Email 4: Would you be interested in buying my book?

Q7: What do authors mess up with the emails they send?

A7: They don't give their emails as much care as they do their books.

Q8: Who should your emails focus on?

A8: Your reader.

Q9: What is Bryan's favorite way to build traffic?

A9: Networking. Connecting with other authors.

Q10: What type of events does Bryan recommend to do to grow your network?

A10: Multi-author Facebook events.

THE SINGLE MOST EFFECTIVE STRATEGY 70 OUT OF 75 SUCCESSFUL AUTHORS PUT TO USE (ERIC VAN DER HOPE)

WHO'S ERIC?

Eric V. Van Der Hope is a publisher, author and speaker who has quietly worked behind the scenes within the Internet Marketing community, developing little-known 'virtual real estate' niches. His passion and desire in helping others find their own 'niche' has been instrumental in their success. Many in the marketing 'arena' respect his 'tell-it-like-it-is' attitude as it brings a breath of fresh air to a competitive market. Eric is the host of the Publishing Success Summit in which he interviewed 75 authors and influencers in the publishing space.
Connect with Eric at https://ericvanderhope.com.

THE GOLDMINE

Alinka: Eric as the host of the Publishing Success Summit you interviewed 75 successful authors, is that right?

Eric: Yeah, almost right. I actually interviewed 86, by the time it all ended I had actually interviewed 86 individuals, you were pretty close.

Alinka: That's incredible. You are just an incredible well of publishing wisdom, we're going to use you now. My question is, what do all these successful people that you've interviewed, successful authors. What do they all have in common or in other words what is the single most effective strategy that most of these authors put to use?

Eric: That's a great question and it was from the time that I started the first interview I got an idea of the general gist of how they started or not just how they started, but what it took for them to become successful in what they were doing. I would say for the most part creating and developing and building a strong platform. That just it entails not just what you think it is but there's a lot more that goes behind what a platform is engagement with your audience, knowing influencers or folks in your genre, in your space, being able to get good feedback from your audience and engagement with your audience.

Successful authors create and develop a strong platform.

There's a number of things that go into that but for the most part I believe it was the platform building and having a solid platform that helped these individuals create what they had and in an easier way. Because anyone can go out there and write a book but it's then when you publish that book are people ready for that book, do they know that you're there? If they don't know you're there then you're going to ...

Crickets, that's all you're going to hear when you publish your book and for the most part, at least most of them. A lot of these individuals try to show and explain and just explain how to develop a platform in the most ... The easiest and the simplest way.

Alinka: When we say platform what exactly do we mean, what is that? Do you mean Amazon, is that being setup on Amazon, other retailers, websites, social media, all of the above?

Eric: Right.

Alinka: Let's get a little bit deeper into this.

Eric: Absolutely, I like to use Michael Hyatt as an example. You probably have heard of Michael Hyatt or know him and he has a pretty good definition of what a platform is. For simplicity he says very simply, "A platform is the thing you have to stand on to get heard, it's your stage but unlike a stage in a theater today's platform is built of people, contacts, connections and followers." That's what it is for the most part.

Alinka: It's a great comparison and it's a great description of a platform. Where would you start? Let's say an author has a book that they're just about to launch and they've been immersed in writing that book and getting it ready for publication so they really haven't thought about what exactly they need to do next. Well, they are starting to think about it now because if you're on this challenge you're a step ahead of everybody else. What would you recommend for authors to start in terms of platform building, what's the first thing people should do?

Eric: That's a good question, first I think that folks who are doing this or they're creating a platform or they're developing their book is they have to ask personal questions to themselves. What is their message, why are they doing what they're doing, what's the what? The why and the what are so important before you even get started because once you can answer those two questions then you're going to know what type of audience that you're going to be seeking out.

You can't publish for everybody.

If you don't know the type of audience that you're seeking out then you're just throwing out a net and you're pretty much catching pretty much everybody and you're not narrowing in on the topic. You can't publish for everybody, you're going to have to publish or talk your message to a specific person otherwise you're not going to get that feedback back. Does that make sense?

Alinka: Yeah, totally, you need to know what your message is, what you're talking about and see if there are people who want to listen to you and get to those people because that's your target audience. Now technologically speaking or when you're sitting in front of your computer what do you do first in terms of creating an online platform? Would it be the website, what exactly in terms of website or what's your recommendation for people to start building that platform like practical things?

Eric: Can you hear me right now because I think I muted myself?

Alinka: Yeah, I can hear you great.

Eric: You can hear me okay because I heard the phone go off and I was hoping that you didn't hear the phone. Yes, from a practical sense the best thing and it's a funny thing is how do you amplify your message, how do you get your reach to go further out? The easiest way of doing that is obviously to create a website before you do anything. The reason for that is because everybody right now in the world when they want to find out information about you where do they go? They go to the internet.

It may seem the simplest thing ever but by putting up a website and it doesn't have to be this big drawn out website. It could be just a one page website or a two page website where it has your information, it has information about your book, what it is that you're trying to explain to others or teach or share whatever goes on there. Then some sort of opt-in so that you're at that point then encouraging people to follow you and engage with you and that's what we call list building.

There's nothing better or more stronger than having that and doing that from the beginning because when you're finally down the road launching your book. You need to be able to have a team of people that can help you and leverage that help because you can't do it all by yourself. It's like you need a small community to help you and you can't do everything all by yourself.

Does that make sense? Simply just a small website, whether it's one or two pages that's all it needs and then a simple opt-in to invite people that want to be part of your message. You need some sort of connection and that's your way of getting those people to connect with you so that you in turn can email them and talk to them about what your message is all about.

Alinka: I totally agree, I think that's the number one strategy every online business should pursue and authors are only catching up now. Whereas business people in other niches have been doing this for years now and just one page, you just need one page, the landing page or in other words a squeeze page. Just a page where you arrive and you can either subscribe or leave. When you subscribe the author gets this amazing opportunity to have a direct channel of communication with the reader and that's when you start bombarding them with the message, "Buy my book," right?

Eric: No, I know you know.

Alinka: You're listening.

Eric: I know you know. Absolutely not. That is your time to connect on a personal level with your audience and until that you feel that you have a connection you still don't say, "Buy me, buy me, buy me." You want to make it a natural fit so that when you say enough people are going to go, "Well, what else can I do?" By making stuff available on your website as you go on and have more experience building websites and stuff you can add more things to your website and then direct people to that.

Connect with influencers.

Another thing too is you can rely on other people. Getting connected with influencers or not just influencers but with people who are really strongly following your message. They can be like your marketer. There's nothing stronger than having a person actually recommend you. That type of marketing is so strong. For example, obviously I had this past summit that went on. A lot of folks shared that information on social media. That's great, absolutely wonderful and I have lots of impressions and hits and all sorts of stuff.

When it doesn't come directly from the person let's say someone saying, "Oh, I recommend you go do the ... Check this out it's great information." People are less likely to catch that and then follow through with that and then do something with it. Whereas if it comes directly from someone like such as yourself or someone else they say, "Hey I've got a recommendation, check them out this has got some great information." That is such a strong connection between ... Because you already have a set up engagement with your audience.

That's what I've found in the past as far as what I learned and I already had an idea that's probably what would happened. You can also connect with obviously through social media but there's nothing more strong than actually having your own email list and bonding and connecting with your audience there and people begin to trust you because they see the information that you're sharing.

What you want to do is you want to go out of your way to share information. You're not giving away information but you're sharing it and people then are more likely to say, "Wow this guy or this girl has got great information." What does this person have to sell because it's got to be even better?" That's the kind of thing you want to develop, does that make sense?

Alinka: Yes, it absolutely makes sense. That's exactly what people should be thinking. We get so much incredible stuff and before you even manage to tell people, "Buy this," they're already thinking, "What does this person have to sell? I want it before you even offer it." That's exactly you want. Eric you mentioned that an integral part of building a platform is networking and you're an incredibly effective networker. The fact that you interviewed 86, 86?

Eric: Yes.

Alinka: 86 successful authors for your summit, you have to be an incredible networker. Can you tell people, can you reach back into the past and tell people how you started building that network?

Eric: Absolutely and that's a great question and I mean for everybody that's listening in you have to start somewhere and that somewhere, it could have been 10 years ago, it could have been five years ago, it could have been a week. If you don't start reaching out, and this is a big thing as far as part of reaching out with just one aspect. There's so many different aspects of networking.

You're going to have to go into it not thinking, "What I'm I going to get out of it. You have to go in there thinking, "What can I do for this person, to help this person do what they're doing or help them spread their message or whatever it is." You can't go in thinking, "What's in it for me?" It's because it's just not going to work that way. They're going to catch on right away, "Well this person is looking for something for me to give him," or "it's the leveraging of my email list, or whatever, there's so many other things, right? Having an unselfish aspect of going into it.

One of the things that I've done over the past and it doesn't happen automatically it takes time. Let's say one aspect or one tactic I guess you could say is, is search out folks in your niche or in your genre and then do like let's say for example you follow a person that you like and you like their post. Go on there and start commenting on their post and say, "Yeah great post," get it like a running conversation going. Do that with your favorites and that's going to start building rapport with that individual.

Sooner or later down the road they're going to say, "Wow I love this guy," and they're going to reach out and say, "Hey, I'd like to talk to you more or whatever." Otherwise and I totally recommend this you've got to go to physical events. There's nothing better than going to physical events. I'm not saying, "Oh yeah go there and suddenly start buying a $1000 products and all that stuff." You've got to go for these networks.

For example my genre, my space is publishing and marketing. I'll go to events like Author 101 University, which is a marketing and publishing event or I'll go to like a speaking event where's people who are learning how to speak. That kind of atmosphere and networking then you get with the folks there that are also trying to learn and you just start making connections and you just build on that.

Like I said if it's a big influencer that you just can't quite reach. The easiest thing to do is just follow them and start just not guest posting but you're not actually guest posting but you're commenting on their blog comments or their blog entry. That's one way that you'll get their attention and there's just a whole different other aspects to it. Is that kind of what you were thinking about?

Alinka: Yeah, perfect. One way that I use also is it if I want to connect with an author. If I'm really passionate about what they're doing, I've read their books, I get their books, I buy their book and I leave a review. I don't do it as a review exchange that's what I recommend but as a reader you review as a reader and the author even if they have 300 hundred reviews. I can tell you I have 300 reviews on my book for authors and every now and then I go and check if the number of review has increased.

I read the recent reviews and I check out the names and I can sometimes match the name of the reviewer with someone who's been emailing so I know that this person has left a review. Even if somebody has hundreds of reviews it doesn't mean that they don't go and check who's been reviewing because your book is always your book. You keep having a really close relationship and you do appreciate. I appreciate a lot when somebody leaves a review. Anybody you want to connect with, that's a really good way to stand out, people notice that.

Eric: Absolutely and that makes me not remember something in my head but it triggered something. Another way of reaching out and growing your audience as well and reaching out to your influencers and that is talk to folks that are around them. Who also have a direct relationship with them and figure out what are their favorite things, what do they like, what are they doing, are they working on a book, stuff like that. Then offer, "Hey, I'd love to do like an advanced review if you don't mind for your book." Just anything you can.

That's another thing but going back to the networking thing too is I know Rick Frishman and David Hancock Author 101 and Morgan James Publishing and the way that I went toto connect with them I was like, "What's the best way that I can," because I wanted to be able to learn from them and be able to. Because these guys are the top of their game, right? I volunteered, I went one day five years ago to Author 101 and said, "Hey," it wasn't Rick that was someone else who was putting on the event for Rick and the coordination and I said, "Hey, what can I do to help out? I'll volunteer, I'll do anything but I want to help you guys out."

By volunteering, that's another way that you can get closer to your future mentor or the folks that you want to get close to as far as influencers. Now again there are two things behind that, You want to go in and say, "Well, because I'm doing this directly so I can get something out of it." Now I knew that I wanted to go in there and I was saying to myself, "If I don't get anything out of it no worries. I don't have a problem with that because but it was just the fact of getting near to him and hearing him and not just hearing him but hearing his sphere of influence of others, I learning from.

I said, "You know what, whatever happens form this I'm going to benefit because I'm going to be able to start associating with other individuals in the space." You just have to make the effort, you have to go out of your comfort because I was uncomfortable, I'm an introvert and most authors are introverts. I was like, "There's no way, I don't like crowds and all these stuff," but it's like, "You know what, you got to punch through it and then do something you're uncomfortable with," when you get out on the other side it's like, "Why did it take this long for me to do this?" Those are some ways to reach out and connect and build and audience.

Alinka: That's the mindset, what can you do for others, what value can you bring to the table? Another thing that comes to mind is once you've made a few connections you can start introducing people to one another. You can say, "Eric meet Alinka, Alinka meet Eric." Say, "You two guy are rocking it, you should know each other," and let the people follow up with each other. Then people think of you as the person who knows people in your niche. That's a really good thing to do.

Even if you just know a few people you can be sure that that person that you connected to somebody else will think of you when they need to connect somebody else to somebody like you, you will be top of line. If you do that every now and then for people, people reciprocate that's normal, it's human nature. You do it for the fun of it and when you do it because it's exciting because that's what you're fortunate about. I think internet really helps introverts because you can hide behind the computer screen and send out emails.

You can do so much just by typing and that's excellent. It hasn't been possible in the past so if you're an introvert you can totally do it and even if you're an introvert you can connect with a huge network of people like Eric like you did. You managed to pull-off this incredible event where you interviewed 86 speakers. There must have been some, you had to get out of your comfort zone.

Like I said going back to how in the world could I have connected with that many people and how in the world was I able to actually, to interview all those people in a small amount of time? Because I did all these within, I don't know, it must have been three to four months. I was doing six interviews a day taking time off work. If you have strong enough why and a strong enough what you can do anything you want.

I hear so many people say, "Well, I can't do that I got this and I got this and I got this." Well prioritize, it's all about prioritizing. How import is it to you? If it's important enough to you you're going to find a way no matter what I guarantee you. If I can do 86 of these things, 86 interviews in this period of time and pull it off, anyone can do anything. Because I'm just this little person that just did this.

How did I get all these people? Well, it's over a period of years that I developed relationships with these folks. They wrote articles, I shared their articles with other folks, I shared their stuff on my social medial. A lot of it was just giving to them as much as I could as far as what I could give as far as what I mean by giving. I did what I could and that was by sharing what they had.

I shared their information with my audience thinking, "Okay, I think this is going to fit with my audience." A lot of that it's just not automatic, you can't just say, "Oh I'm going to do this one thing today and tomorrow I'm going to be suddenly interacting with this person." It has to be a slow ... It doesn't have to be but for me and a lot of the folks that I interviewed and they did it the same way, it takes time.

This is not like an overnight success and I don't consider this like a total success. In every business there's the next step, right? You got to do something else and then do something else and do something else. But yeah it takes time but you got to start somewhere. Start now by reaching out to just one person and doing something for them.

Alinka: Excellent I love this actionable advice. Eric I have a chicken and egg question for you?

Eric: Oh no.

Alinka: What comes first, the platform or the book?

Eric: Both at the same time. No, that's actually a good question because a lot of people have a book in their mind and a lot of folks they get the book, they write the book and then they publish the book, right? A lot of times when that happens they're not as successful because no one notice them. That goes back to the platform and a platform doesn't have to be this heavy thing that's just like.

I know it is because when people hear this keyword they're like, "Oh," and they're suddenly like collapsing through their chair because it's like, "Well, I've got to do this marketing, I've got to do my website and I've got to begin the social and I've got." They've got all these clabbering marketers coming down on them to get 20, 40 different things.

It comes back simply to just doing one thing your website and then creating and opt-in. That website like you said it would be a simple squeeze page with an opt-in where basically people that come to your website if they see what they … If they like what they see then they're going to opt-in if you're sharing something. If there's not something there that they don't like they're going to leave. It makes it simple just a one, two thing.

Platform I feel strongly about, you really have to be able to reach out to folks so that when you ultimately go out and you publish your book you'll have a following, you'll have people that are like, that love your message already. Then there are going to be people ... A launch takes time but as that launch goes then you're going to have people that really like you and they're going to tell others. It's a lot of word of mouth marketing going on too.

Chicken or the egg, platform by far and large is the biggest gorilla in the room. You got to get that done part and then go from there and it's just things become a lot easier to do because you can just grow your … As you're growing your platform you can start writing your book or if you've already written it you can start doing the process of getting your files uploaded to whatever site to get your book published.

The publishing part is the easiest part, that's the part you can do within one day. You can have your book published and listed on Amazon in less than one day. That publishing part is the easiest thing, it's the platform that takes the time but you've got to take the time to do it but that is the hardest of the two. It makes sense?

Alinka: Yes, excellent. It's perfect. Eric this was incredible but no wonder because you interviewed 86 successful authors and you know what these people all have in common. Just recapping it's the platform, the website, the networking and we've got some incredible golden nuggets in this interview for people who have been listening and paying attention. Eric I know we just scratched the surface of everything but how can people connect with you and pick your brain more about everything that we've talked about?

Eric: Absolutely my official website is ericvanderhope.com that's the easiest way to connect with me. I've got a blog there, if folks are interested in the information there they can sign in or they can sign up to my newsletter. Social media facebook/ericvanderhope.com twitter/ ericvanderhope.com. If you put Google my name you'll find plenty of ways to connect me. That would be the easiest way to connect with me.

Alinka: Awesome, just one last thing.

Eric: Absolutely.

Alinka: Our challenge participants are action takers.

Eric: I love that.

Alinka: What's the one thing that they should do right now to make sure that they publish a book that will launch them on a five figure author career path?

Eric: The first thing I'd do, well can I enlarge it from one to three?

Alinka: Go ahead, big homework everybody.

Eric: The first thing is expectations. You've got to understand that publishing a book, there's a lot more to than publishing a book. You have to look back at your expectations and know that you can't expect the world, you can't expect, "Okay, I'm going to publish this book and I'm going to suddenly make. I'm going to suddenly sell thousands in copies." It's for the most part probably not going to happen unless you have a solid foundation that you've already built upon.

The second thing I would say is the most important. I would say just you've got to get started. If you don't have a book started then you have to start writing the book, right? Get the book written and then take steps to publish. Again like I said publish is the easy part so written the book first. If you haven't written the book write the book.

The third thing that I would say is and it's a two-parter. Build your website, whether it's a one or two page website I would say the simplest just one page like you indicated earlier, make it a squeeze page or an opt-in page. You at least have some information there of what your message is and if people are resonating with that type of message then provide a way, this is the second part, of building your email list.

Have an opt-in there so people can opt-in to you, follow you and then that's how you're growing your platform. That's as simple as I can get without really going into a lot of detail because there's a lot of details here but those are the simplest things to get started and there's a number of ways you can do that.

Alinka: Perfect, excellent. Well, thank you so much Eric. Everybody big homework from Eric Van Der Hope but it will definitely help everybody get started on this early exciting path to a five figure author career. Thank you so much Eric this has been incredible.

Eric: Thank you for having me, it's a privilege and I found it really fun obviously. We had the opportunity of meeting back when you were down here in Long Beach. Again this goes back to and I don't know if you want this little extra information provided for your folks here in the audience and that's by connecting. This is a big example of connecting is by reaching out and finding folks that you resonate with and then take the steps of actually meeting folks.

Alinka: Yeah, we've actually had lunch together.

Eric: That's right, that relationship becomes stronger and then there's more to it than just the internet things. Obliviously it's hard to meet someone who's around the world, a actually you are around the world. You're in Italy right now, right?

Alinka: Yeah, I am right now.

Eric: Take that opportunity of reaching out to friends, to influencers whatever. Start now, stat reaching out, start connecting in a real world sense and that's going to start growing your platform just that in of itself.

Alinka: So true, words of wisdom. Thank you so much Eric.

Eric: You're welcome, my pleasure.

WERE YOU PAYING ATTENTION?

Q1: What do the most successful authors have in common?

Q2: What is a platform according to Michael Hyatt?

Q3: What is the question you should ask yourself first?

Q4: Where should you start when creating a platform?

Q5: What do you do when a visitor subscribes do your list?

Q6: What else does Eric recommend you do to build your platform?

Q7: What does Eric recommend you do to make an impression on your audience?

Q8: What's the most effective way of connecting with people?

Q9: What's a practical tip Eric gives to connect with people?

Q10: What offline recommendation does Eric give for connecting with people?

Q11: What recommendation for connecting with authors does Alinka give?

Q12: What's something you can do to stand out at physical events?

Q13: What else does Alinka recommend you do to make an impact with influencers?

Q14: Platform or book first?

CHALLENGE

From Eric:

1) Manage your expectations.
2) Get started.
3) Get a website with an opt-in form.

From Alinka: Pick one influencer and start commenting on their blog post, review their books, follow them on social media.

THE GOLDEN NUGGETS

Q1: What do the most successful authors have in common?

A1: They created and developed a strong platform.

Q2: What is a platform according to Michael Hyatt?

A2: "A platform is the thing you have to stand on to get heard, it's your stage but unlike a stage in a theater today's platform is built of people, contacts, connections and followers."

Q3: What is the question you should ask yourself first?

A3: What's your message?

Q4: Where should you start when creating a platform?

A4: With a simple website with an opt-in form.

Q5: What do you do when a visitor subscribes do your list?

A5: You connect with them on a personal level. You engage with them.

Q6: What else does Eric recommend you do to build your platform?

A6: Network. Get connected with influencers.

Q7: What does Eric recommend you do to make an impression on your audience?

A7: Share information.

Q8: What's the most effective way of connecting with people?

A8: Reaching out and asking how you can help them.

Q9: What's a practical tip Eric gives to connect with people?

A9: Comment on their blog posts.

Q10: What offline recommendation does Eric give for connecting with people?

A10: Go to physical events.

Q11: What recommendation for connecting with authors does Alinka give?

A11: Buy and review their books.

Q12: What's something you can do to stand out at physical events?

A12: Volunteer.

Q13: What else does Alinka recommend you do to make an impact with influencers?

A13: Introduce people to one another.

Q14: Platform or book first?

A14: Platform.

PART 4: YOU, MY NEXT BEST-SELLING AUTHOR?

Have you met Jane? She's an author too. When she first published her book she was dreaming of her name on the New York Times Best-seller list, because she knew that what she wrote could change her readers' lives.

She was giddy with excitement when she first saw her name and her cover available on Amazon. "This is my big break," she thought.

She was checking her sales dashboard and she couldn't believe her eyes. One day had already passed and she didn't make a single sale. She emailed her publisher to ask if the system was working. And her heart sank when she got the reply. The system was tracking correctly.

She still didn't believe it so she bought her own book herself. And there it was: 1 sale on her dashboard.

But Jane wasn't easily discouraged.

She woke up the next day with new hope in her heart. She logged into her dashboard and there it was again: 1 sale - her own.

While Jane's hopes of landing on the NYT list faded, her determination to get her message into the hands of readers who need it, did not.

She started hunting the net for tips on book marketing and she was overwhelmed by what she found: "try blogging, join Facebook groups, join Tweet teams, create merchandise, join a forum, create an RSS feed, create a YouTube channel, make a book trailer, donate your books…"

Jane did ALL of it. She spent $2,000 on the book trailer, another $2,000 on merchandise related to her book and she donated $1,000 of her books.

She also realized that 6 months had passed and she sold 131 copies, making $262 in royalties.

She was $4,738 in the red and ready to call it quits.

She never told anybody about this because she was ashamed.

She didn't want her family and friends to see her as a failure. She was a writer after all, an educated smart woman. How could this be happening to her?

She failed at reaching the NYT best-selling list. She failed at fulfilling her life long dream of making a career as an author. She even failed at making a return on her book marketing investment!

She felt miserable and borderline depressed… and puzzled how other authors whose books were no better than hers…were actually making a great living as authors!

Is it possible that Jane might be…***you?***

If so, you must hear about **R.A.C.E.** Because R.A.C.E. is what will pull you out of this swamp of author mediocrity.

If you've participated in the 5-Figure Author Challenge, you've already got the R.

R=Reach

This is the first step to winning the author race.

It means that you need to reach your readers. Before they can form a life-long relationship with you, they need to know you exist. And there are ways to do it right and ways to completely bomb it.

Reaching is like walking into a bar and making eye contact with that stunning individual that takes your breath away.

If you've been paying attention during the challenge, you know what type of romance works best to seduce your readers.

But that won't get you anywhere near your full potential as an author.

What you need now is the A, C and E.

A=Acquire

Once that stunning individual from the bar looks you deeply in the eyes for one second too long, your next goal is to get their number (or have them come over and get yours).

That's what acquire stands for.

Once readers know that you exist, you want a way to keep seducing them, because if you fail here, it's game over.

C=Convert

This is a huge milestone that will completely change your relationship with your reader. In our bar situation, this is when you get to first base.

Now remember that the steps that lead to this are crucial. You can't just kiss a stranger and expect to get anything more than a hard slap in the face. But if you go through steps R and A, C is where you start reaping rewards.

E=Engage

This is the culmination of the R.A.C.E. methodology. This is where you marry your stunning individual from the bar, or in other words, this is when that casual reader who had no idea who you were a few steps ago is now your hard-core true fan.

A true fan is someone who will plow through a snow storm for 3 hours barefoot just to see you. Just like a true love.

So now that you know all this, **how do you win the book sales R.A.C.E?**

I have an unprecedented opportunity for you.

It's for my mystery package recipients only.

For a limited time, I'm opening the doors to 100 determined authors who are serious about making the best-seller list.

I'm going to guide you exactly from where you are now, all the way to best-seller status.

I'm only accepting the first 100 authors and then the doors are closing because I want to give those of you who make it my undivided attention.

Go here for a chance to join the best-selling authors club: authorremake.com/club

This has transformed struggling writers like Jane into profitable authors who make a full time living from their books.

To your best-selling success!

Alinka

P.S. Jane was $4,738 in the red and borderline depressed before she discovered R.A.C.E. Now she's in the best-selling authors club. Go here to have what she's having: authorremake.com/club